IMAGES
of America

Prallsville Mills and Stockton

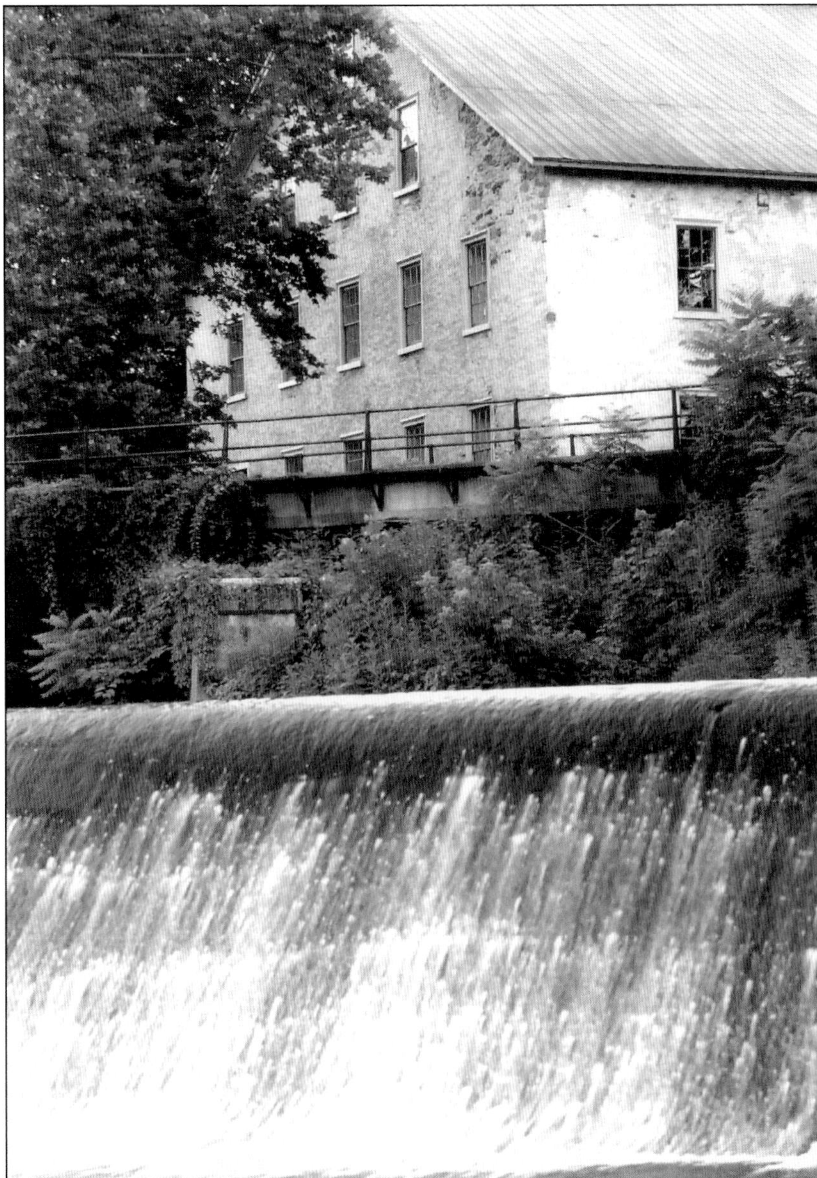

Three levels of technology spanning over 250 years can be seen in this view of Prallsville Mills in Stockton. In the foreground, the spillway of the Delaware and Raritan Canal forms a soft fall of water into the Delaware River. At one time, the bridge above carried railroad cars full of freight and passengers over the Wickecheoke Creek that provided waterpower to the gristmill to produce feed and flour. (Courtesy of the Delaware River Mill Society.)

On the cover: Stockton attracted many skilled stonecutters, its quarries producing some of the finest sandstone of the "brownstone era." This early-1900s photograph from the collection of Carl Cathers includes his grandfather, James Sillery (fifth from right, back row) and "Johnny New York," known for his striking resemblance to Charlie Chaplin (second from right, front row). His coworkers, unable to pronounce his last name, simply used his hometown in its place and the name stuck. (Courtesy of Carl Cathers.)

IMAGES
of America

PRALLSVILLE MILLS AND STOCKTON

Keith Strunk

ARCADIA
PUBLISHING

ISBN 978-0-7385-5690-1

Published by Arcadia Publishing
Charleston SC, Chicago IL, Portsmouth NH, San Francisco CA

Printed in the United States of America

Library of Congress Catalog Card Number: 2008921940

For all general information contact Arcadia Publishing at:
Telephone 843-853-2070
Fax 843-853-0044
E-mail sales@arcadiapublishing.com
For customer service and orders:
Toll-Free 1-888-313-2665

Visit us on the Internet at www.arcadiapublishing.com

To Carl Cathers, whose passion and dedication to the history of his home have made this book possible.

Contents

Acknowledgments

My mom and dad loved a good cemetery. My brothers and I would spend hours with them walking around and reading the names and dates and figuring out the stories behind the tombstones. It was like spelunking the caverns of history looking for a bit here or a piece there that would unlock some long-held mystery. I would like to start by acknowledging my mom and dad, thanks Blaine and Liz, for my sense of curiosity around history.

Putting a book like this together requires a great deal of support and understanding from a lot of people. First and foremost I want to thank my fiancée, creative muse, and partner in all things, Laura Swanson, who edits all my ugly first drafts and also Trevor and Caitlin Rose for teaching their father the importance of telling a good story.

My thanks to my editor at Arcadia, Erin Rocha, without whom this never would have been possible and Edie Sharp, executive director of the Delaware River Mill Society, who has allowed me access, provided countless hours of discussion and help, and has written a wonderful introduction.

My deepest thanks to Carl Cathers, who has been my indispensable link to Stockton's past and a fascinating font of stories that have breathed life into the pages of this book. My thanks to Pieter Prall and Jeanie Prall Wing for access to so much of the Prall family history.

My thanks to Austin L. Davison, Wesley Hendricks, Edith McCloughan, Ashley Haughton, the Delaware and Raritan Canal Commission, Iris H. Naylor (for her book published by the Stockton Centennial Committee *Stockton, New Jersey, 300 Years of History*), Marfy Goodspeed, Emmert Wilson, Egbert T. Bush, the Writers Corner U.S.A. in Doylestown, Pennsylvania, Chris Wildgen, my agent Sara Crowe, and my good friend Jonathan Maberry for their support over the years.

INTRODUCTION

The historic Prallsville Mills complex in Stockton is a surviving example of the 18th-, 19th-, and early-20th-century American industrial village complex. It provides significant insight into the interdependence of agricultural and manufacturing concerns with the advancements in transportation that have spanned our nation's history. At its core is the story of an industrious resiliency throughout the changing eras.

Long before European settlers discovered the plentiful natural resources and benefits from river transportation, it was the native Leni-Lenapes that thrived along the beautiful shores of the Delaware River Valley. In 1677, John Reading, at 20 years of age, purchased proprietary share in the new Colony of West Jersey. He came to the colony in 1684 with his wife, Elizabeth, and daughter Elizabeth and settled in Gloucester County along the Delaware River. This was part of the settlement of Quakers organized by William Penn.

By 1686, he was a wealthy and influential member of the Council of Proprietors of West Jersey, a captain of the county militia, the first recorder of deeds for West Jersey, and a justice on the Colonial Supreme Court. In 1702, Reading made his first purchase of land in an area that would become Hunterdon County. In 1709, he bought 1,440 acres, which would become the structural nucleus of his Mount Amwell plantation and would later become the village of Stockton. As Reading held the ferry rights for both the Delaware River and Gloucester River crossings, this section of the Delaware River Valley was soon referred to as Reading's Landing, with the ferry operation at the site of present-day Ferry Street in Stockton Borough. In 1713–1714, a section of northern Burlington County was set off and established as Hunterdon County, including a large tract of land along the Delaware River, north and south of the Wicheckeoke Creek.

Reading's daughter Mary married Daniel Howell of Bucks County, Pennsylvania, around 1710. Reading presented his daughter and her husband with a tract of land about a mile square on the south side of the Wicheckeoke Creek and constructed a sawmill and a gristmill for them—the first establishment of this kind in the area. Mary and Daniel inherited Reading's 70-acre plantation two years after his death in 1717. In 1733, Daniel bequeathed the gristmill, land, water rights, gears, and associated utensils to his two oldest children, Daniel Jr. and John. The two sons maintained ownership for only a few years, selling the tract to Charles Woolverton Jr. in 1750.

After Woolverton's death in 1765, his sons Morris and John were given control of the estate. Morris received a plantation of 268 acres, and John received the 70 acres along the river and creek where the gristmill was located. Shortly before his death in 1773, John drew up a will, which mentioned several structures including a mill, a quantity of lumber, a crosscut saw, and sawmill irons. In 1792, his sons Charles and George purchased the mill property from their father's executors for £1,500.

In 1794, the sons sold their recent acquisition for the exact price of their purchase to a successful Revolutionary War lieutenant, John Prall Jr. Two years prior, Prall had purchased the former Reading-Howell plantation of 280 acres. This tract of land lies from present-day Ferry Street in Stockton Borough along the Delaware River to the mouth of the Wickecheoke Creek.

Combining natural resources with developing modes of technology and transportation allowed Prall to expand the small mills to the size of the larger stone structures that remain today. The Prallsville gristmill, commercial fisheries, stone quarries, sawmill, linseed mill, plaster mill, general store, post office, and Prall's plantation all prospered. His growing family built several stone manor homes and became an influential New Jersey family. Prall maintained ownership of the site until his death in 1831, when the mill complex was sold.

Successive owners Hoppock and Wilson, Kessler, and Stover continued to prosper from the bountiful opportunities the location provided. Stone, fish, good soil, and lumber were in abundance, as was the waterpower necessary for mill technology. The gristmill ground local farmers' grain for market. Limestone, a component for local buckwheat farmers, was milled by the plaster mill. Local commerce guaranteed a customer base for the general store and post office, and advancements in transportation proved vital to getting goods to larger markets.

Italian stonecutters and Irish canal builders, drawn to jobs endowed by area natural resources, brought an influx of an industrious population with a strong work ethic. In the 1830s, the Prallsville Mills complex had the good fortune to be located on the banks of the newly built canal system. Running along the canal, the 1850s railroad brought another wave of prosperity, as did the construction of the Center Bridge to Pennsylvania. A cinder from a railroad steam engine ignited the gristmill fire of 1874, and Kessler, the current owner, sold the property to Stout Stover, who rebuilt and reopened the gristmill in 1877.

The property was sold to Joseph and John Smith in 1883. By the end of the 1800s, the Borough of Stockton was formed. The railroad, canal, river, roads, and bridge enabled Stockton to provide products to a growing nation. Life in this river town prospered until the early 1930s. Although the Depression brought many changes, the mill continued to function under the Smith family's ownership until 1955. Combining other enterprises was attempted in the final years, including a hardware store.

In the late 1960s, the beauty of the area was almost responsible for the Prallsville Mills' demise. Citizens struggled to save the historic site from developers. A visionary, Donald Jones purchased the property in 1969 and gave it to the State of New Jersey in 1973. The formation of the Delaware and Raritan Canal State Park provided walking and bicycle paths along the banks of the old canal from Trenton to Frenchtown, with the Prallsville Mills complex located in the center.

In 1976, the Delaware River Mill Society was formed as the private, not-for-profit organization responsible for the continued restoration, maintenance, and operation of the Prallsville Mills, and the complex was placed on the National Register of Historic Places in 1979. Today a thriving center for cultural, educational, arts, and ecotourism activities, the Prallsville Mills lay at the center point of New Jersey's Delaware River Scenic Byway, bordered by the federally protected Wild and Scenic Delaware River. The Prallsville Mills complex provides an opportunity for all to enjoy the beauty and natural resources of the location and learn its amazing history.

This is the story of a community that has had the courage, industriousness, and resiliency crucial to meeting the challenges that the changing world presents. Forefathers who led the way with innovation are followed by present-day preservation efforts. Stockton enjoys the good fortune of still having most of its historic buildings and charming homes. As Shakespeare said, "what's past is prologue," and the Prallsville Mills has once again been established as a centerpiece for local activity.

It is an honor and privilege to be even the smallest part of bringing the history and natural beauty of this area to your attention.

Edith Shreiner Sharp
Executive Director of the Delaware River Mill Society

One

The Mills Complex

Gentle as a mother's caress and as powerful as a thousand locomotives, a river is a watery dichotomy that draws people in, excites their senses, and pulls at the very core of their humanity. For some, it is the river's beauty that awes them, its meditative serenity that calms, and for many, it is its power that seduces.

The Delaware River draws a dividing line between Pennsylvania and New Jersey and is fed by hundreds of smaller streams along its length. During the early times of settlement by the Europeans, hundreds of mills were built taking advantage of the ample waterpower the streams and river provided. In 1794, John Prall Jr. acquired such a property that included "a Corn or Grist Mill & Saw Mill with the Full Custom Benefit in Grinding and Sawing."

Prall took the small mill nestled next to the Wickecheoke Creek at the point where it flows into the Delaware River and used the power of the water to develop a village industrial complex. He rebuilt and expanded the gristmill and built a linseed oil mill and a sawmill. He built a stone store to serve as the center of his developing village and commercial concerns, and built houses for his family, farmed the land, developed two fisheries on the Delaware River, and opened a sandstone quarry.

The prosperity that the expansion provided was relatively short lived, and the fortunes of the mills complex would not turn until after the Prall family had sold the property to William Hoppock and John Wilson. The factor that revitalized the mill's business was the building of the feeder canal for the Delaware and Raritan Canal, which provided convenient transportation for goods. In 1852, the building of the railroad further enhanced the mill's commercial viability. Through a variety of owner and management changes, the Prallsville Mills complex continued to prosper well into the middle of the 20th century.

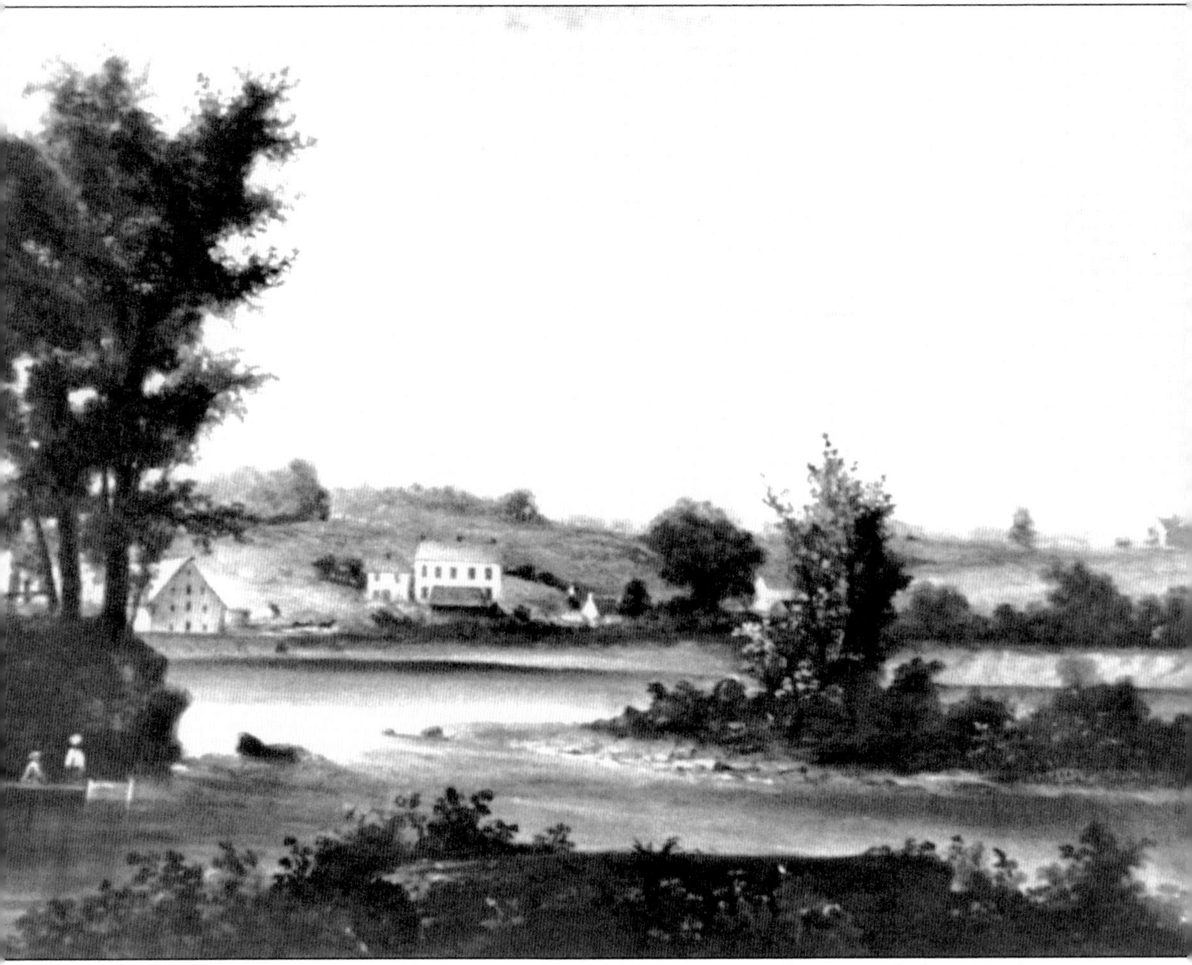

John Parker Prall, grandson of John Prall Jr., had spent good time with his grandparents in Prallsville. In his memoirs, *Historical Family Sketch*, written in 1876 in New York City, he wrote, "In order to preserve for myself and my children a remembrance of the dear spot where I had seen such happy days, I took with me an artist by the name of [Thomas] Whitley, to Prallsville where the three sketches now in the parlor were taken." Prall has provided, by way of three oil paintings, a snapshot of 19th-century Prallsville from three different perspectives. Here Prallsville is seen from across the Delaware River in Pennsylvania. In the foreground, Hendricks Island is on the left, and Snake Island is on the right. From left to right, on the opposite shore, can be seen the gristmill, the store house, the manor house, and the roof of the sawmill, which hides the base of the manor house. At the top of the hill is the plantation house (currently the Woolverton Inn). (Courtesy of the Delaware River Mill Society.)

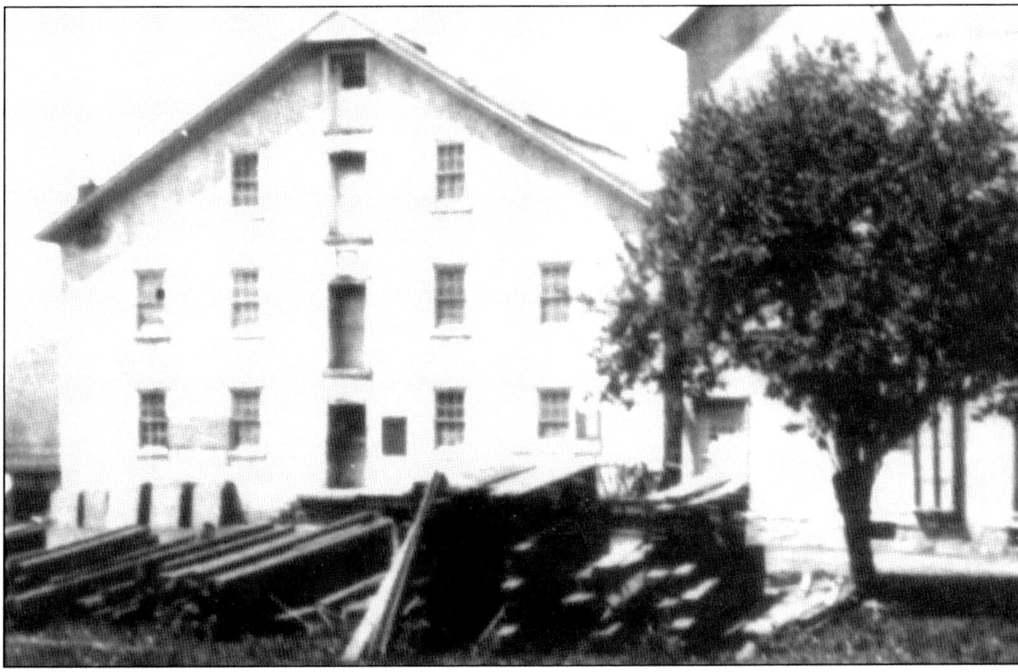

In the 1930s, the mill property was owned and operated under the name J. W. Smith's Sons. The business included milling flour and mixed feed grains and selling fertilizer. Adaptability was the key to success, and in addition to selling lumber, seen stacked in the foreground, they sold a variety of building supplies and continued operation until 1968. (Courtesy of Carl Cathers.)

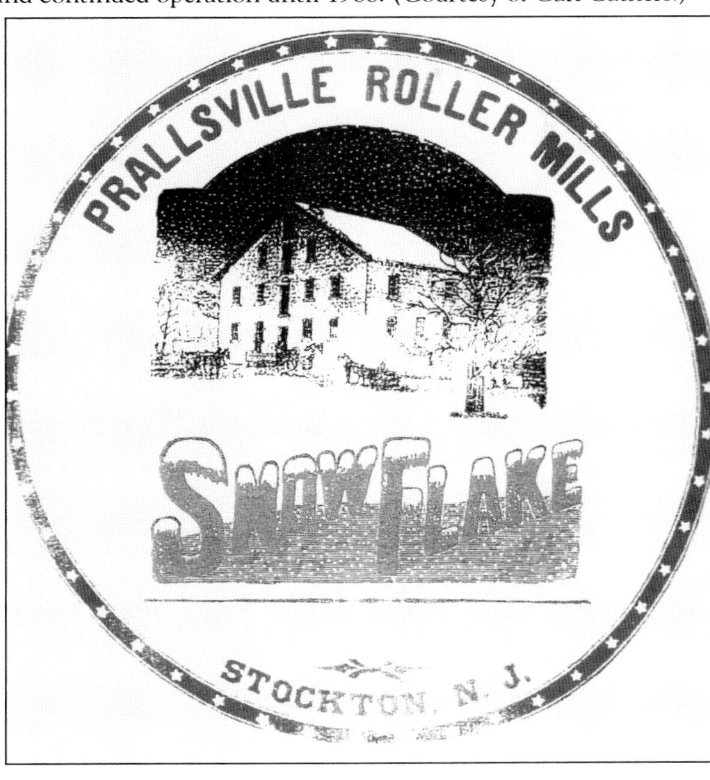

Each line of flour had its own brightly colored seal that marked the bags in which it was sold. In fact, designing and painting the seals was done by designers who traveled among the various mills throughout the northeast. Each designer had their own style. Similarities can be found in seals from different mills that used the same designer. (Courtesy of the Delaware River Mill Society.)

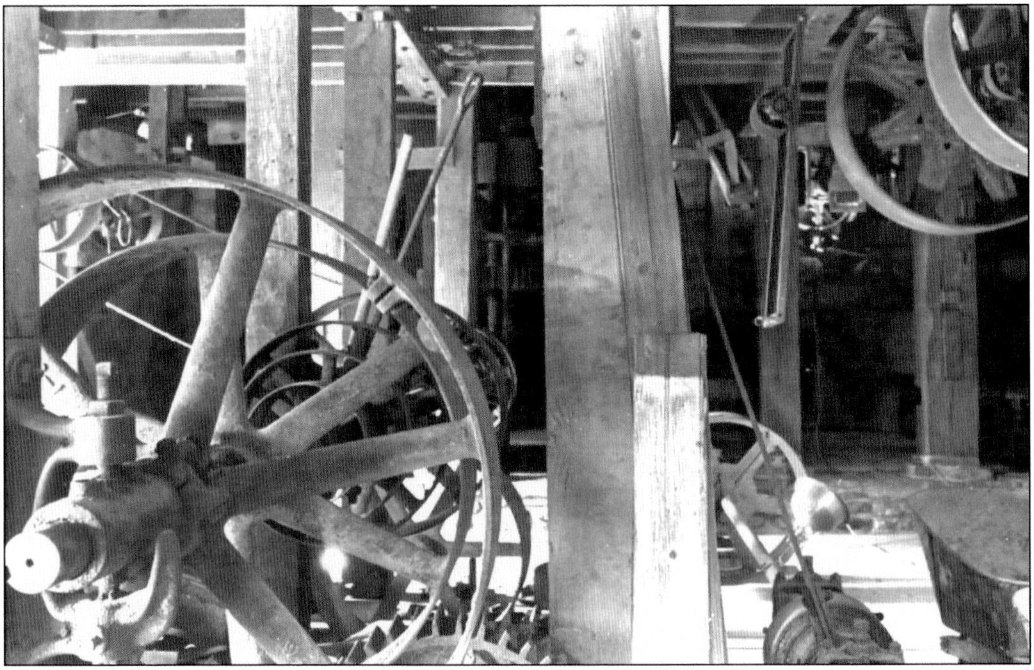

This current photograph shows part of the gears, rollers, and belts that harnessed waterpower. During periods of low water, millponds provided a backup power source. In the latter years of the mill operation, backup power was provided using a tractor to power a belt fed through a hole in the mill wall to turn the wheel in the foreground. (Courtesy of the Delaware River Mill Society.)

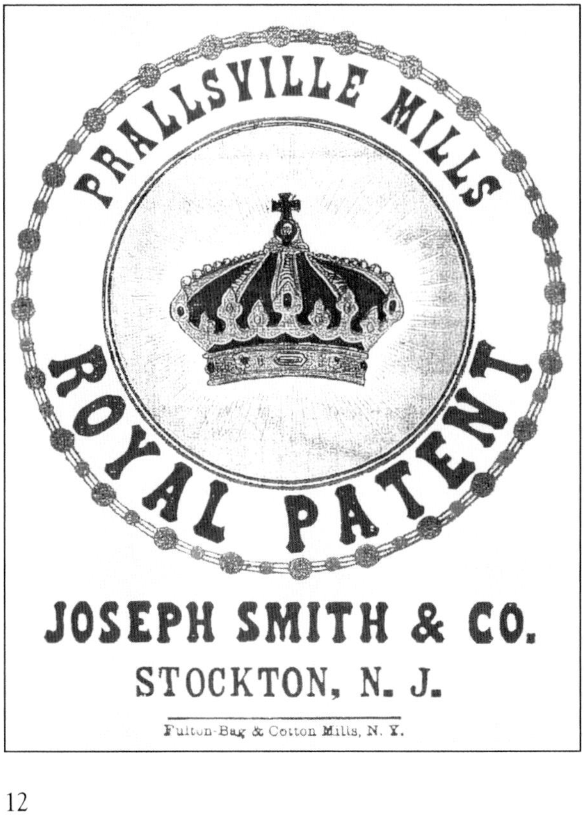

Here is another example of the colorful seals used on the flour bags. The ink used for the printing provided a vibrant and eye-catching color that did not fade easily. In fact, bags found on the mill property many years after it had ceased operations were still marked with seals that had not faded at all in the many years since they were printed. (Courtesy of the Delaware River Mill Society.)

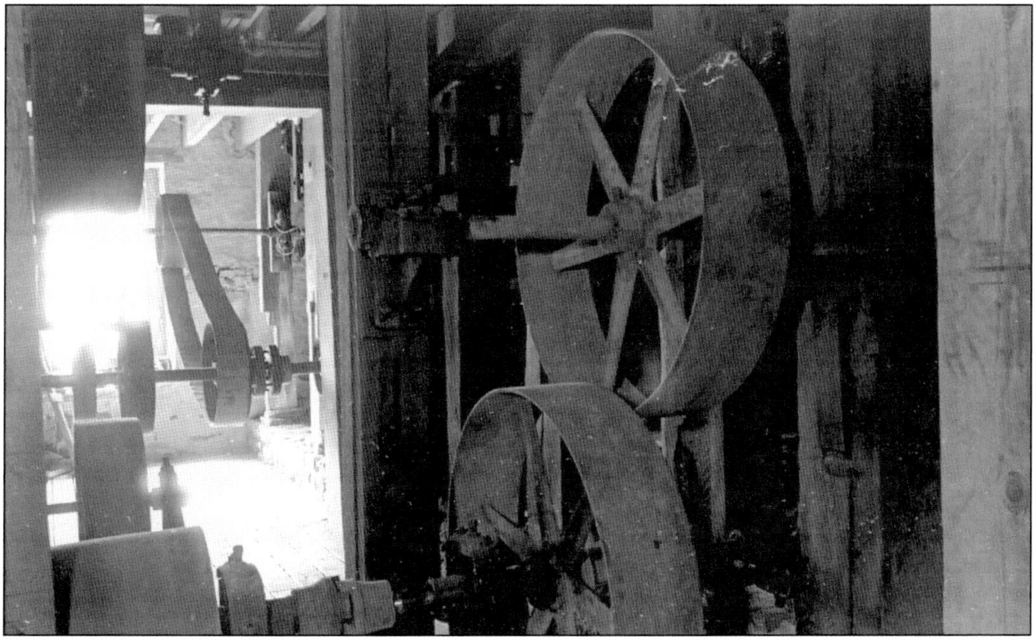

The race channeled water past the waterwheel and later, after 1877, turbines housed in the mill basement. Rollers and belts were used to transfer power through the four levels of the mill in order to run the grain elevators and turn the heavy millstones that milled the grain into flour. As metal rollers became available, they would be used to replace the older wooden rollers when they wore out; however, the mill operators saw no need in replacing wooden rollers that were still functioning. This explains why both wooden and metal rollers are found in the mill today. In the photograph below, there is a paned window with a deep-set stone arch. This is the fore race where the water used to enter to provide power when the mill was in operation. (Courtesy of the Delaware River Mill Society.)

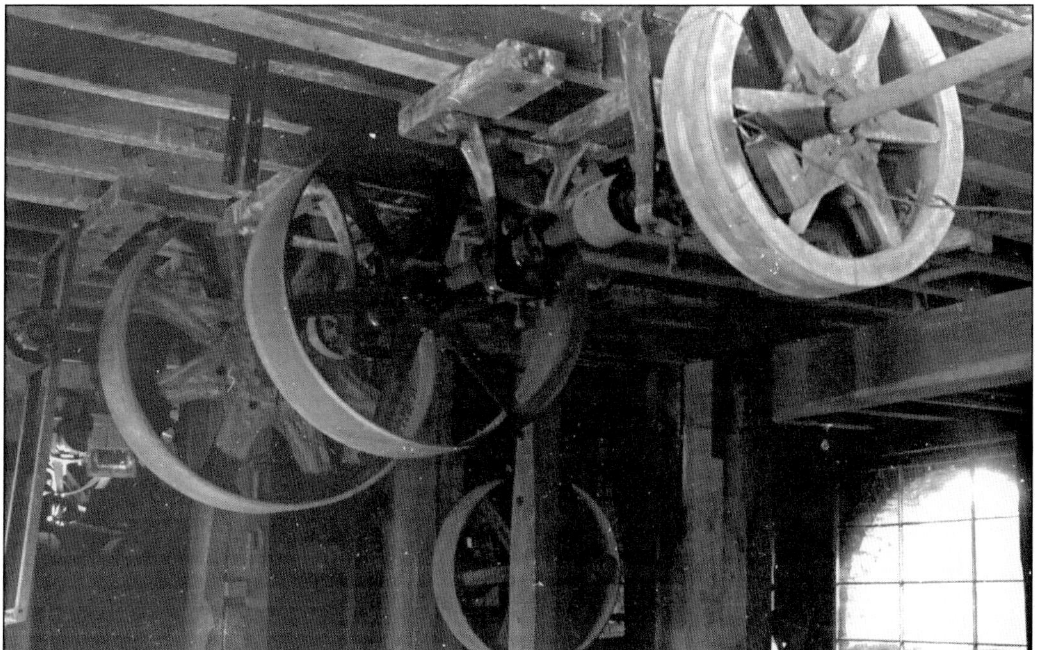

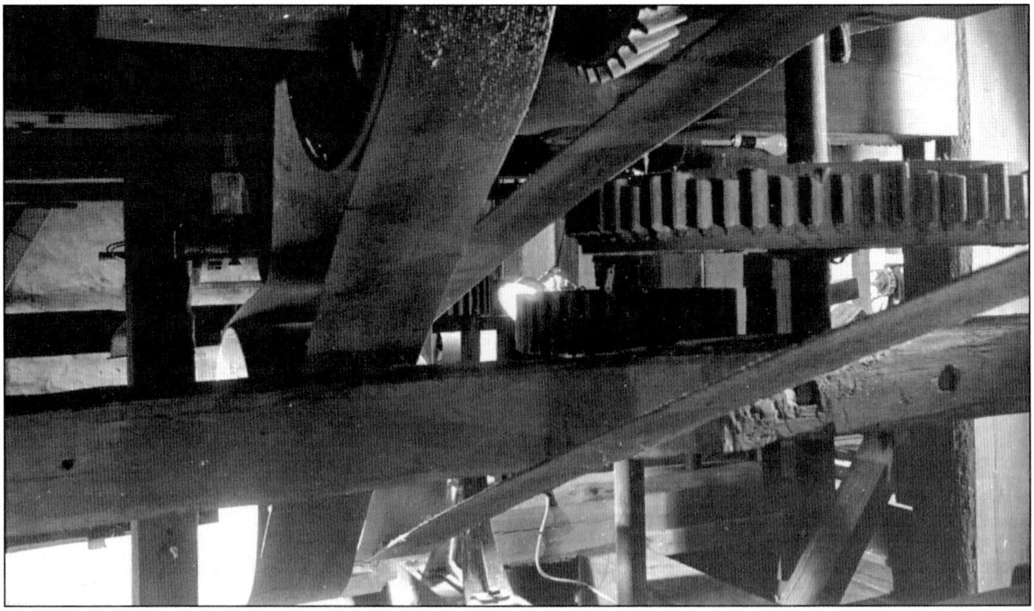

Another challenge in managing waterpower was converting horizontal power into vertical power. The short belt in this picture turns the roller with the attached pinion gear, which then turns the horizontal gear on the right. The shaft of the horizontal gear was directly attached to the grinding stone located on the floor above and turned the stones to grind the grain. (Courtesy of the Delaware River Mill Society.)

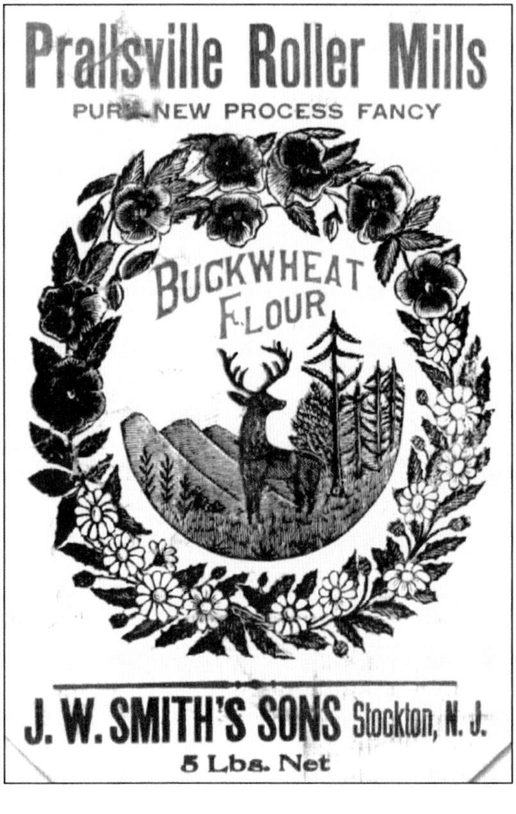

A major crop for nearby Kingwood Township was buckwheat, which the mill used to produce buckwheat flour. George Smith, who was not related to the Smiths that owned the mill, was put in charge of the gristmill in 1914 and remained the miller through 1946 when he retired. During that period of time, the mill used roller mill technology to mill flour. (Courtesy of the Delaware River Mill Society.)

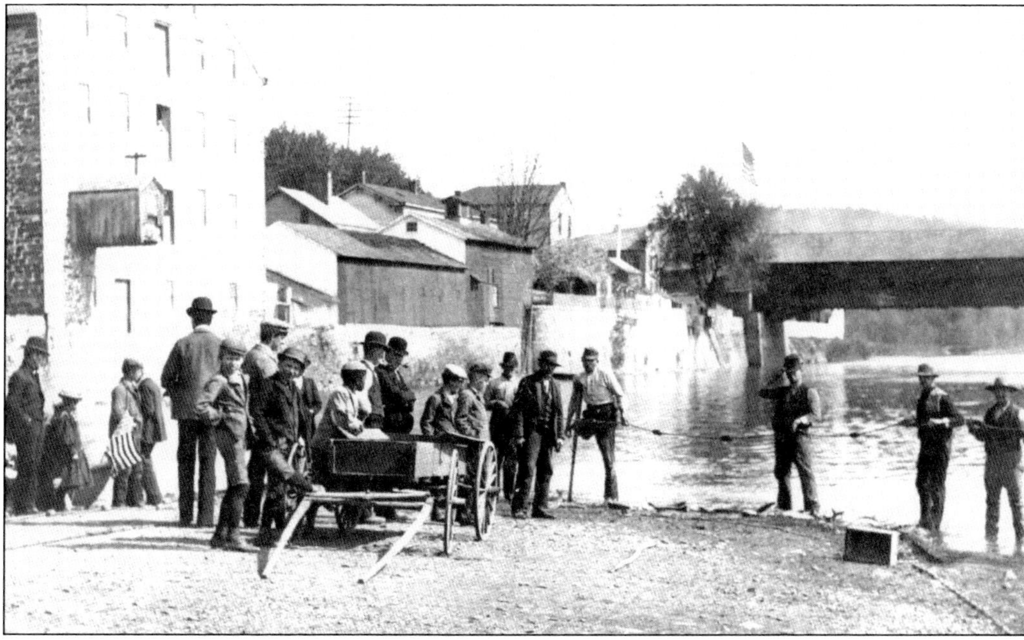

A group of men are shad fishing near the Lear Mill in Lambertville in this 1898 photograph. The wooden structure protruding from the second floor of the building was a "Chic Sale." Charles "Chic" Sale was a vaudevillian famous for having written a play about an outhouse builder, which resulted in his name becoming a euphemism for outhouses. The second picture is looking at the back of the silo and gristmill at Prallsville. While the mill never had a Chic Sale, the small cube-shaped object in the second story window on the left side of the silo (the center building) was the exhaust for the Sifter Sorter, which sorted debris such as sticks and stones from the grain and spewed it out to the ground below. (Above, courtesy of Carl Cathers; below, courtesy of the Delaware River Mill Society.)

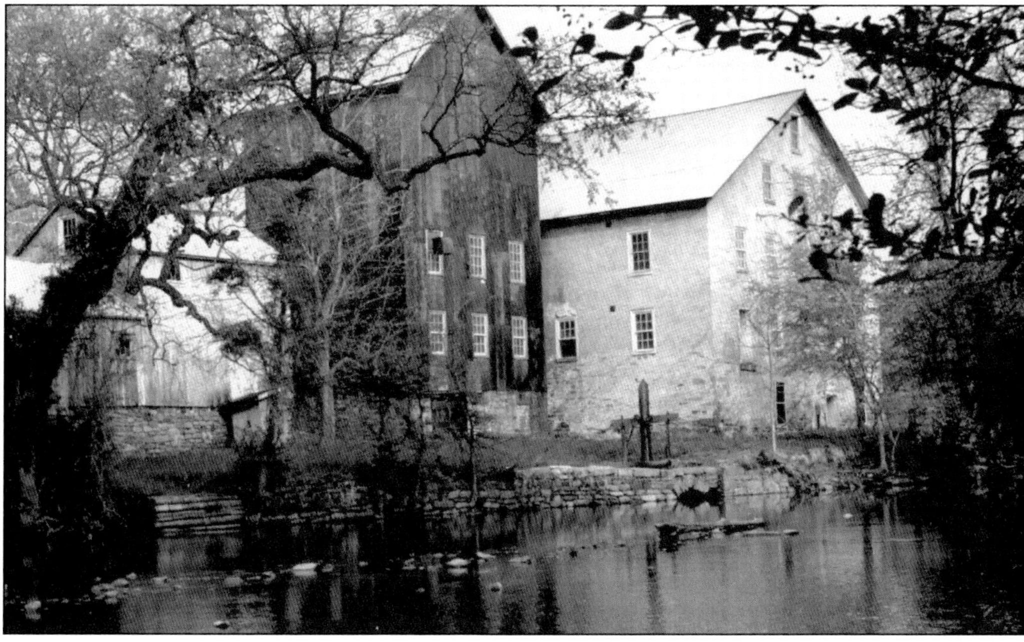

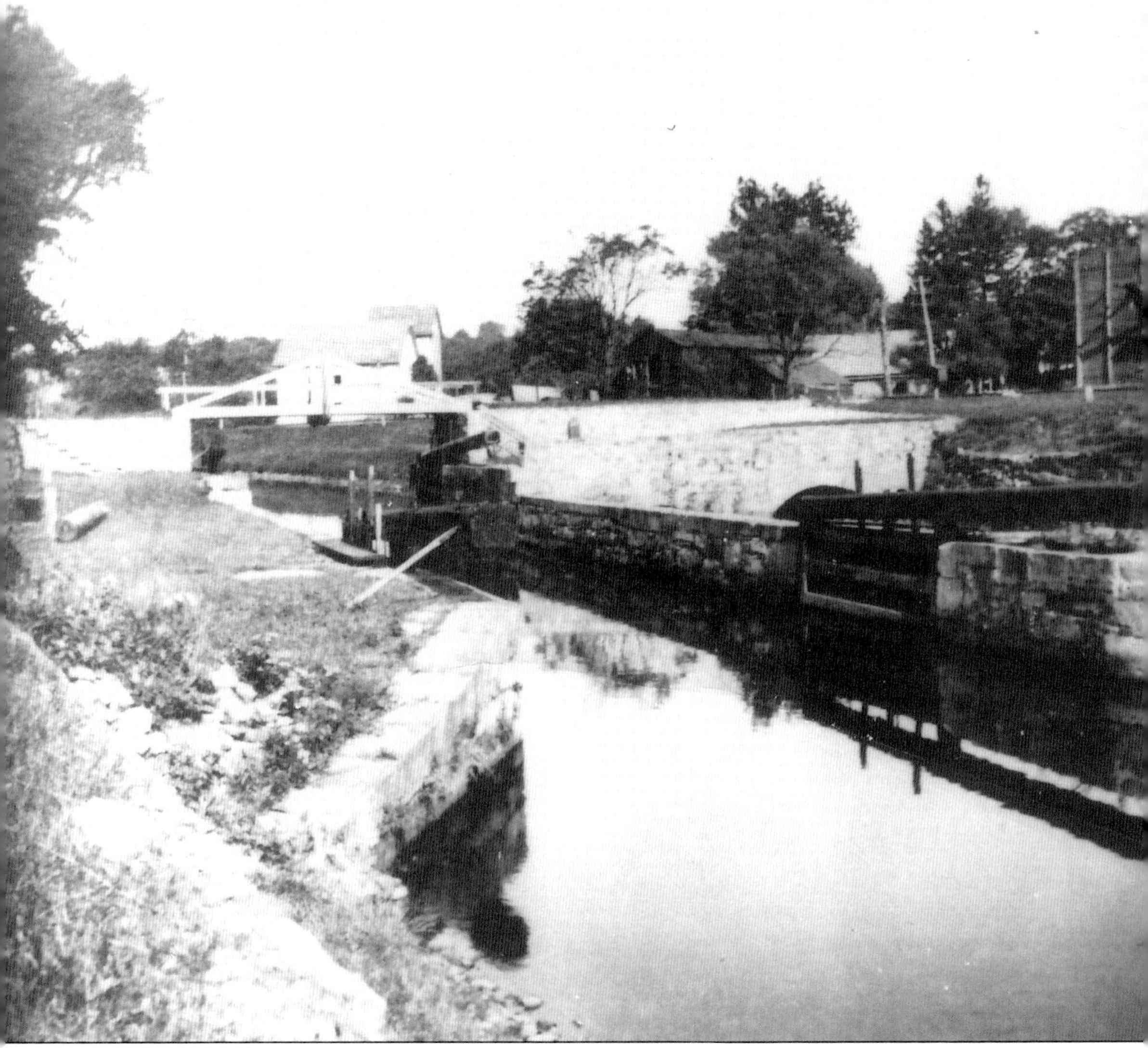

The canal that passes behind the Prallsville Mills was the feeder canal for the Delaware and Raritan Canal. It originated at Bull's Island near Raven Rock and continued onto Trenton. It was navigable along its entire course and had only three locks. The lock seen here is the Prallsville Lock and is constructed of Stockton sandstone. The wooden gates were operated by using the long wooden handles seen on top of and running parallel to the right side stone wall. The gristmill and silo can be seen in the distance behind the canal bridge. To the right, in the center of the picture, are the sawmill and linseed oil mill. On the far right is the stone crusher, which was only in use for a short period of time and places the picture in the 1920s. (Courtesy of the Delaware and Raritan Canal Commission.)

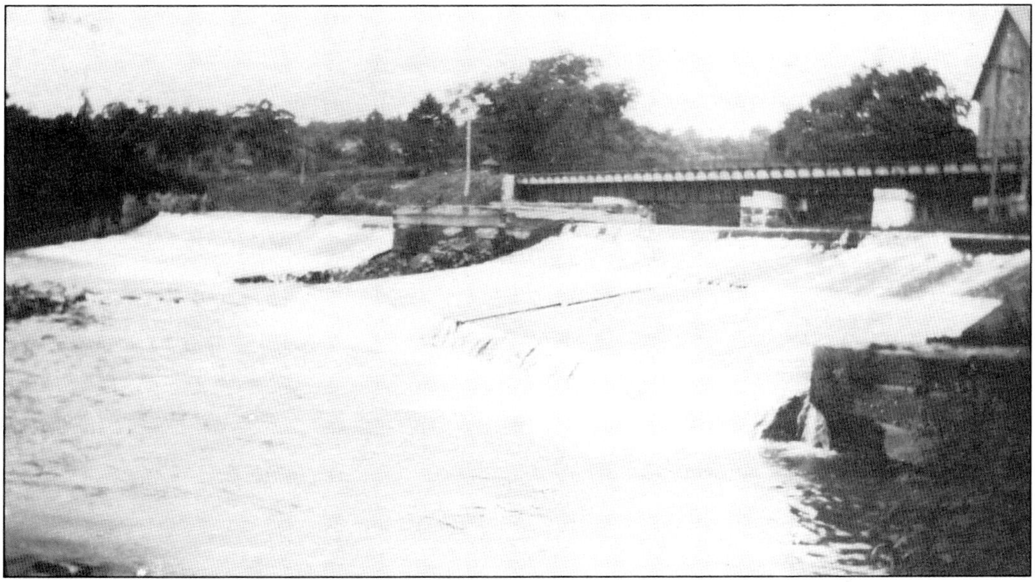

The canal spillway is seen here from the Delaware River side. The spillway, or "overflow" as the residents call it, was designed to regulate the water level of the canal. This is also the point where the Wickecheoke Creek flows into the feeder canal. The railroad bridge that used to carry the trains across the creek now serves bicyclists and hikers. (Courtesy of Carl Cathers.)

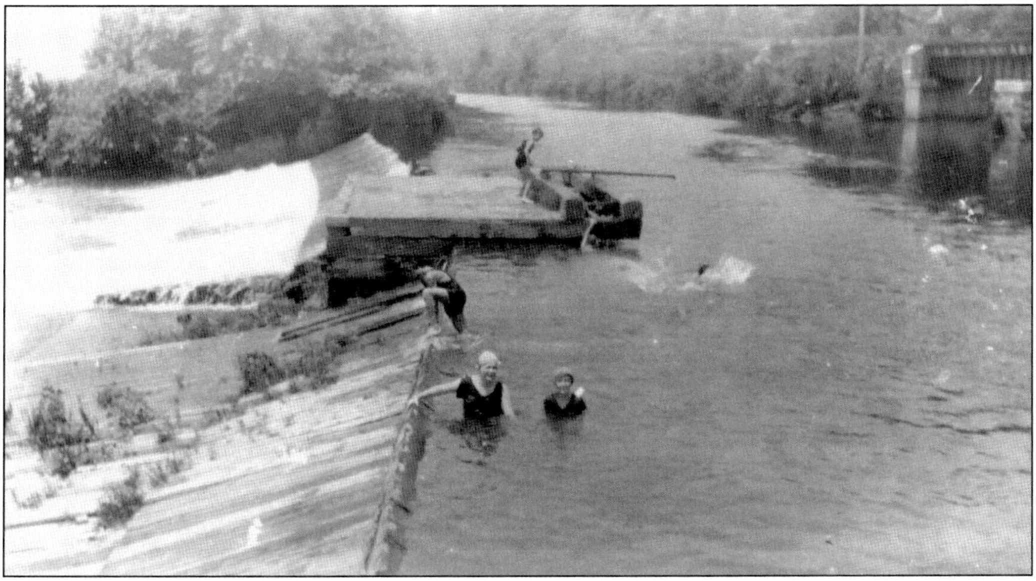

Long before it became a state park, the canal served as a recreational area for the local residents. The structure in the middle housed the control gates for the canal, which could be used to drain water from the canal if necessary. Known by the residents as the "stone box," it was a popular swimming and meeting place during the warm summer months. (Courtesy of Carl Cathers.)

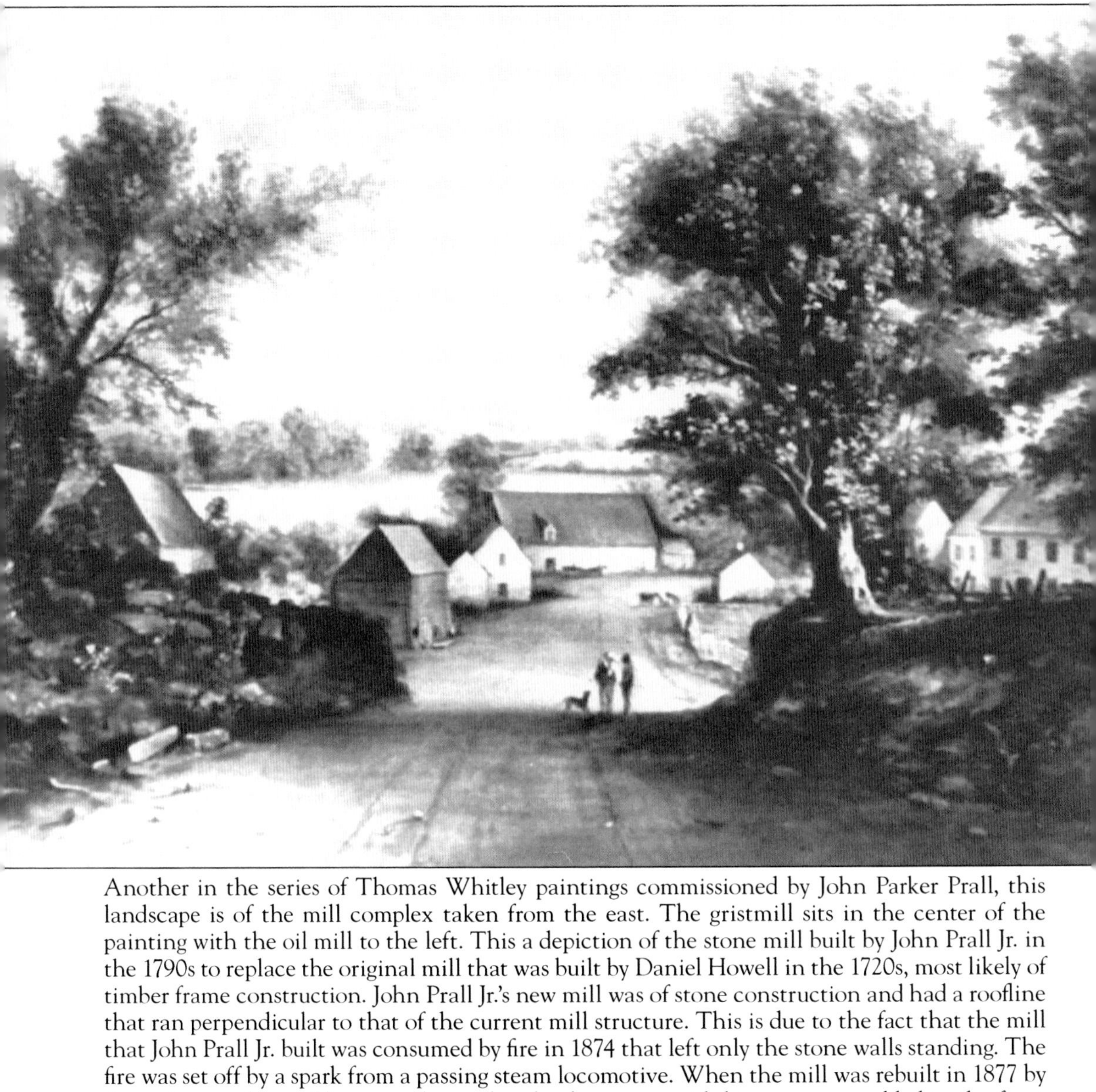

Another in the series of Thomas Whitley paintings commissioned by John Parker Prall, this landscape is of the mill complex taken from the east. The gristmill sits in the center of the painting with the oil mill to the left. This a depiction of the stone mill built by John Prall Jr. in the 1790s to replace the original mill that was built by Daniel Howell in the 1720s, most likely of timber frame construction. John Prall Jr.'s new mill was of stone construction and had a roofline that ran perpendicular to that of the current mill structure. This is due to the fact that the mill that John Prall Jr. built was consumed by fire in 1874 that left only the stone walls standing. The fire was set off by a spark from a passing steam locomotive. When the mill was rebuilt in 1877 by Stout Stover, the roof line was changed and a date stone with his name was added to the front wall facade. (Courtesy of the Delaware River Mill Society.)

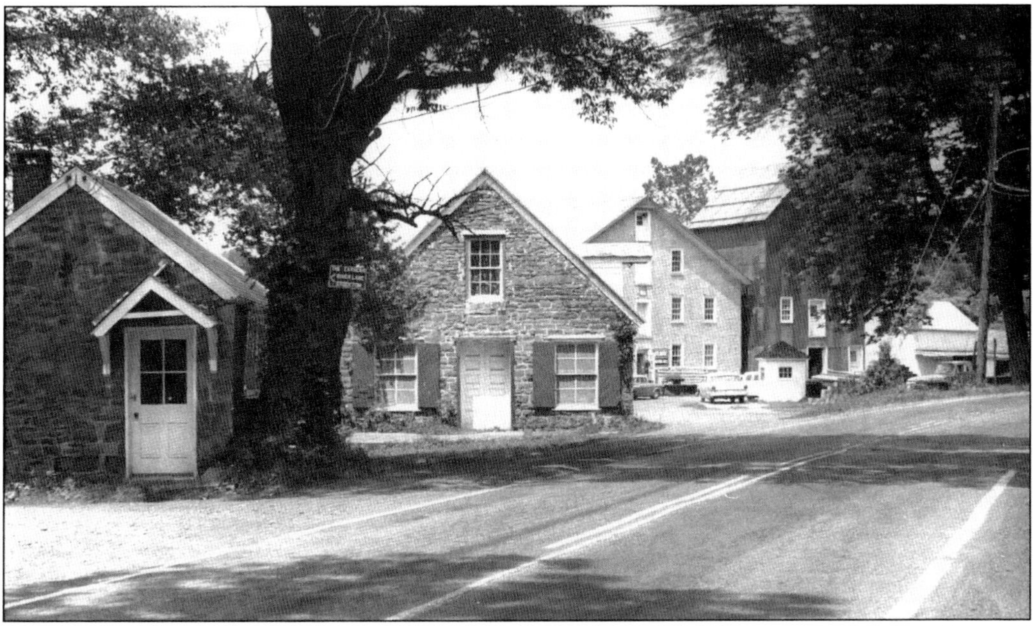

The picture above in this pair was taken during the mid-1950s, when the mill was still in full operation. Although they had stopped milling flour at this point, the Smith family continued to grind feed for farm animals and expanded the mill offerings to include a hardware store that provided lumber, building supplies, paint, and glass. The gristmill housed the hardware store, while the linseed oil mill served as storage for roofing materials and fertilizer. The smokehouse on the far left was empty. The neat appearance of the property stands in stark contrast to the second photograph taken in 1973, which shows the mill complex abandoned and deteriorating. The dark, square objects in front of the oil mill are pipes being used for the sewers installed in Stockton in 1973. (Courtesy of the Delaware River Mill Society.)

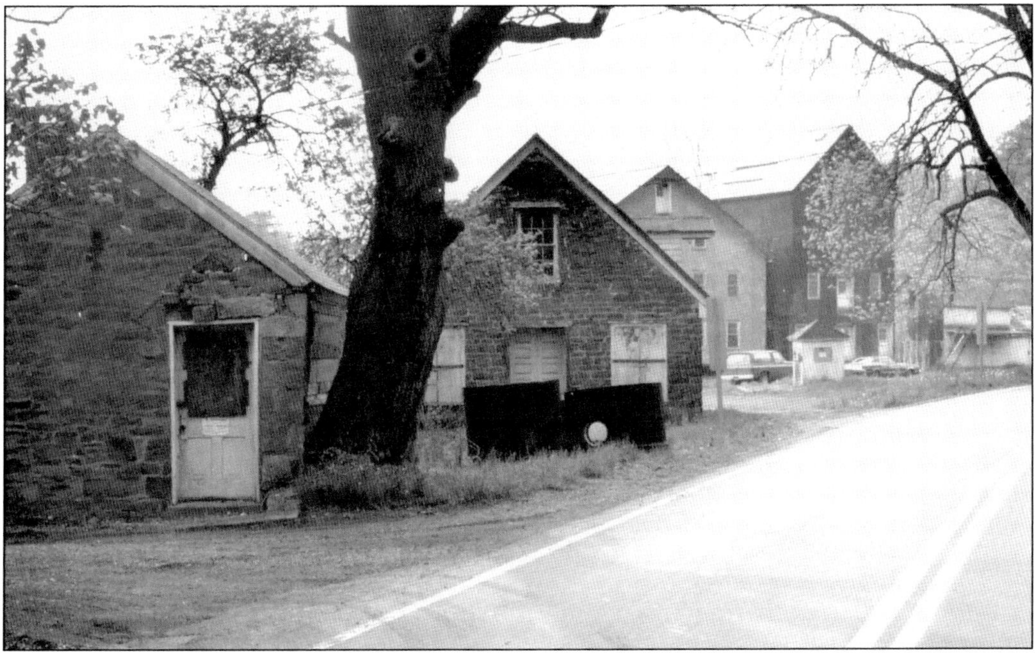

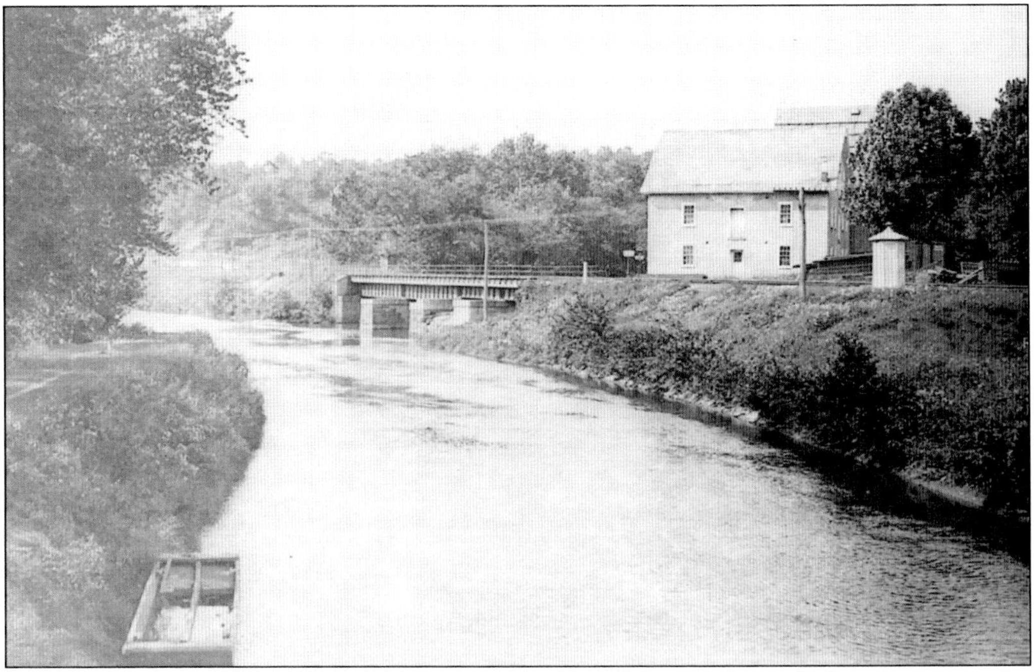

Lock tender George Price's boat can be seen in the lower left in this pre-1936 view of the feeder canal. He operated the boat by pushing a long pole to the canal floor while standing at the front of the boat and then walking to the back to propel it forward. (Courtesy of the Delaware River Mill Society.)

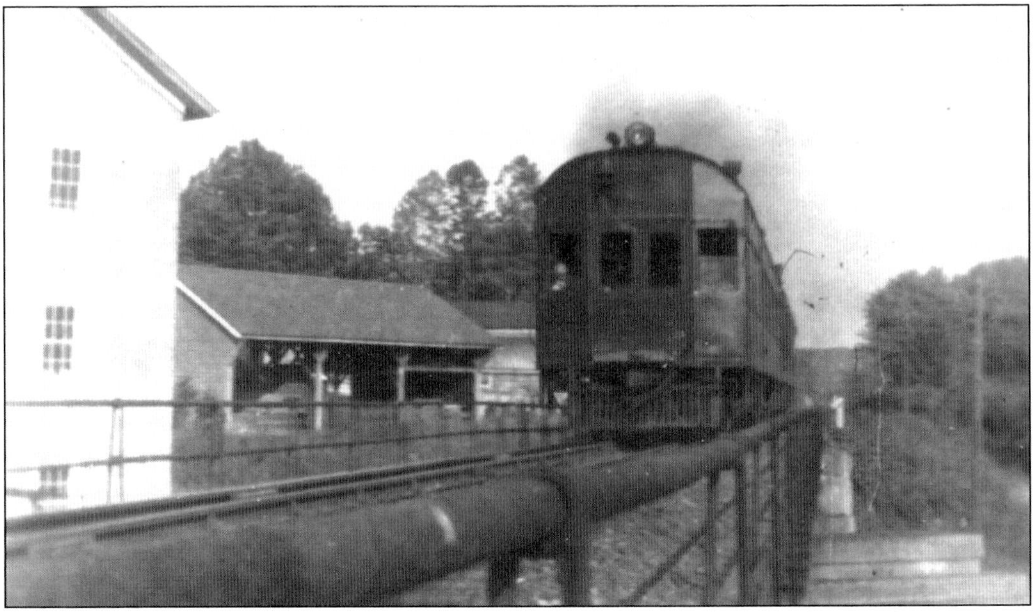

Although the era of the steam locomotive ended in the 1950s, the use of trains for passenger service was still very much alive. In order to contain costs, the railroad started using self-propelled passenger cars, which were more economical to run than larger diesel engines with cars. Known as "Doodlebugs," this one is northbound past the Prallsville Mills on its way to Phillipsburg from Trenton. (Courtesy of Carl Cathers.)

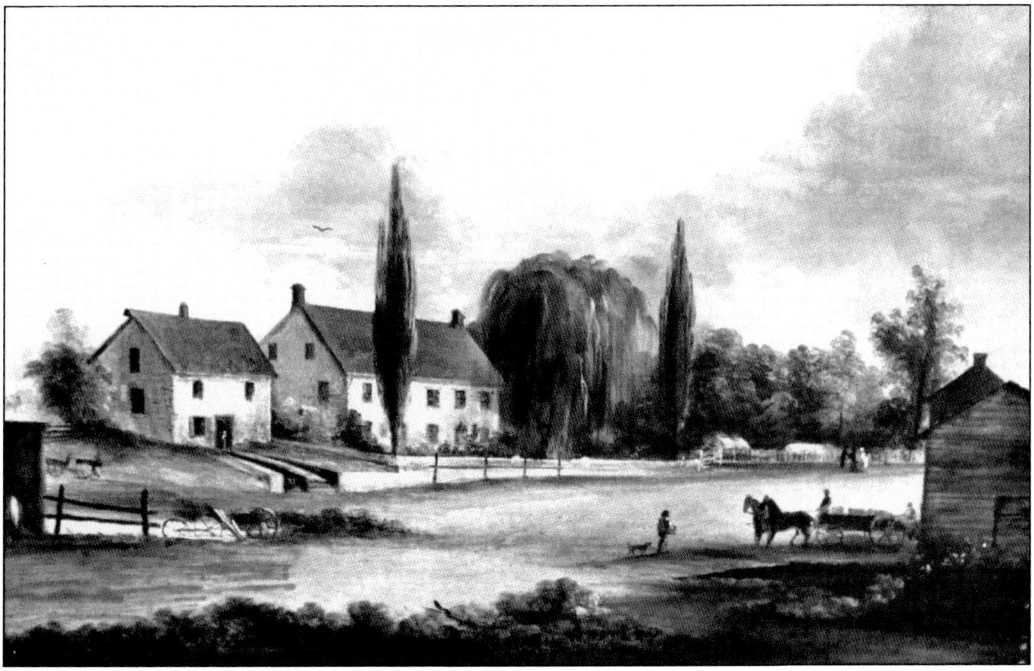

This final painting of the Thomas Whitley series shows the manor house in the center with the store to its left. The oil mill is in the lower left corner, and the millpond, which provided power for the oil and sawmills, is on the left below the store. The millpond no longer exists on the property. (Courtesy of the Delaware River Mill Society.)

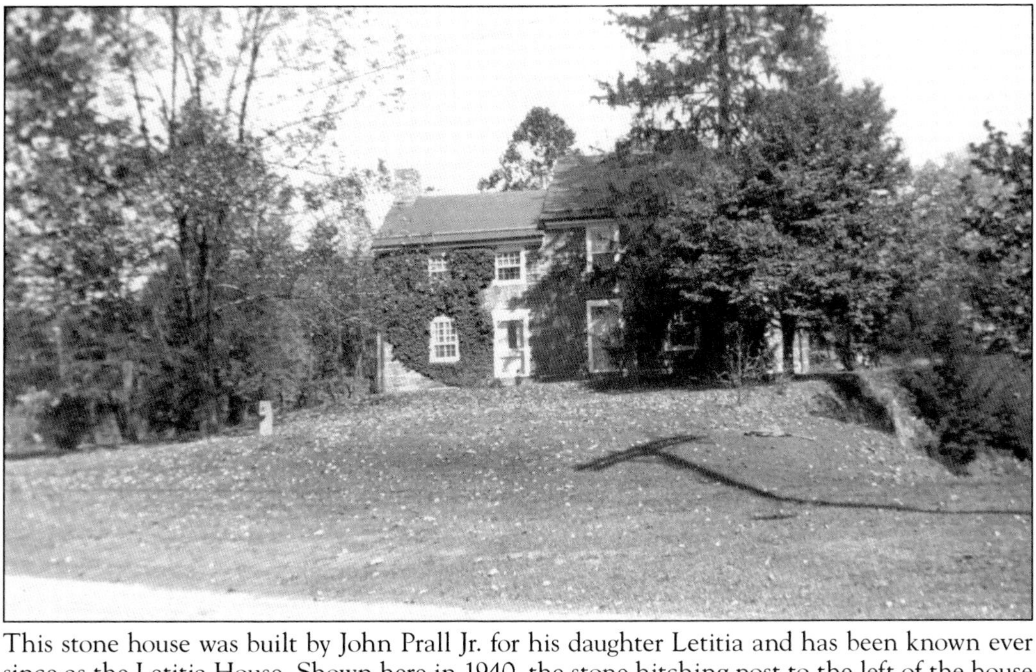

This stone house was built by John Prall Jr. for his daughter Letitia and has been known ever since as the Letitia House. Shown here in 1940, the stone hitching post to the left of the house is the last remaining evidence of the road that once ran past the house and up the hill to the plantation house, which is now the Woolverton Inn. (Courtesy of Carl Cathers.)

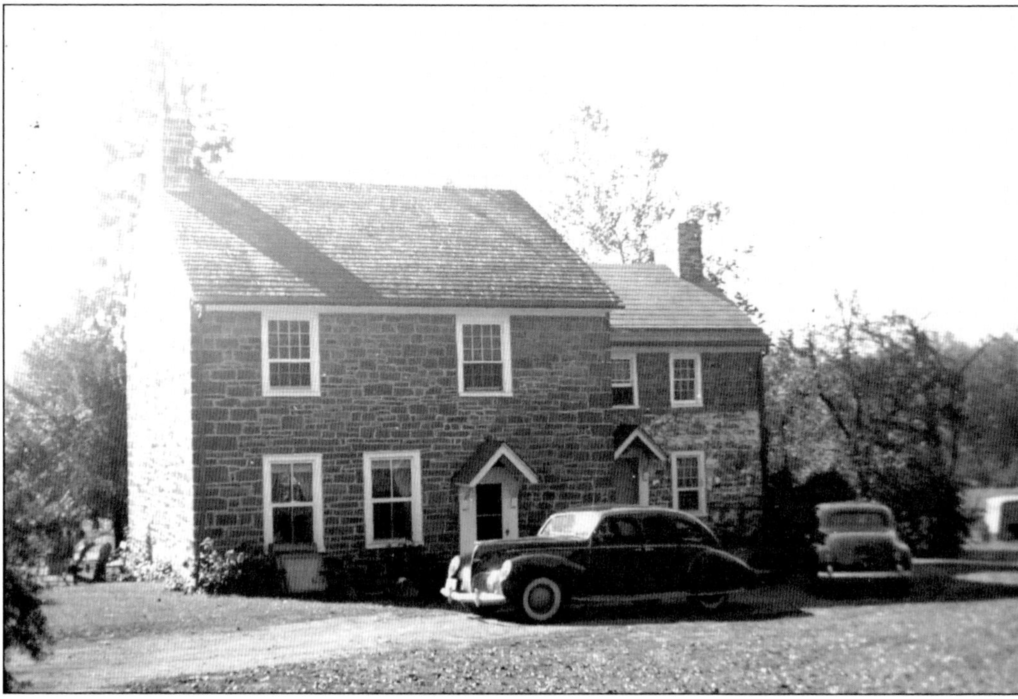

This view of the back of the Letitia House was taken after Anne and Jack Matthews had bought the house in 1940 for $10,000. Anne was the actress who played radio soap heroine Stella Dallas. She commuted from Stockton to New York everyday by car and train and only missed two performances in the 18 years that the show was on the air. (Courtesy of Carl Cathers.)

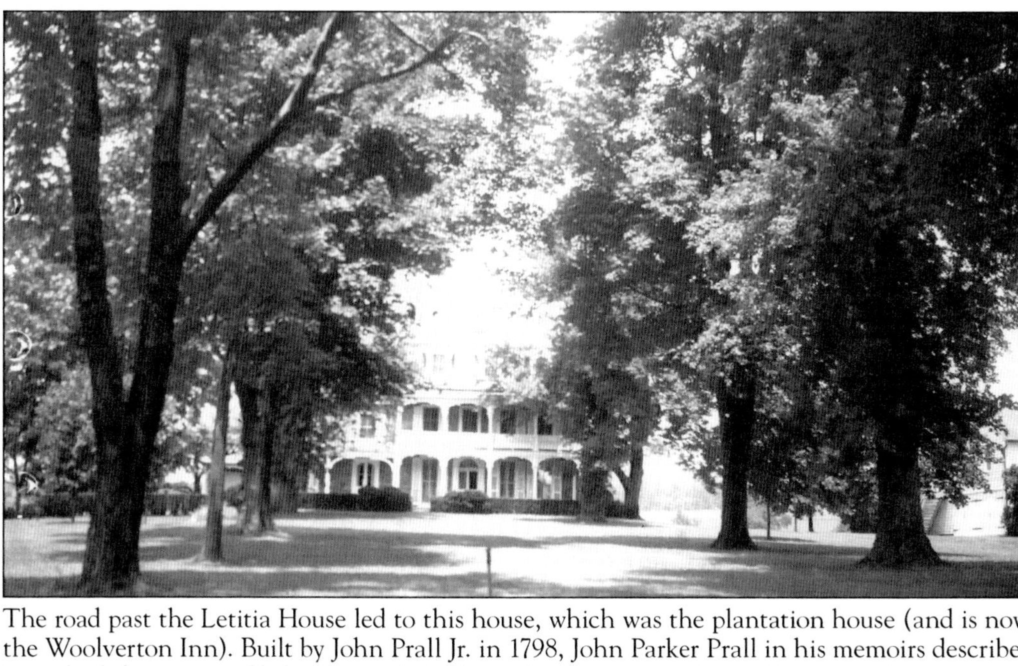

The road past the Letitia House led to this house, which was the plantation house (and is now the Woolverton Inn). Built by John Prall Jr. in 1798, John Parker Prall in his memoirs describes it as "built by my grandfather; entirely in dressed stone, except the walls around the doors and windows, which were chiseled smooth." (Courtesy of Pieter Prall and Jeanie Prall Wing.)

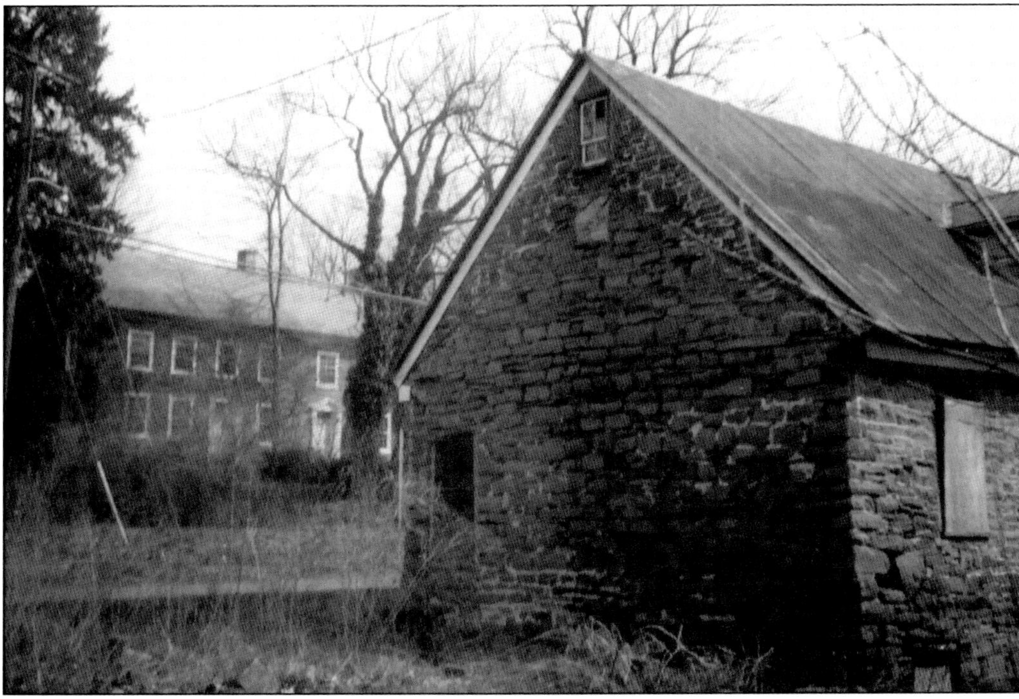

This 1978 photograph of the linseed oil mill was taken soon after the Delaware River Mill Society took over the property. The Prall manor house can be seen across River Road (Route 29), and the run-down condition of the oil mill is apparent. In fact, the roof leaked, and the corner of the foundation in view was crumbling. (Courtesy of the Delaware River Mill Society.)

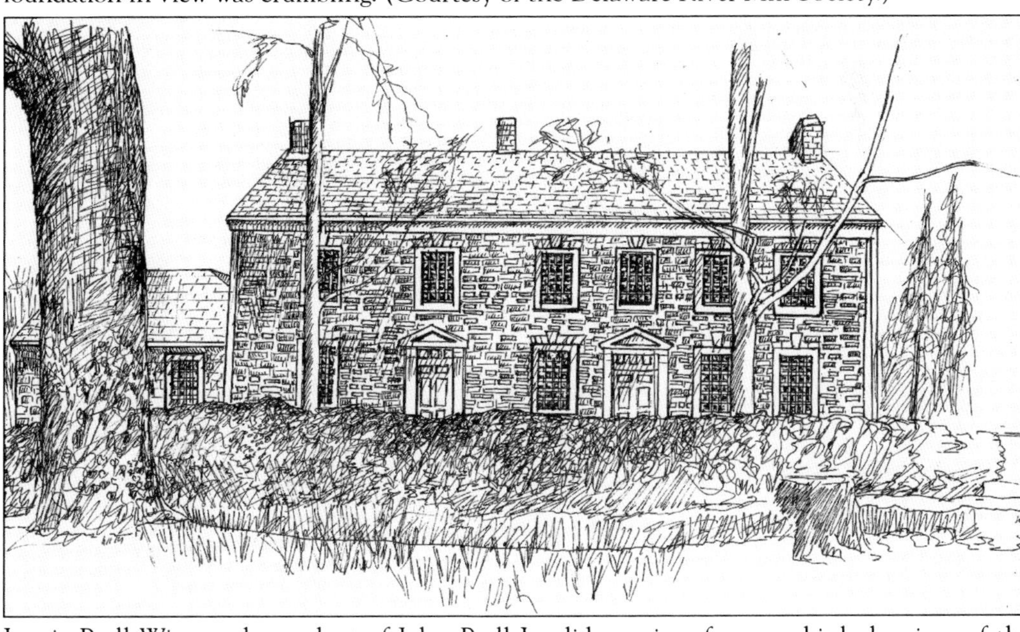

Jeanie Prall Wing, a descendent of John Prall Jr., did a series of pen-and-ink drawings of the Prallsville buildings that captured the simple beauty of the structures. This is the rear of the Prall manor house in which John Parker Prall was born in 1819. (Courtesy of Pieter Prall and Jeanie Prall Wing.)

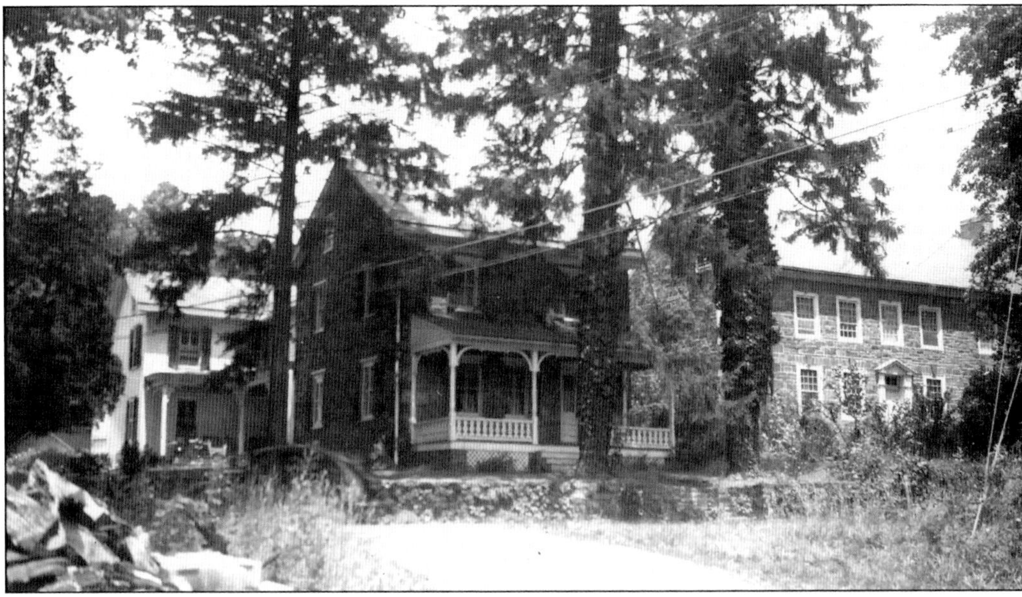

This stone house was built originally by John Prall Jr. as a general store and was the focus of his commercial activities and eventually served as the first Prallsville Post Office. William Hoppock converted the store into a residence around 1848 and moved the Prall store and post office to the linseed oil mill. (Courtesy of Pieter Prall and Jeanie Prall Wing.)

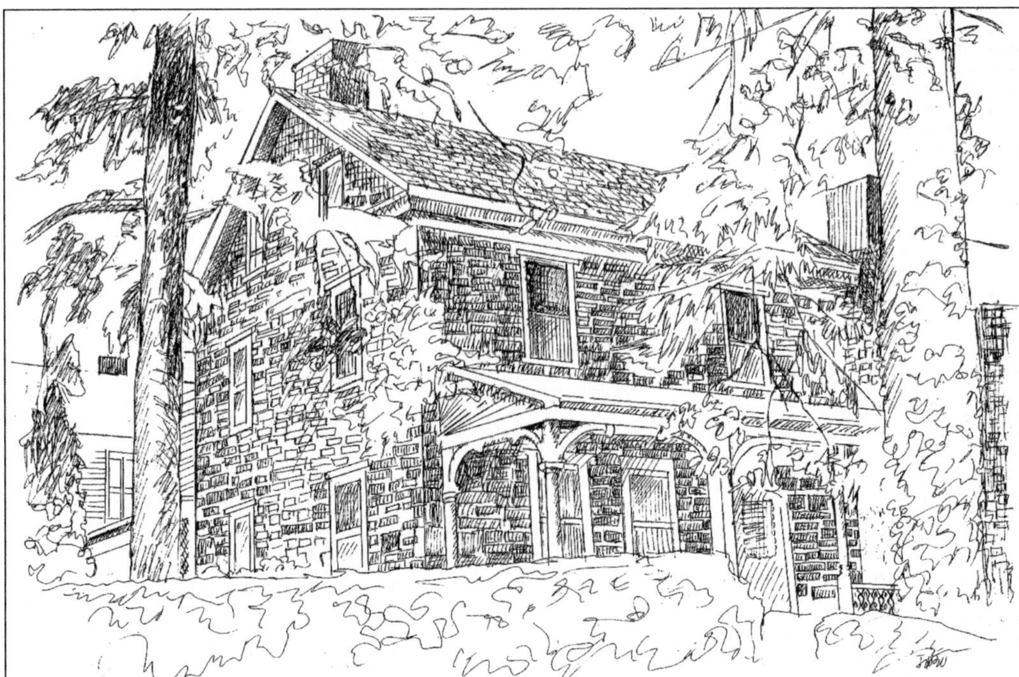

Soon after purchasing the mill property with his uncle Joseph Smith, John W. Smith added a wooden addition to the stone store and used it as his residence until his death in 1923. The era of the Smith family ownership would prove to be a prosperous one for the mill complex. (Courtesy of Pieter Prall and Jeanie Prall Wing.)

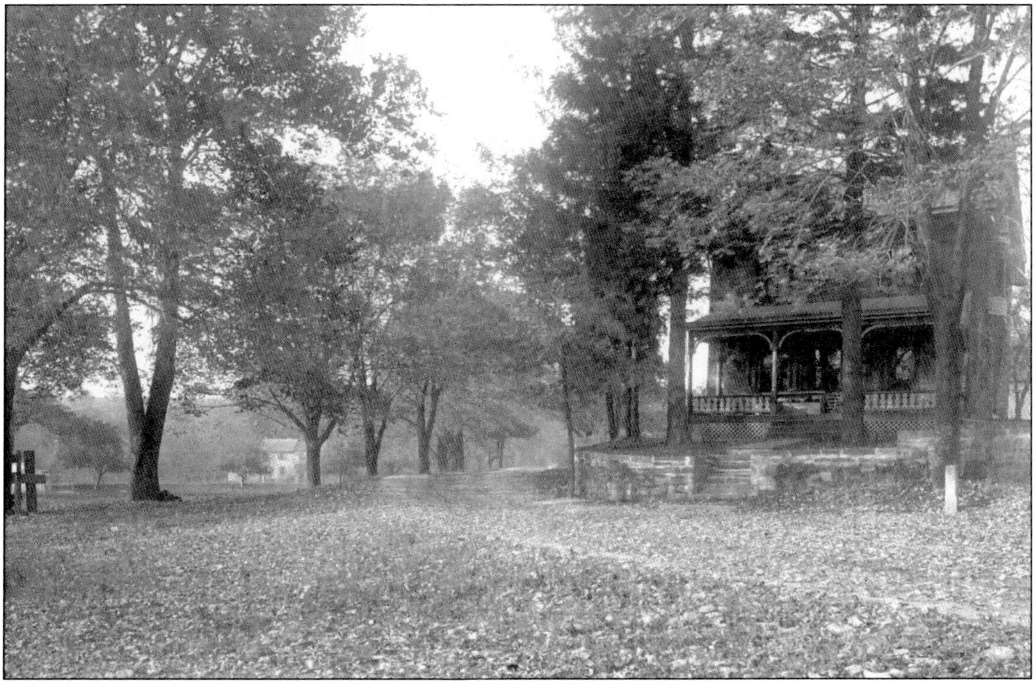

This tree-lined dirt road is the 1920s view of present-day Route 29 or River Road as the locals still call it. On the right is the Prall stone store, which has long since been converted to a residence. The miller's house is off in the distance on the left side of the photograph. (Courtesy of the Delaware River Mill Society.)

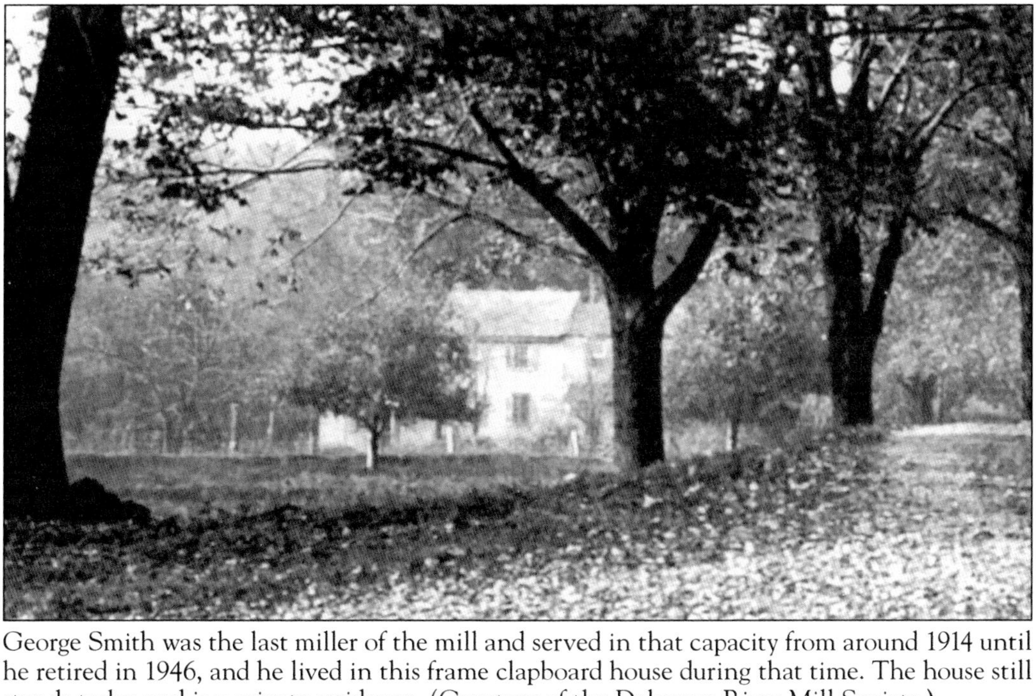

George Smith was the last miller of the mill and served in that capacity from around 1914 until he retired in 1946, and he lived in this frame clapboard house during that time. The house still stands today and is a private residence. (Courtesy of the Delaware River Mill Society.)

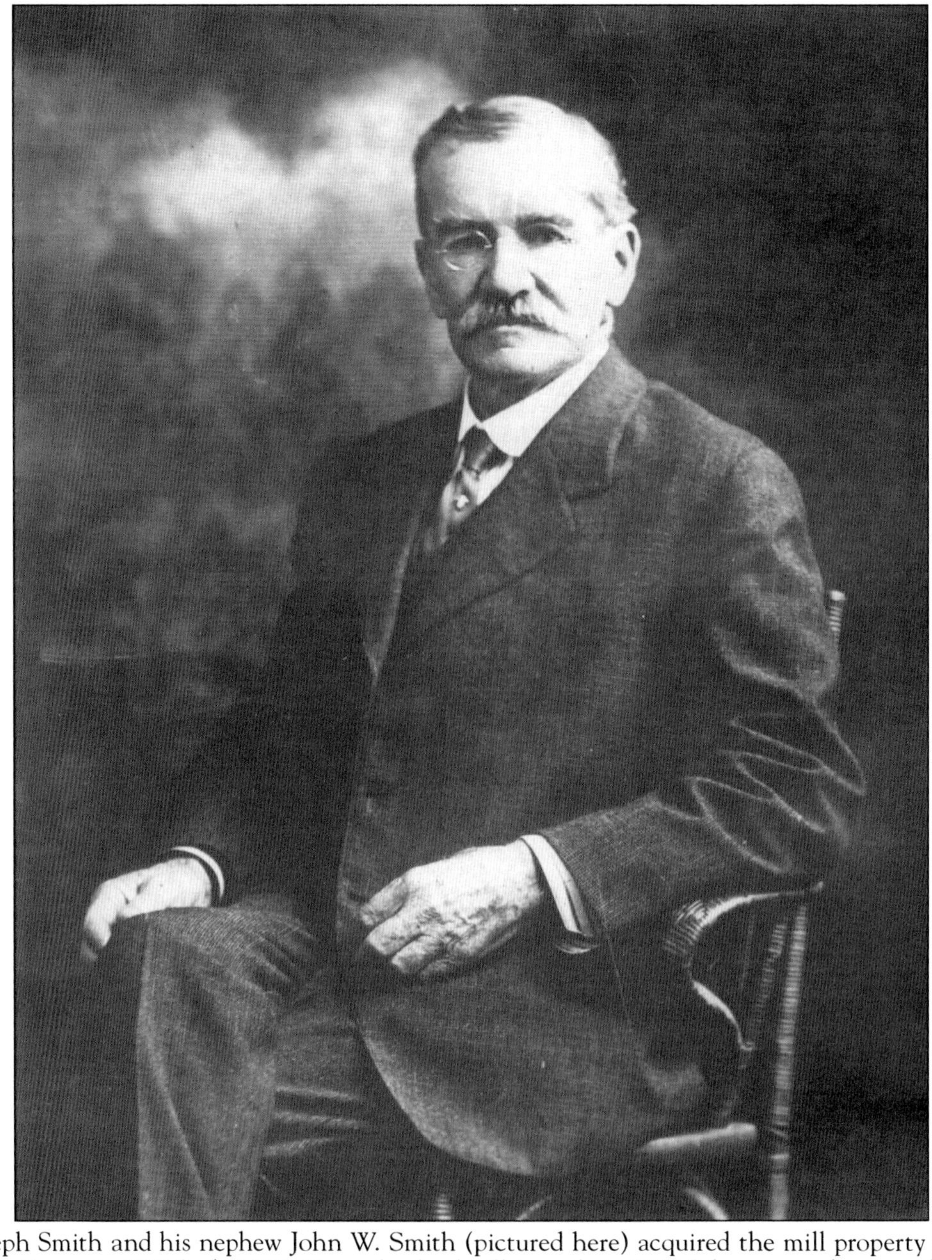

Joseph Smith and his nephew John W. Smith (pictured here) acquired the mill property from Stout Stover in 1883 for $19,000. Upon the death of his uncle in 1888, John assumed responsibility for the Joseph Smith and Company's industrial and commercial pursuits. John's sons, Charles and Joseph, were active in the business, which flourished during the decades before and after 1900. Among the improvements, a large frame granary was constructed, and an addition to the sawmill was built to increase its capacity. A bit of the Smith's business philosophy can be gleaned from the last sentence of a letter written during the Depression to a farmer who owed the company a large sum of money and could not pay. It read, "As I see it I cannot take any money with me when I leave this abode so why hasten the time (AS I have done before) by overwork. Under this new rule for my life I do what I can and the rest just goes over." (Courtesy of the Delaware River Mill Society.)

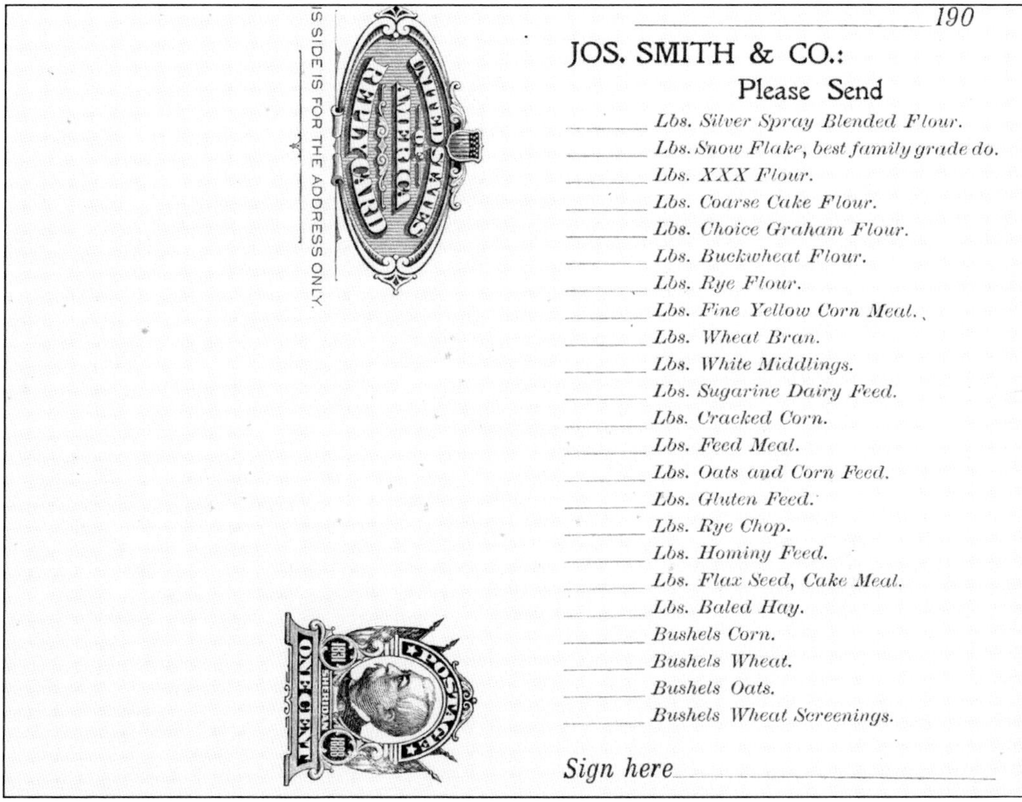

IS SIDE IS FOR THE ADDRESS ONLY.

UNITED STATES OF AMERICA REPLY CARD

POSTAGE SHERIDAN 1831 1888 ONE CENT

_______________190

JOS. SMITH & CO.:

Please Send

_______ *Lbs. Silver Spray Blended Flour.*

_______ *Lbs. Snow Flake, best family grade do.*

_______ *Lbs. XXX Flour.*

_______ *Lbs. Coarse Cake Flour.*

_______ *Lbs. Choice Graham Flour.*

_______ *Lbs. Buckwheat Flour.*

_______ *Lbs. Rye Flour.*

_______ *Lbs. Fine Yellow Corn Meal.*

_______ *Lbs. Wheat Bran.*

_______ *Lbs. White Middlings.*

_______ *Lbs. Sugarine Dairy Feed.*

_______ *Lbs. Cracked Corn.*

_______ *Lbs. Feed Meal.*

_______ *Lbs. Oats and Corn Feed.*

_______ *Lbs. Gluten Feed.*

_______ *Lbs. Rye Chop.*

_______ *Lbs. Hominy Feed.*

_______ *Lbs. Flax Seed, Cake Meal.*

_______ *Lbs. Baled Hay.*

_______ *Bushels Corn.*

_______ *Bushels Wheat.*

_______ *Bushels Oats.*

_______ *Bushels Wheat Screenings.*

*Sign here*_______________

An example of early direct mail marketing, Joseph Smith and Company sent these prestamped order cards to their potential and established customers in the first decade of the 20th century. The preprinted 1¢ stamp featured Civil War Union general Philip Henry Sheridan. (Courtesy of the Delaware River Mill Society.)

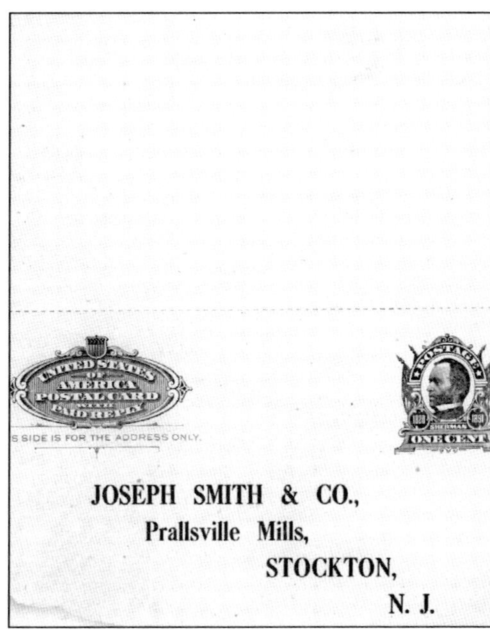

UNITED STATES OF AMERICA POSTAL CARD WITH PAID REPLY

S SIDE IS FOR THE ADDRESS ONLY.

POSTAGE SHERMAN 1820 1891 ONE CENT

JOSEPH SMITH & CO.,

Prallsville Mills,

STOCKTON,

N. J.

On the flip side of the mailer's order form was a preaddressed and stamped reply card that was perforated to be easily torn off and returned by mail to the mill. The 1¢ stamp on this side of the card featured Civil War Union general William Tecumseh Sherman. (Courtesy of the Delaware River Mill Society.)

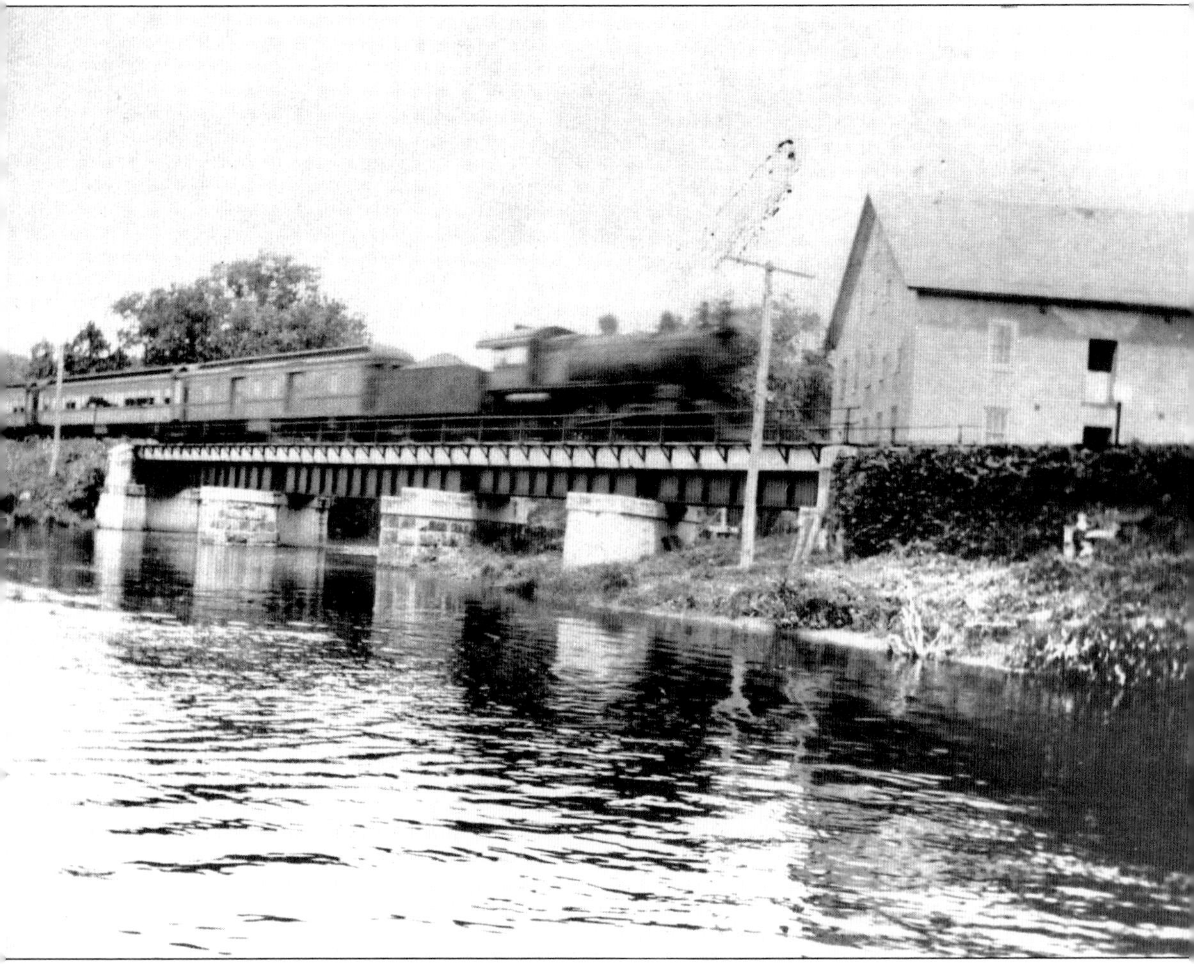

This *c.* 1920s shot of a passenger train rushing past the mill is the midday train. The family cook at Austin Davison's home would not start lunch until she heard the whistle of this train sound as it left Raven Rock at 11:00 a.m. If the train was running late, lunch would be late as well. The steam locomotives threw hot cinders and ash into the air as they passed close by the mill buildings. On one occasion, the cinders ignited the roof of the sawmill, threatening the building and the lumber stored within it. Although the local fire chief, who owned the bakery, could not respond right away because he had just put a fresh batch of bread into the ovens, quick action by the mill workers saved the building. In an effort to protect the buildings from such a calamity from happening again, the roofs of the building as well as the wooden sides of the silo were covered with metal siding to protect them from the hot cinders of the passing trains. (Courtesy of Carl Cathers.)

When they acquired the mill from Stout Stover, Joseph and John Smith agreed to assume full responsibility for an $8,000 mortgage held by Samuel Stover. This receipt, dated April 10, 1883, and signed by Stout Stover, is for $100 to cover the interest on the mortgage for the first quarter of 1883. (Courtesy of the Delaware River Mill Society.)

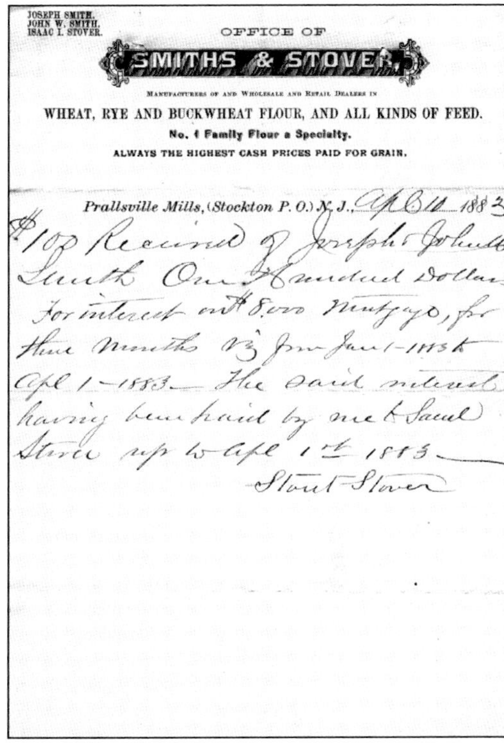
JOSEPH SMITH.
JOHN W. SMITH.
ISAAC I. STOVER.

OFFICE OF
SMITHS & STOVER,
MANUFACTURERS OF AND WHOLESALE AND RETAIL DEALERS IN
WHEAT, RYE AND BUCKWHEAT FLOUR, AND ALL KINDS OF FEED.
No. 1 Family Flour a Specialty.
ALWAYS THE HIGHEST CASH PRICES PAID FOR GRAIN.

Prallsville Mills, (Stockton P. O.) N. J., Apl 10 1883

$100 Received of Joseph & John Smith One Hundred Dollars For interest on $8000 Mortgage, for three months viz from Jan 1-1883 to Apl 1-1883 — The said interest having been paid by me to Saml Stover up to Apl 1st 1883 —

Stout Stover

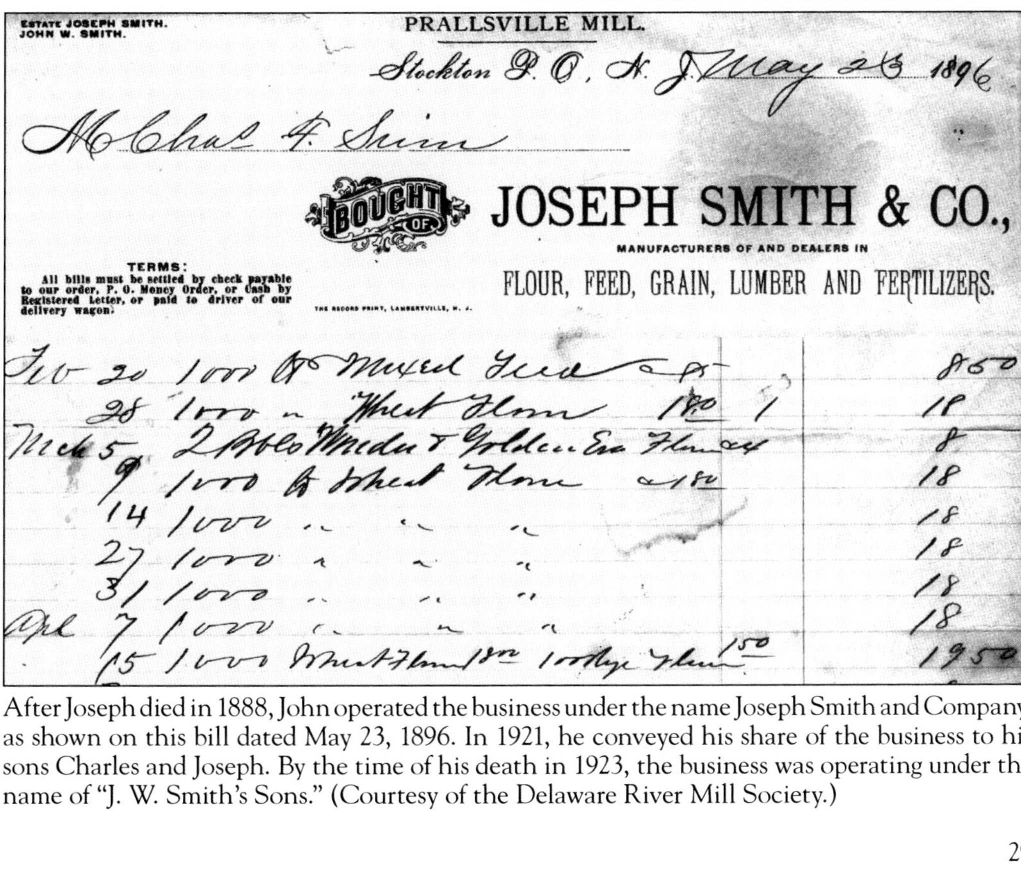
ESTATE JOSEPH SMITH.
JOHN W. SMITH.

PRALLSVILLE MILL.
Stockton P. O., N. J. May 23 1896

M Chas F. Sinn

BOUGHT OF JOSEPH SMITH & CO.,
MANUFACTURERS OF AND DEALERS IN
FLOUR, FEED, GRAIN, LUMBER AND FERTILIZERS.

TERMS:
All bills must be settled by check payable to our order, P. O. Money Order, or Cash by Registered Letter, or paid to driver of our delivery wagon.

THE RECORD PRINT, LAMBERTVILLE, N. J.

Feb 20 1000 lb Mixed Feed @ 85 — 850
28 1000 " Wheat Flour 180 — 18
Mch 5 2 Bbls Meadow & Golden Era Flour @ 4 — 8
9 1000 lb Wheat Flour @ 180 — 18
14 1000 " " " — 18
27 1000 " " " — 18
31 1000 " " " — 18
Apl 7 1000 " " " — 18
15 1000 Wheat Flour 180 1000 Rye Flour 150 — 1950

After Joseph died in 1888, John operated the business under the name Joseph Smith and Company, as shown on this bill dated May 23, 1896. In 1921, he conveyed his share of the business to his sons Charles and Joseph. By the time of his death in 1923, the business was operating under the name of "J. W. Smith's Sons." (Courtesy of the Delaware River Mill Society.)

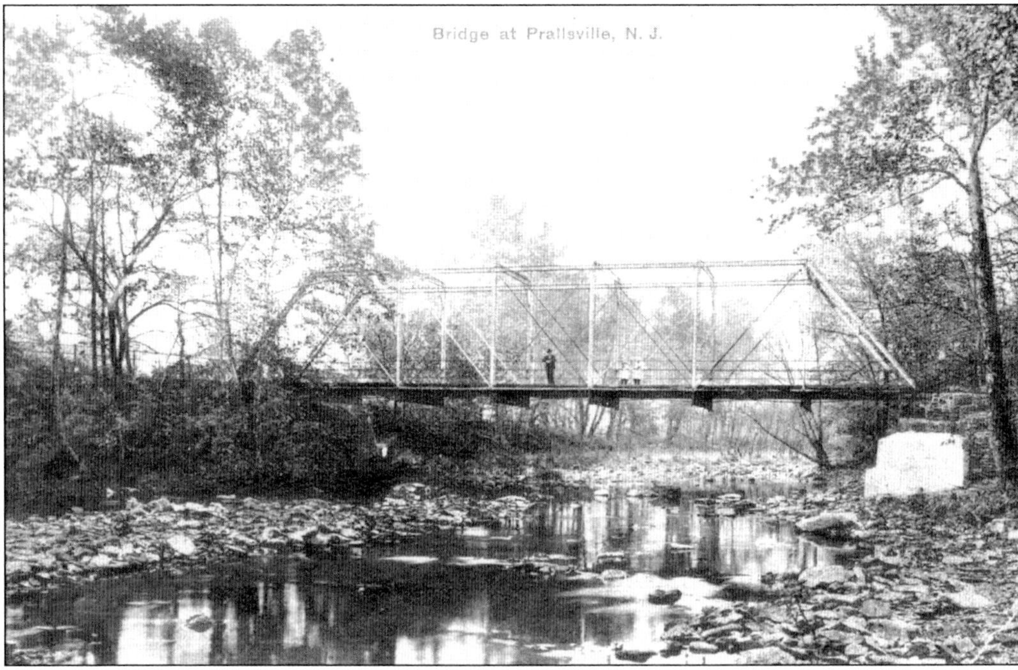

The "Bridge at Prallsville, N.J." as seen in this early-1900s postcard was the crossing for River Road over the Wickecheoke Creek just north of the mills complex. Although the bridge no longer exists, the stone foundations for the bridge can still be seen on the banks of the creek. (Courtesy of Carl Cathers.)

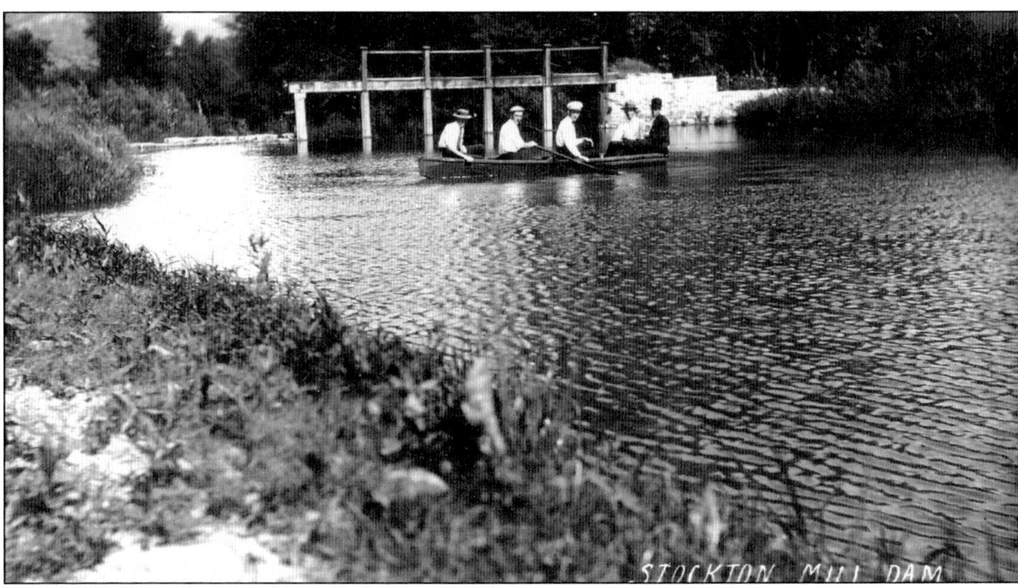

Although this 1920s postcard showing a group of men in a boat indicates that the location is the Stockton Mill Dam, it is not certain that this is correct. The date is somewhat easier to place as the man sitting third from the right is probably wearing a World War I campaign hat. (Courtesy of the Delaware River Mill Society.)

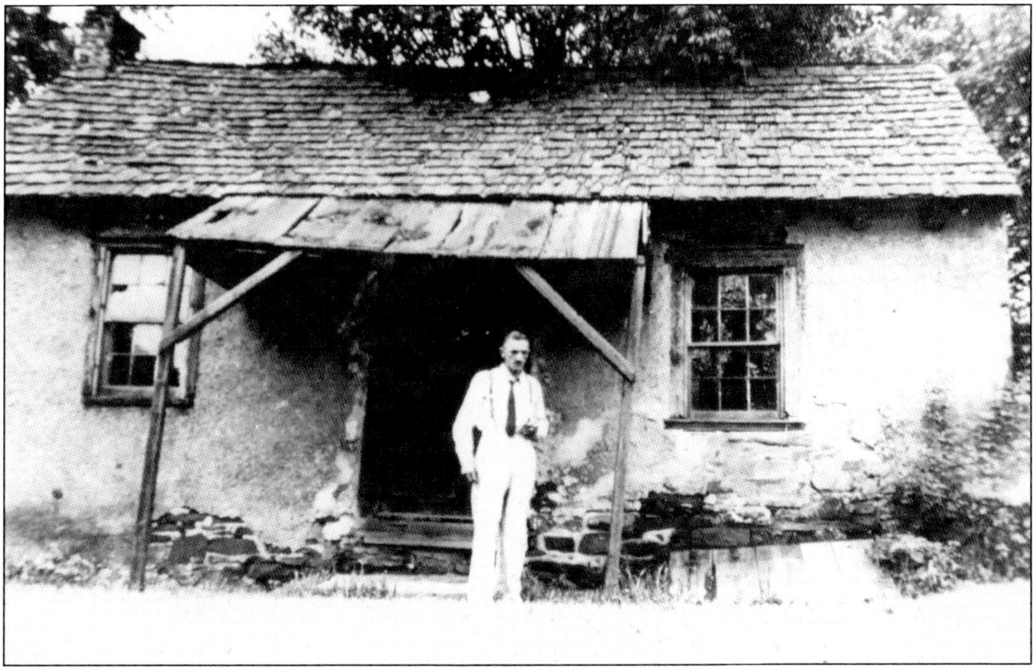

This 1936 photograph of the servant's quarters next to the Prall manor house shows Joe Russo Sr. standing in front of his birthplace. He was born February 18, 1895, and, according to the inscription on the back of the photograph, "his father built [the] railroad for the quarry." (Courtesy of Carl Cathers.)

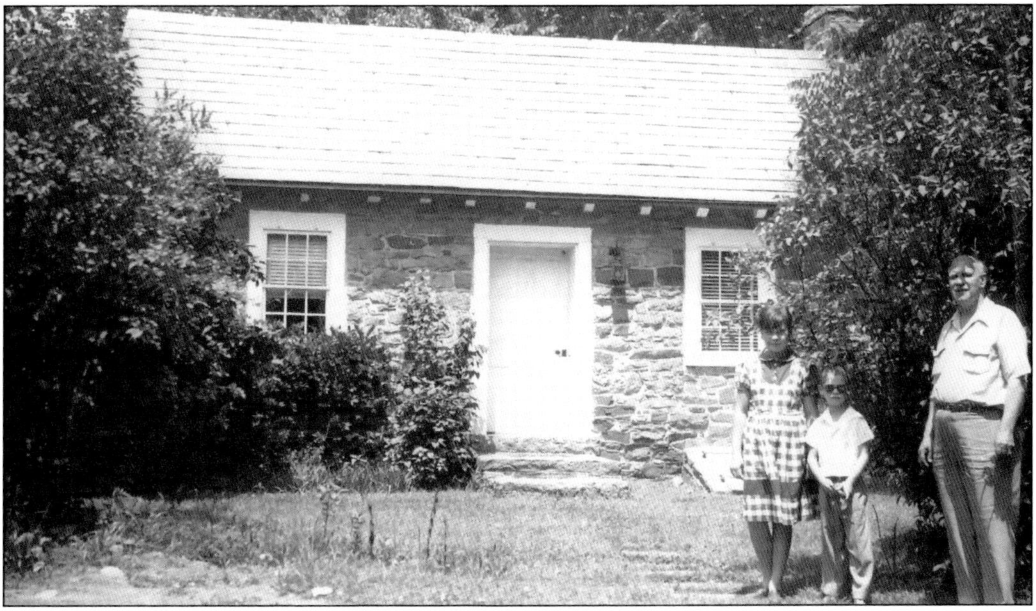

The servant's quarters had been completely refurbished by the time this early-1950s picture was taken. On this beautiful summer day, John Prall Jr.'s great-great-grandson William Russell Prall Jr. explored the mills complex with his grandchildren, Jonathan and Jeanie Prall. Some 20 years later, Jeanie would create the drawings of the buildings that appear in this book. (Courtesy of Pieter Prall and Jeanie Prall Wing.)

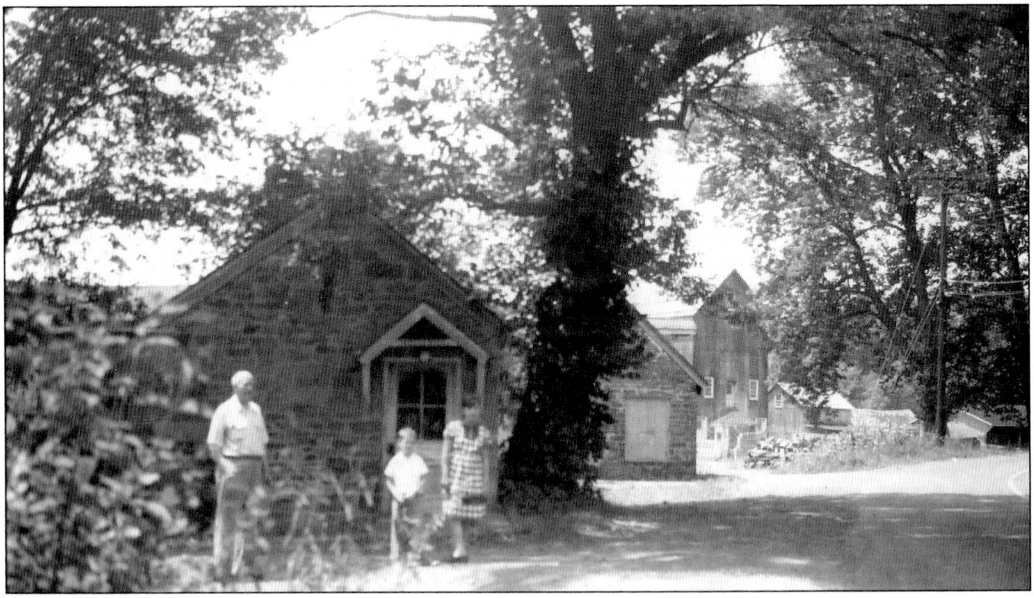

Here William, Jonathan, and Jeanie Prall stand in front of the smokehouse. Behind them can be seen the corner of the linseed oil mill and the silo, which at the time of the photograph, was operating as a hardware and building supply store. (Courtesy of Pieter Prall and Jeanie Prall Wing.)

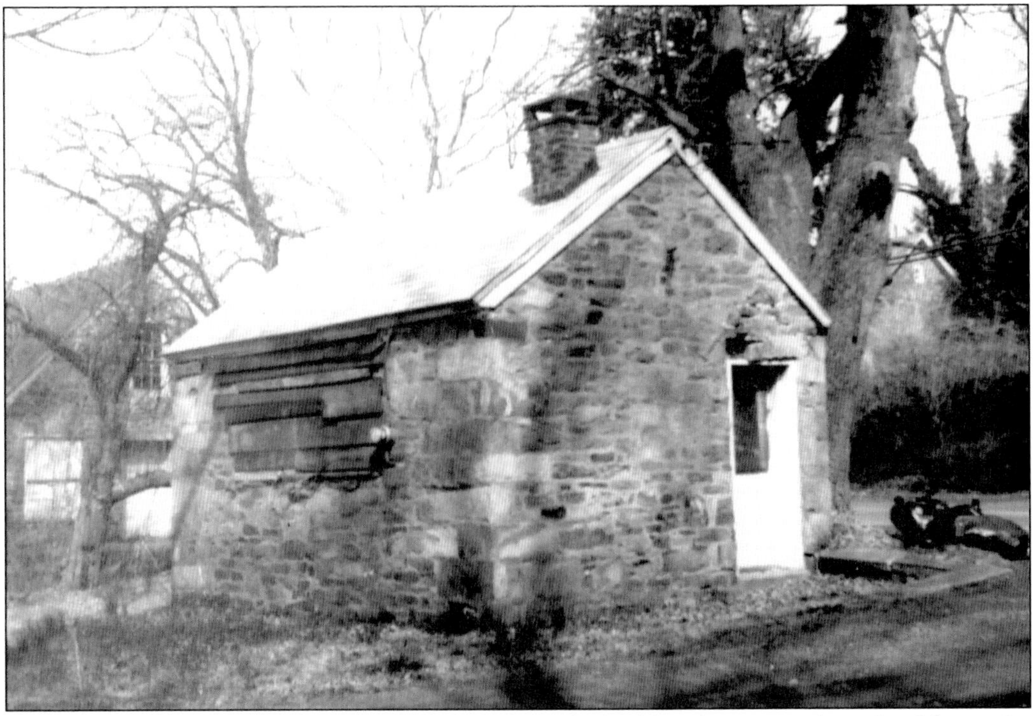

Having not only served as a smokehouse in its past, the building later served as a bunkhouse for the Italian immigrants who worked as stonecutters in the quarry and finally, an office for the last operators of the quarry. By the time of this photograph in 1976, the smokehouse, its windows boarded up, had fallen into disrepair. (Courtesy of the Delaware River Mill Society.)

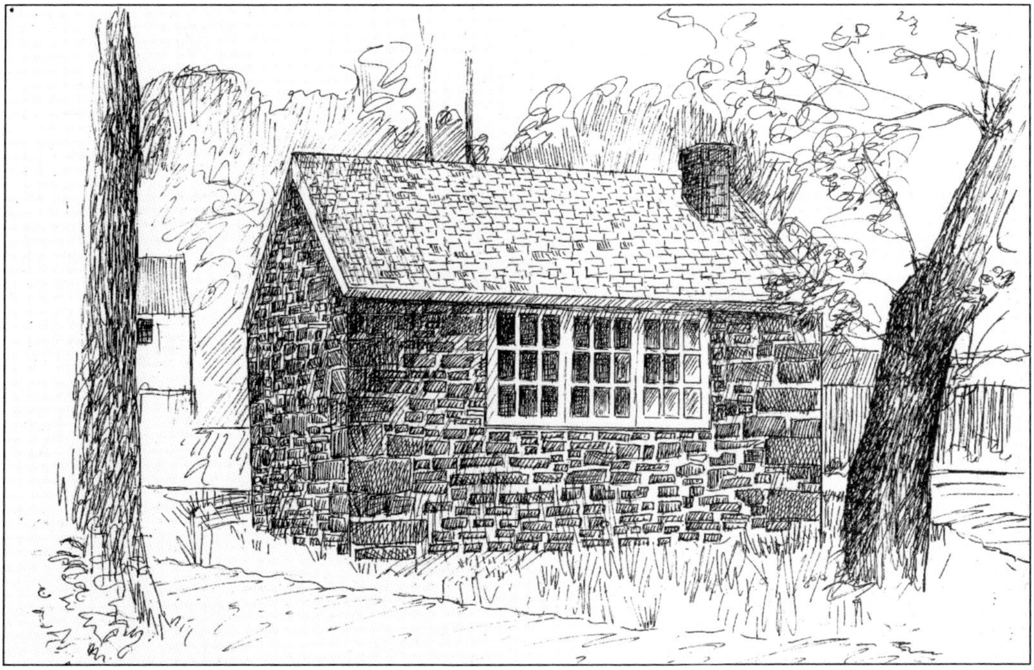

Refurbished by the artist's hand in this early-1970s drawing by Jeanie Prall Wing, the building, which was described in the November 10, 1823, edition of the Trenton newspaper the *True American* as "a frame smoke and pork house and large stone smoke house," is now the visitor center for the Prallsville Mills. (Courtesy of Pieter Prall and Jeanie Prall Wing.)

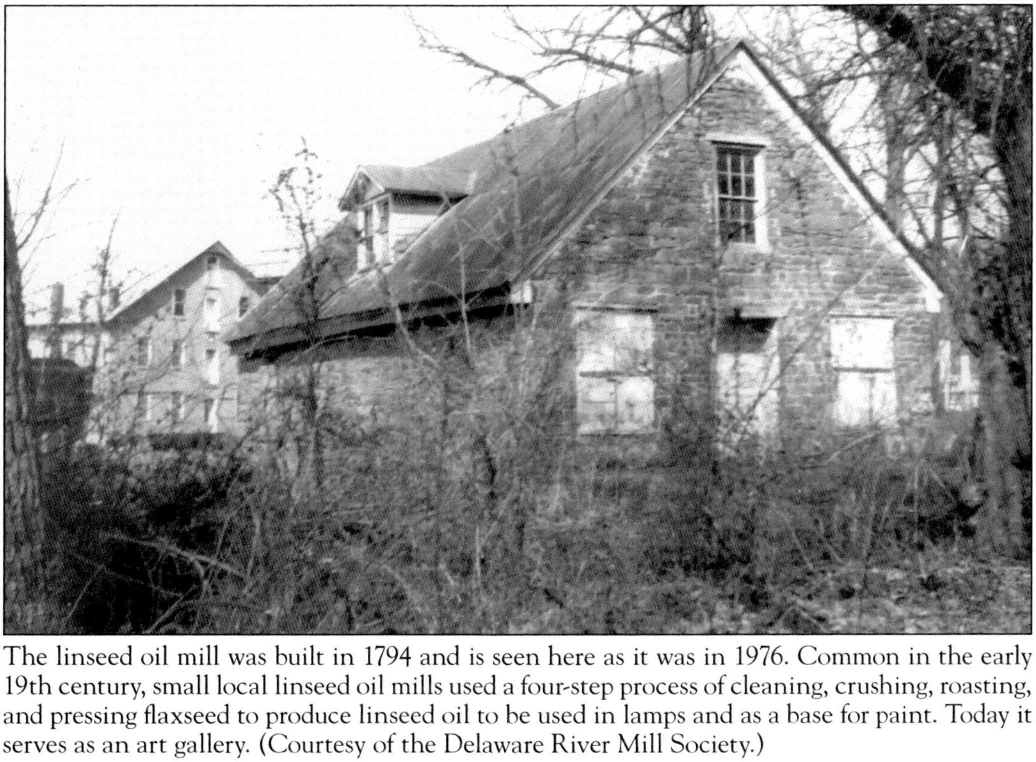

The linseed oil mill was built in 1794 and is seen here as it was in 1976. Common in the early 19th century, small local linseed oil mills used a four-step process of cleaning, crushing, roasting, and pressing flaxseed to produce linseed oil to be used in lamps and as a base for paint. Today it serves as an art gallery. (Courtesy of the Delaware River Mill Society.)

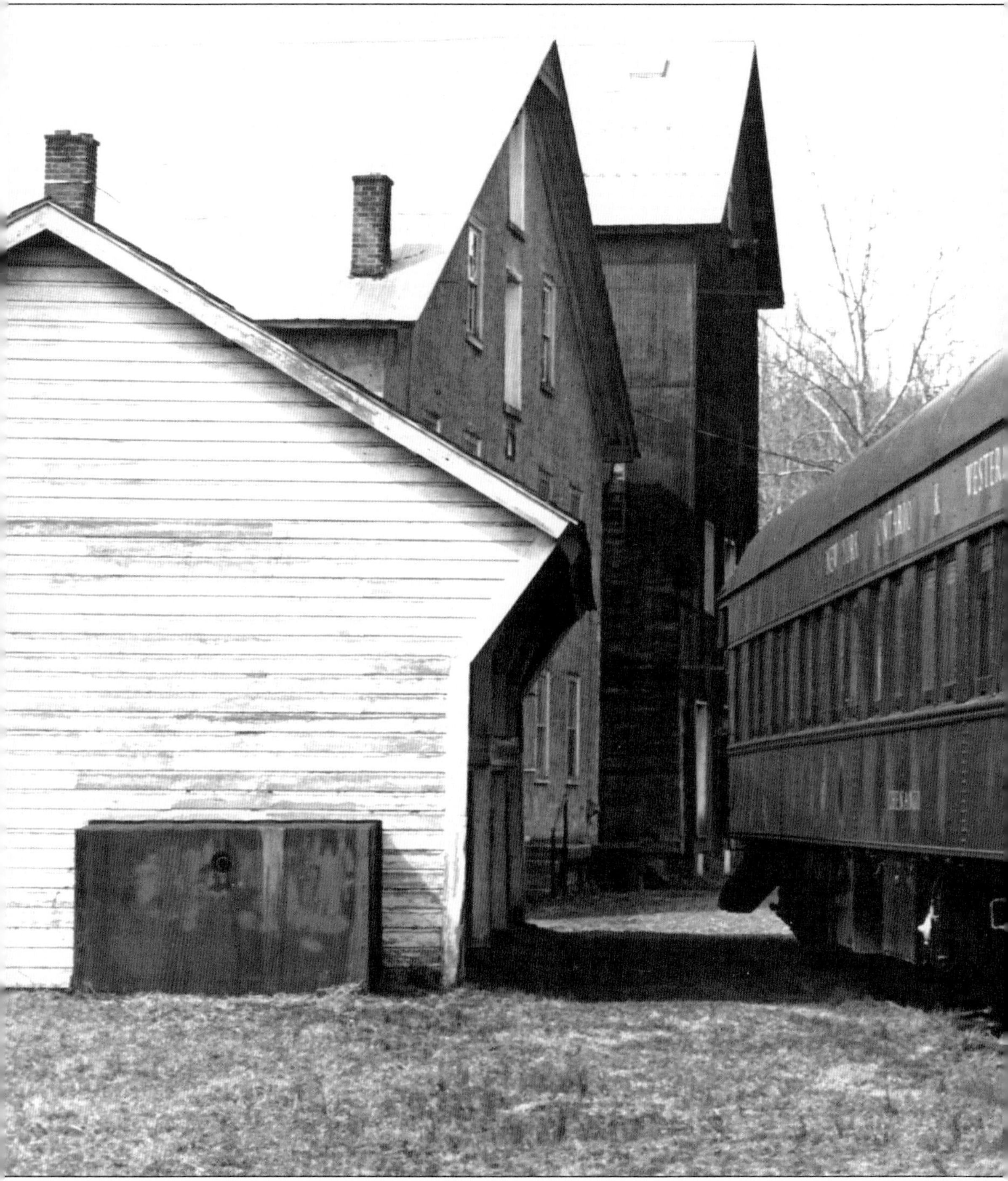

By the late 1960s, the mill buildings and this passenger railroad car were relics of an age that had been passed by as the larger world rushed into the future. Fortunately for all, there were those who paused long enough to preserve these pieces of society's collective history, so the lessons of the past could continue to provide wisdom and perspective for the future. At the time of this photograph, a gentleman was working to restore the passenger car that was moved to a larger

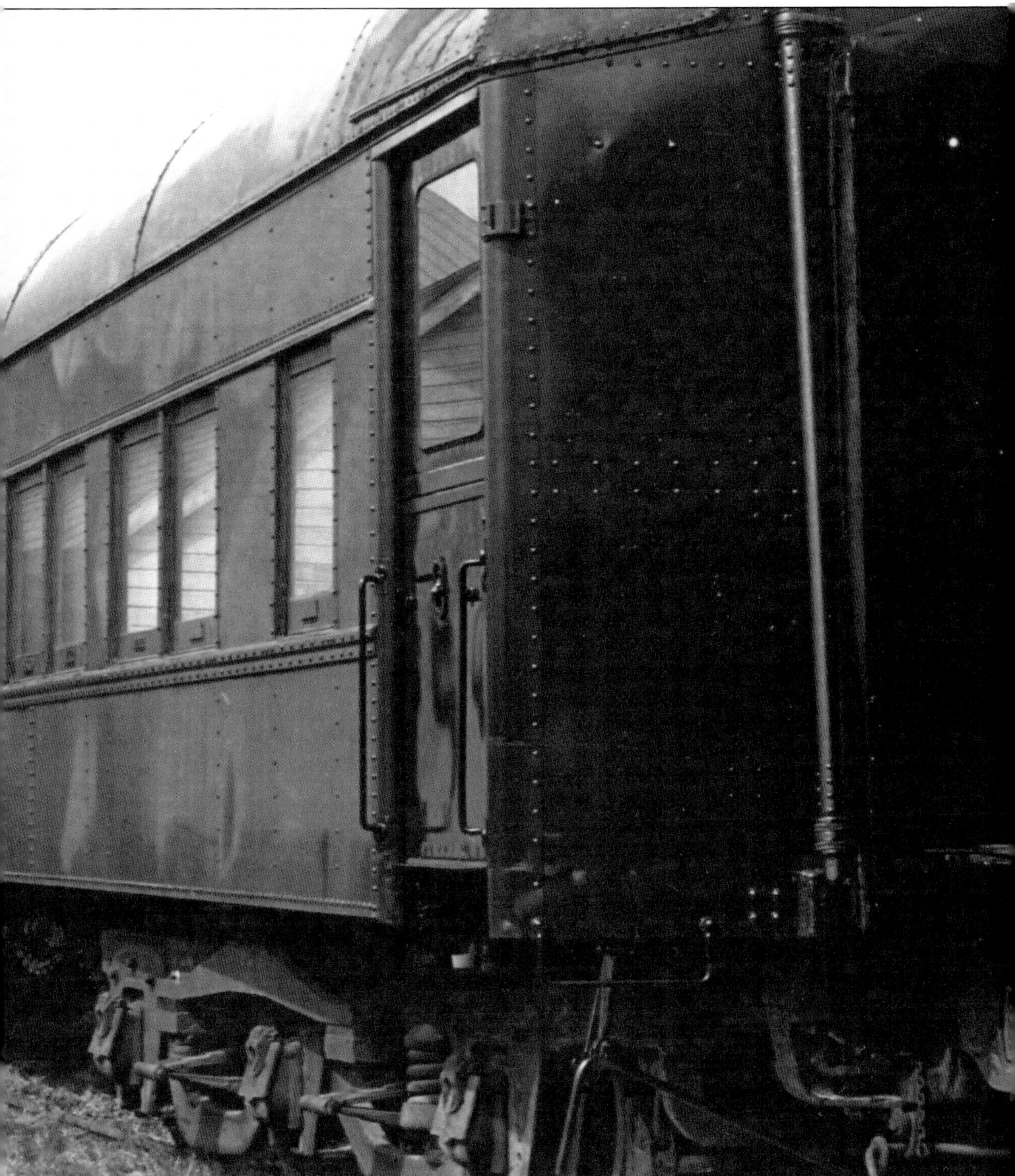

train yard so he could continue his work after the state acquired the mill property. In the case of the Prallsville Mills, it was the vision of conservationist Donald B. Jones that saved it from being lost among the turned pages of time. (Photograph by Michael Slack, courtesy of the Delaware River Mill Society.)

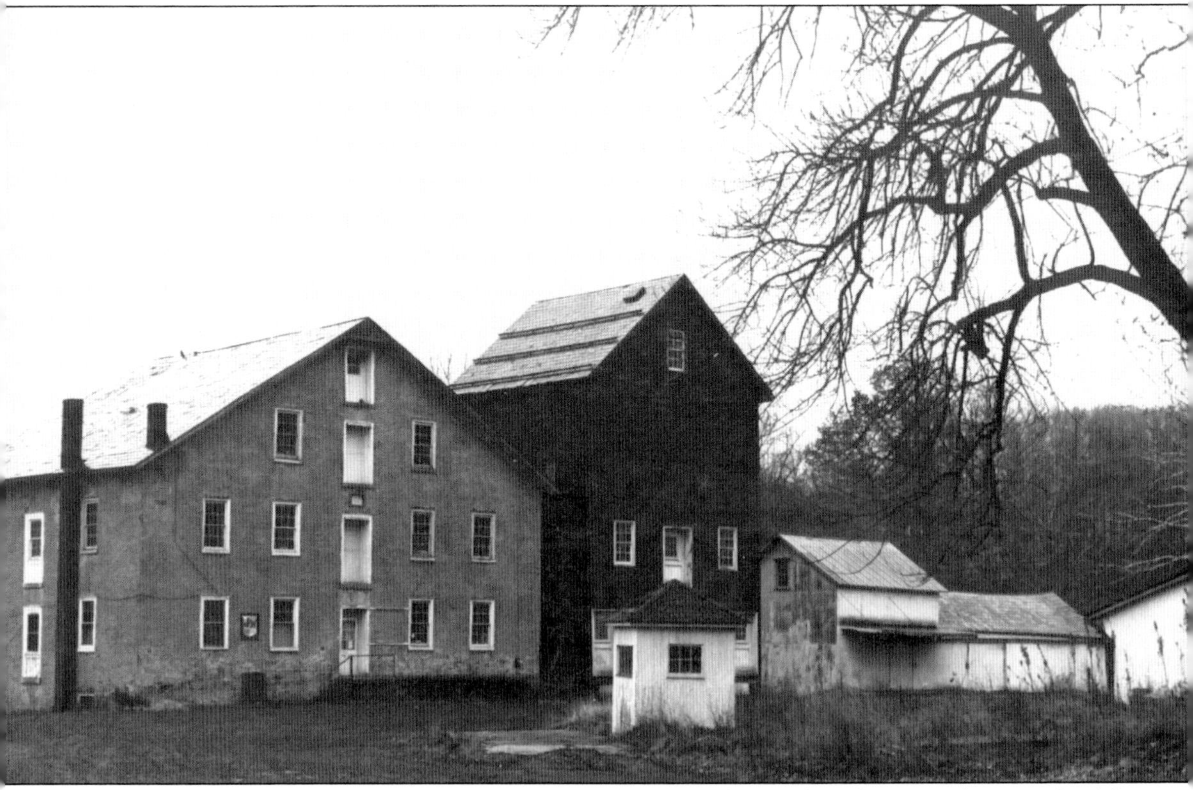

By 1968, the mill's commercial businesses were shut down for good. In this 1976 photograph of the property the gristmill (left), the silo next to it, the small scale house (foreground), and the stables (right) stand abandoned, the only visible remnant of its commercial past is the S&H Green Stamps sign hanging on the gristmill wall. In 1969, the property was sold to Donald B. Jones by the three grandchildren of John W. Smith, Edgar S. Smith, Joseph Smith Jr., and Eva Graham. Jones's purpose in purchasing the property was to transfer ownership to the state so it could be preserved. In 1973, the property was transferred to the New Jersey Department of Environmental Protection (NJDEP) for that purpose. Starting in 1976, the NJDEP entered into lease agreements with the Delaware River Mill Society, which had been formed to further the preservation of the mill complex. In this photograph, the Prallsville Mills complex stands poised to move into the next chapter of its nearly 300-year story. (Courtesy of the Delaware River Mill Society.)

Two

THE PRALL FAMILY

Pieter Prall is the great-great-great-great-grandson of John Prall Jr. He opens this chapter on his family with some personal recollections and his observations about history:

> I remember my great aunt Marion Prall showing my younger brother Jamie and me treasures that she had in her attic: an original copy of the Declaration of Independence and letters that George Washington wrote to my great-great-great-great-grandfather John Prall Jr. There were the pistols that he had used during the American Revolution and the hand-written record that he kept, relating to the fateful event in 1776, when members of the New Jersey Militia and the greater Delaware River community saved the American Revolutionary effort by helping to get Washington's beleaguered army across the Delaware River to a successful rout and capture of the Hessian garrison at Trenton, Christmas night 1776.
>
> There were stories having to do with John Prall Jr.'s activities during the revolution. How he fought at the Battles of Germantown and Monmouth. How he worked with Bray, the Coryells, and others at the Christmas night crossing and stories of other accomplishments.
>
> A friend who used to listen to my brother Jamie speak quite proudly of our family history in class has since told me that she "could have died" back then, wanting to have been there with our ancestors at "the crossing." Our being related to other historic moments added to the intrigue for her.
>
> History is important to all. It is an agglomeration of moments that have somehow been recorded. My ancestors were here and their activities were recorded. We are fortunate here in the United States to have the opportunity to participate in forming the future.
>
> My family itself is fortunate, as people like the late Austin Davison and Donald Jones and the Delaware River Mill Society have preserved the picturesque place called Prallsville—a place that we as a family left so long ago.
>
> Thank you,
> Pieter Prall.

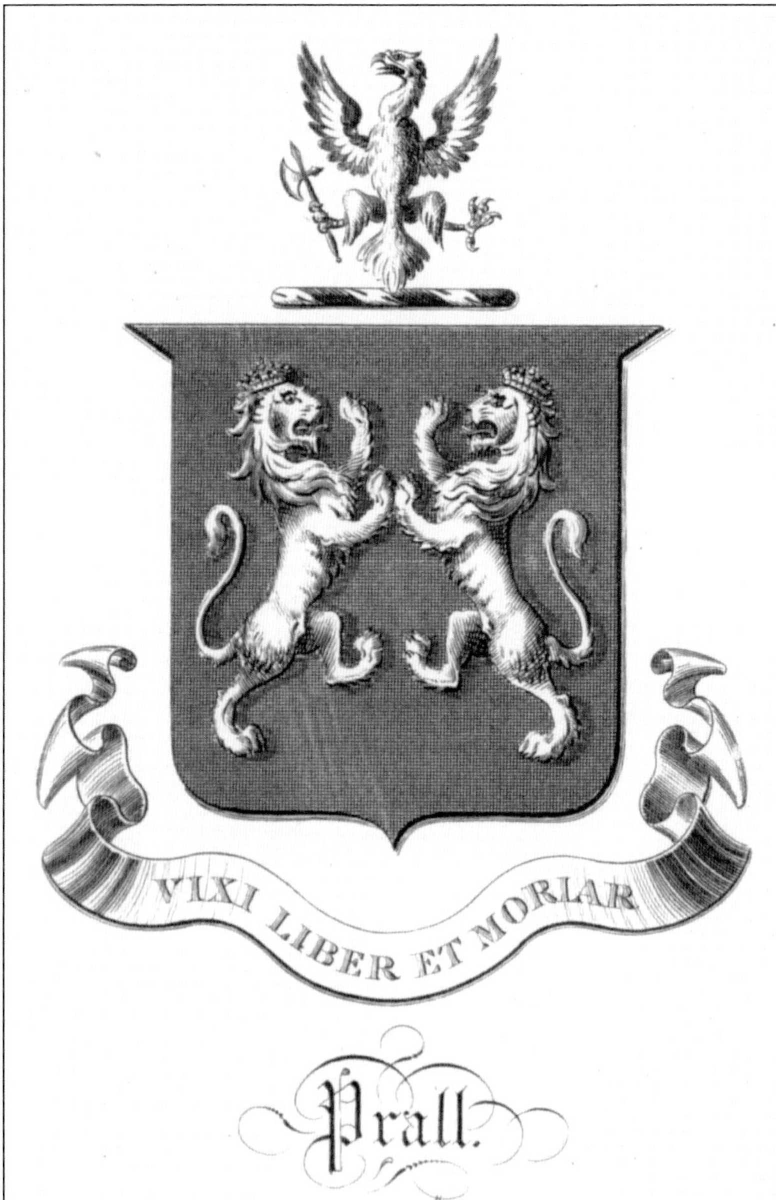

Brought to America in 1660 by Arendt Praal who was the first member of the family to arrive here, this coat of arms is one of the earliest French coat of arms, consisting of a sable shield with two silver lions and is the coat of Clovis. The arms and motto were added much later, and like the current spelling of the family name, are most likely English. The motto *Vixi liber et moriar* translates as "I have lived and will die a free man." John Prall Jr. was born on September 20, 1756, in Hunterdon County and was the fifth generation of Pralls in America. He fought in the Revolutionary War, rising through the ranks to lieutenant, was wounded at the Battle of Millstone, and later returned to duty to fight at the Battles of Germantown and Monmouth. Prall married Amelia Coryell in 1785 and had seven children, Letitia, William Livingston, Elizabeth (who died at age two), Sarah, Frances (who died at age four), Elizabeth, and John Coryell (who died at age nine). (Courtesy of Pieter Prall and Jeanie Prall Wing.)

Amelia Prall, granddaughter of Emmanuel Coryell, daughter of John Coryell, and wife of John Prall Jr., was born in 1758 and died in 1845. Her grandfather's ferry, which ran between present-day Lambertville, New Jersey, and New Hope, Pennsylvania, was known as Coryell's Ferry. Brother George's tombstone in nearby Lambertville indicates that George was a pall bearer at George Washington's funeral. (Courtesy of the Delaware River Mill Society.)

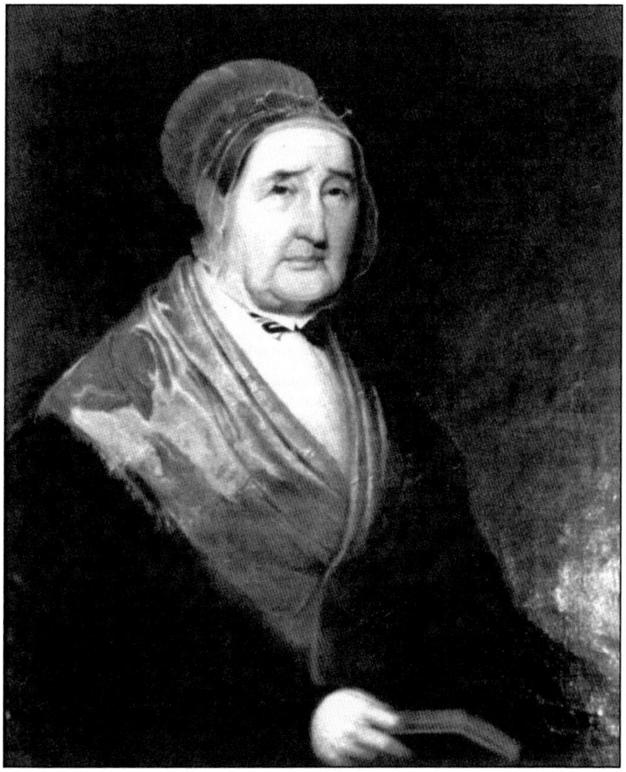

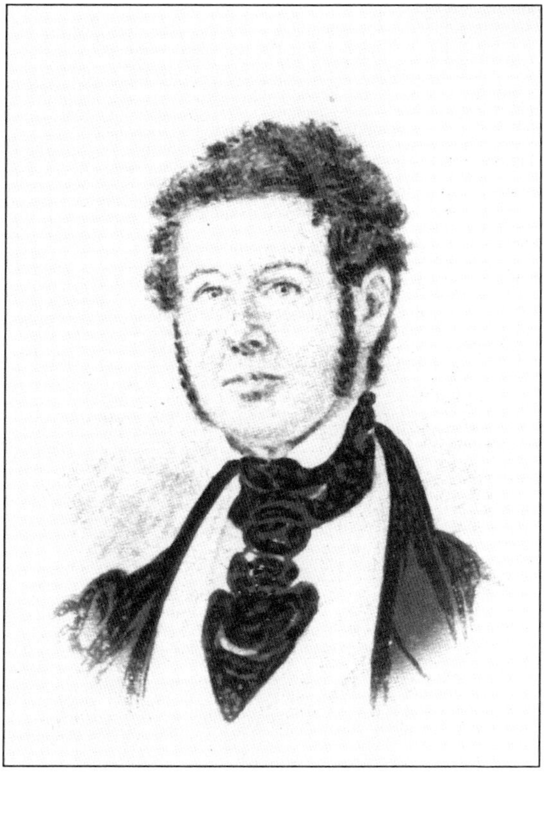

William Livingston Prall, son of John and Amelia, was born in Prallsville in 1788. He was a member of the state legislature and acting governor of New Jersey on a number of occasions. William published the *True American* in Trenton and later moved to New York City. He died in 1848 and is buried in the Green-Wood Cemetery in Brooklyn, New York. (Courtesy of Pieter Prall and Jeanie Prall Wing.)

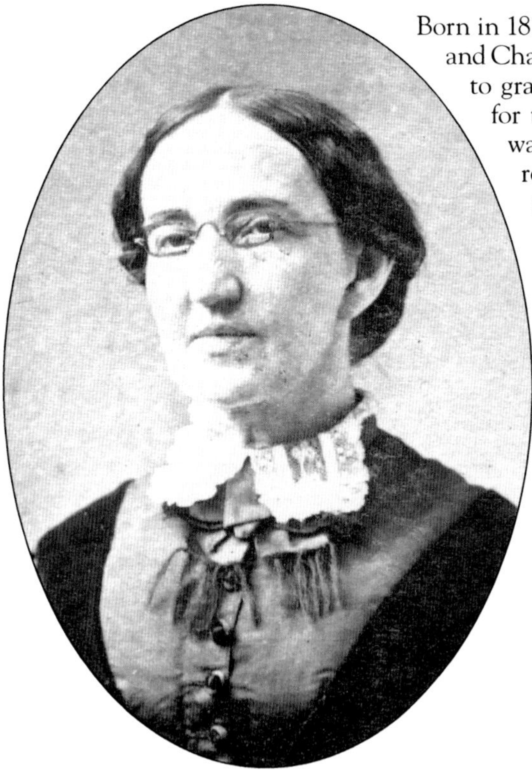

Born in 1816, Elizabeth Smith Prall, daughter of William and Charlotte Prall, was part of the first class of women to graduate from Oberlin College and salutatorian for the commencement on August 25, 1841. She was among the first women in this country to receive bachelor's degrees and to graduate from a coeducational college course. Elizabeth died in 1869. (Courtesy of Pieter Prall and Jeanie Prall Wing.)

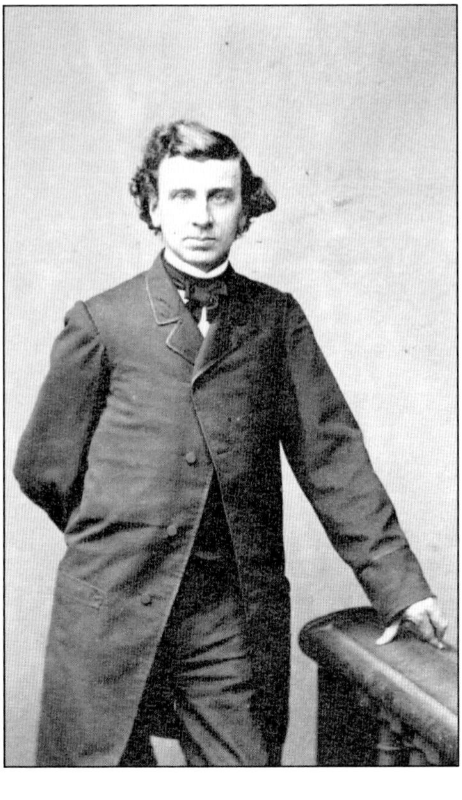

John Parker Prall, son of William and Charlotte, was born in 1819 in Prallsville. In 1844, he married Elizabeth Mary Wheaton. He became a publisher in New York City, was very active in the Presbyterian Church, and wrote a memoir about his childhood in Prallsville. He died in 1891 and was buried in Green-Wood Cemetery in Brooklyn, New York. (Courtesy of Pieter Prall and Jeanie Prall Wing.)

Pictured here at age 70, John wrote of Prallsville, "the stone mill and store [John Prall Jr.] built as if intended for forts. The fisheries, 'Quickstep' and 'Tadpole,' below the mills on the Delaware, in those early days yielded large quantities of shad and other fish, and in our boyish days were full of interest to us." (Courtesy of the Delaware River Mill Society.)

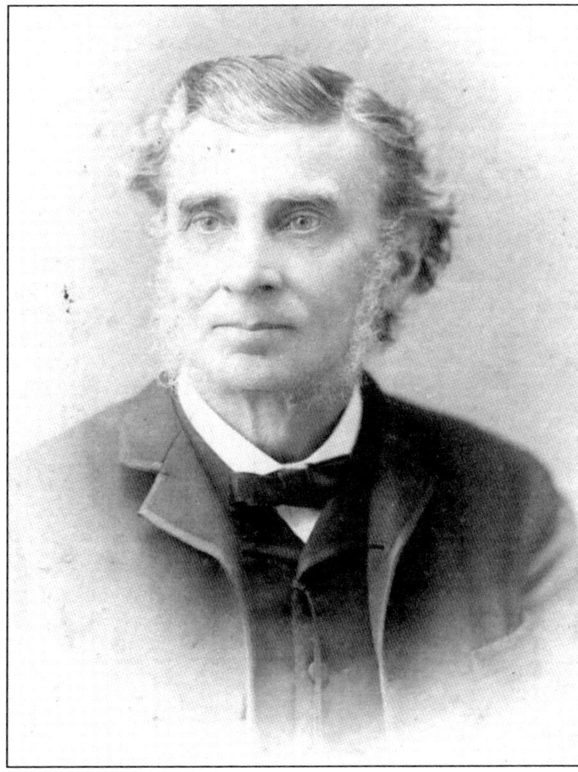

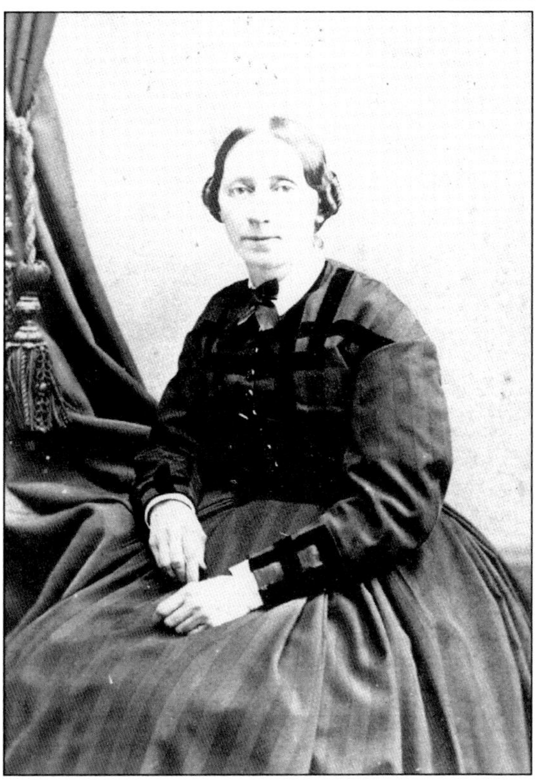

John's wife, Elizabeth, is pictured in this c. 1860 photograph. Family legend has it that her brother Rufus Wheaton went to San Francisco in search of gold. From there, he followed the gold rush to Alaska and was never heard from again. (Courtesy of Pieter Prall and Jeanie Prall Wing.)

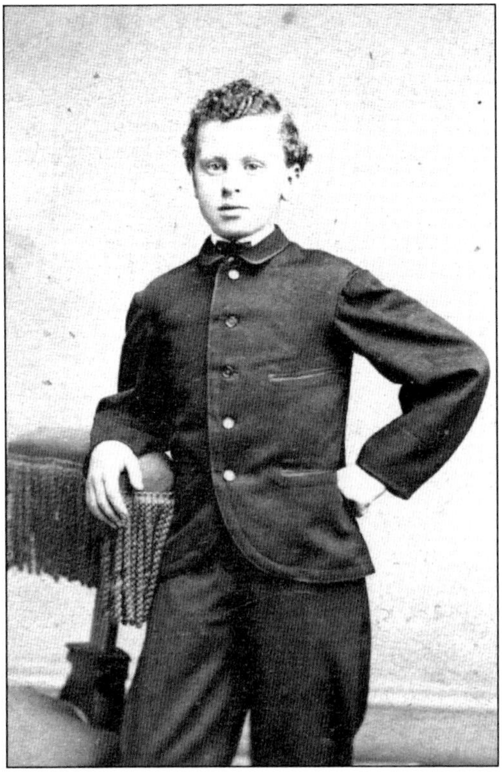

John Howard Prall, son of John Parker Prall, was born in 1855 and grew up to own a seat on the New York Stock Exchange. Known for holding his deep understanding of the markets close to the vest, John Howard earned the moniker the "Sphinx of Wall Street" after the mythical creature that knew much and shared little. He died on March 13, 1918. (Courtesy of Pieter Prall and Jeanie Prall Wing.)

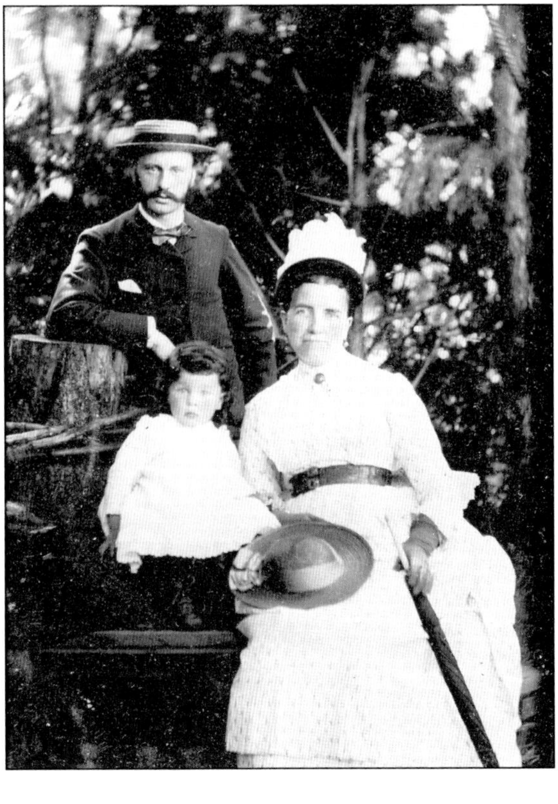

This tintype, from around 1883, pictures John Howard and his wife, Sarah Goldsmith Prall, whom he married in 1881, with their son John Goldsmith Prall. Sarah, born in 1844, only outlived her husband by five months, dying on August 21, 1918. Their son John Goldsmith, born in 1882, died at the age of 24 on April 22, 1907, in a tragic horse-riding accident. (Courtesy of Pieter Prall and Jeanie Prall Wing.)

Mary Coryell Prall, daughter of John Parker, was born on July 5, 1859. These photographs show Mary at ages 7 and 26. Extremely photogenic, she seems to have an intuitive understanding of what was for her a new technology, giving her a startlingly modern look. She married Abram Proctor Jr. on June 18, 1884. They had two children, Mary Elizabeth Proctor, born in 1889, and Laura Prall Proctor, born in 1890. Mary Coryell died on April 1, 1949, a few months before her 90th birthday. (Courtesy of Pieter Prall and Jeanie Prall Wing.)

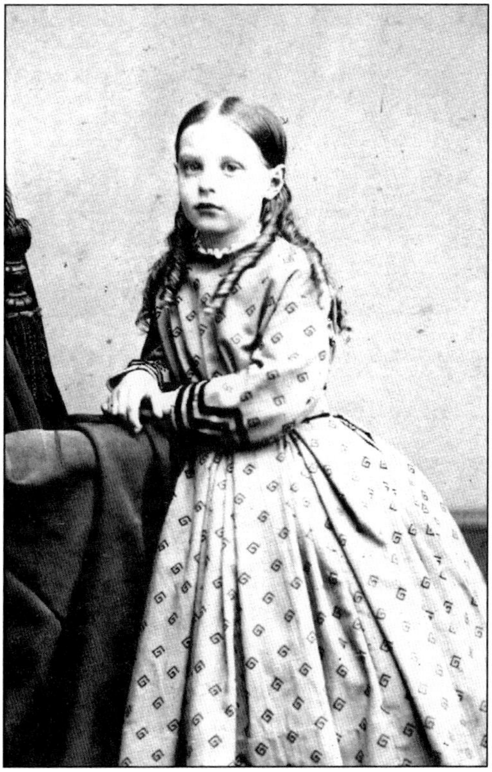

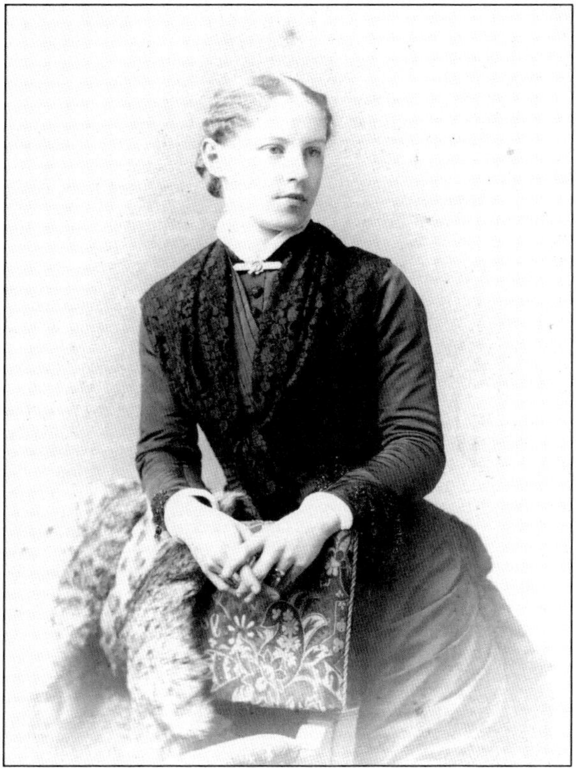

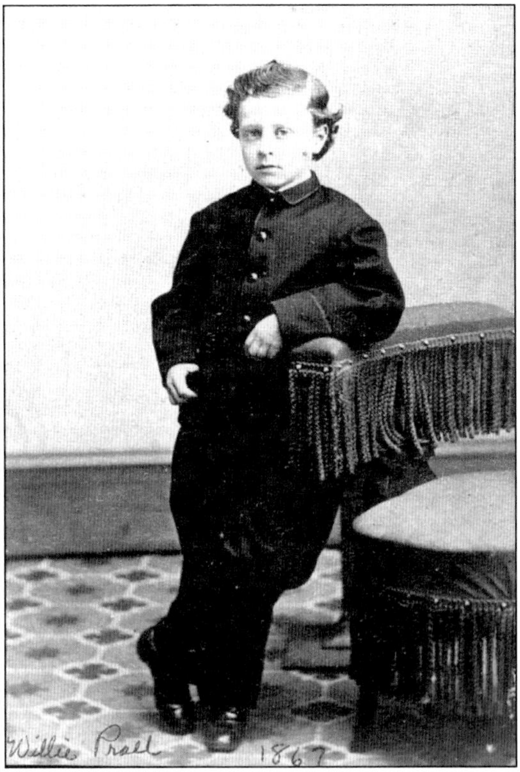

William Russell Prall Sr., son of John Parker Prall, was born in 1857 and was a member of the New York Mercantile Exchange. After moving to Boonton, he founded the fire department and donated the department's first fire engine. Named after his wife, Jeanie, it is now housed at the Boonton Fire Department Museum. He died on September 6, 1937. (Courtesy of Pieter Prall and Jeanie Prall Wing.)

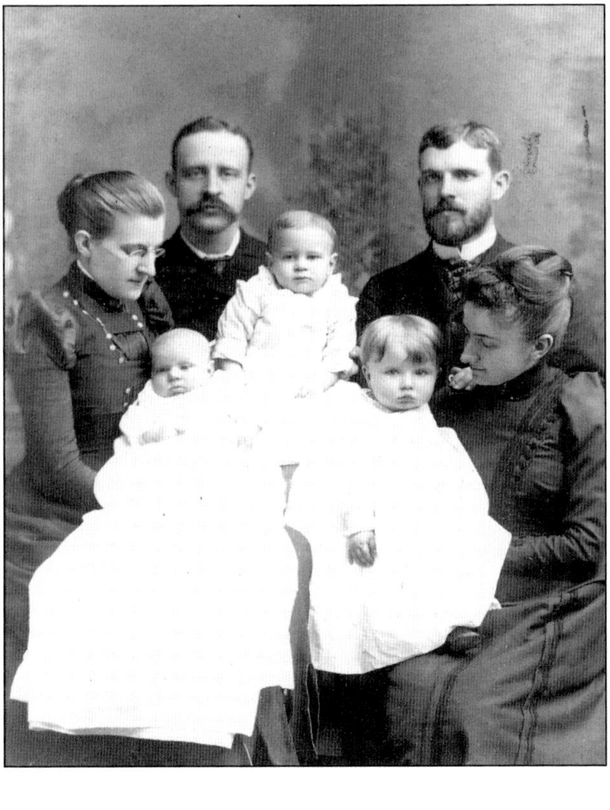

William married Jeanie Cochran Carter (both seated left) in 1889. They had two children, William Russell Prall Jr. (seen on his father's lap), born in 1890, and Marion Cochran Prall, known as Maddie, born in 1891 (on her mother's lap). Also in this photograph are Jeanie's brother Jim Carter with his wife, Carrie Carter, and daughter Miriam (on Carrie's lap). (Courtesy of Pieter Prall and Jeanie Prall Wing.)

While in school at Worcester College, William Jr., known as Russ, and Cole Porter were roommates and members of the glee club. A singer by avocation and a banker by trade, he married Florence Grace Cooley in 1914 and had four sons, their youngest son dying before the age of two. His father had given him the Apperson Jack Rabbit seen in this 1920 photograph for use while attending college. This photograph was taken in front of the garage of the Prall home in Montclair. Pictured are, from left to right, Florence's brother Frank Cooley and William and Florence Prall's sons William Russell Prall III and Robert Cooley Prall. (Courtesy of Pieter Prall and Jeanie Prall Wing.)

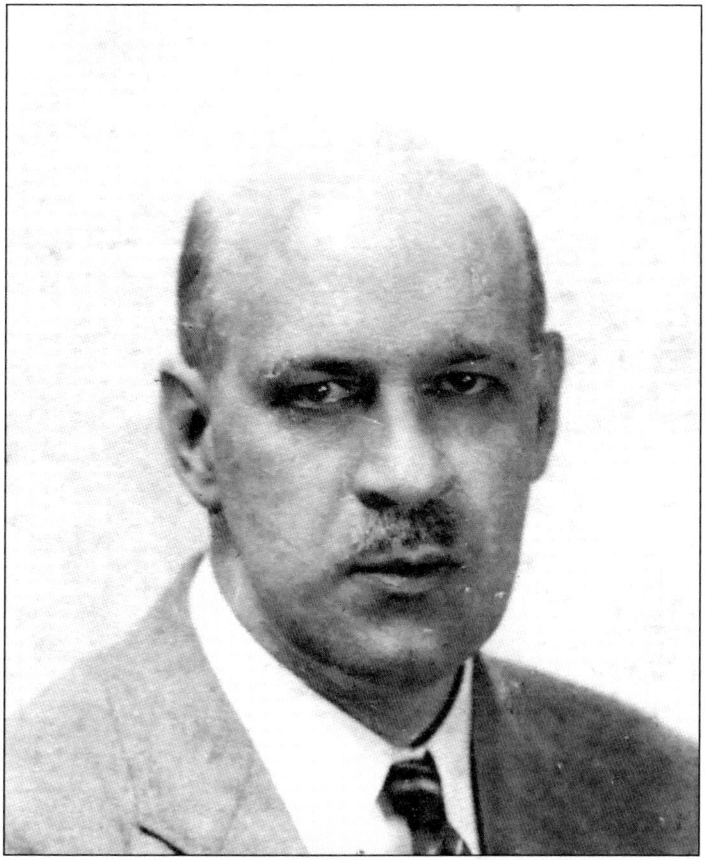

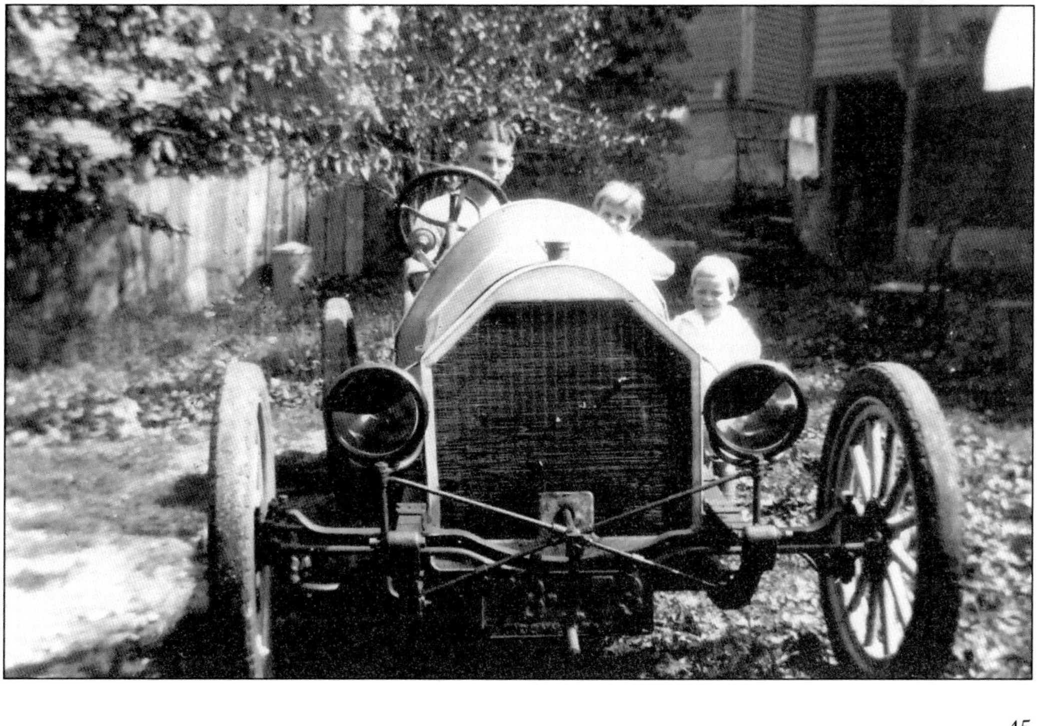

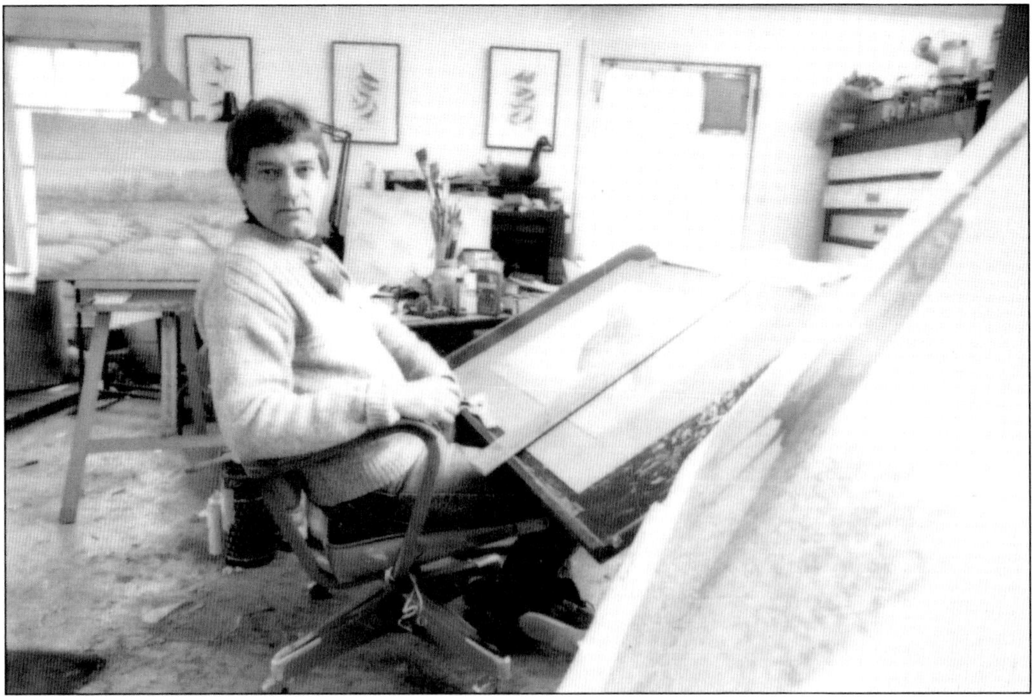

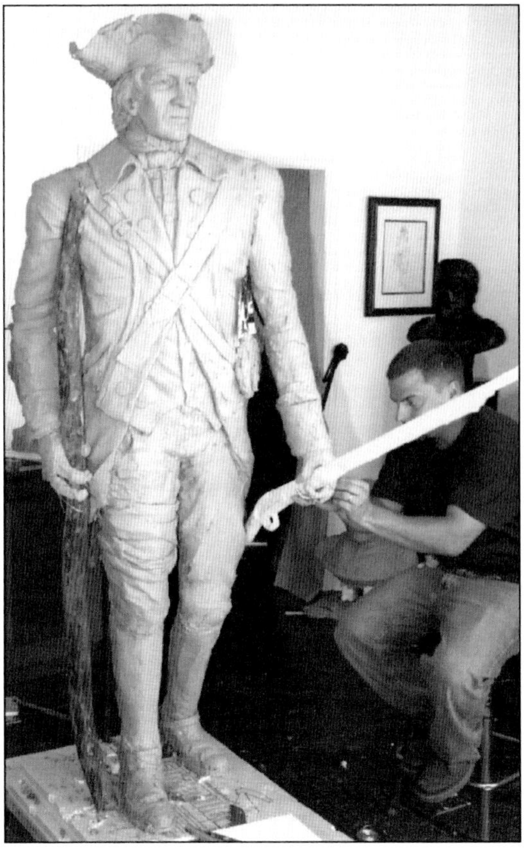

William Russell Prall III married Elsie Elizabeth Brown in 1938 and had five children, Jonathan Cresse Drummond Prall, Pieter Donald Prall, Jamie William Prall, Dana Robert Prall, and Jeanie Carter Prall. Pictured above is Pieter in 1988. He is a naturalist-artist, author, and conservationist and was used as the model for the face and hands of a statue of his great-great-great-great-grandfather John Prall Jr. The statue is the first in a series called *American Patriots in Bronze*. Shown here is sculptor Gregory Marra working on the clay model for the bronze casting. Pieter brought with him an actual cartouche belonging to John Prall Jr. for the sculptor's reference. The clay statue was displayed at the Prall homestead at the Prallsville Mills complex in late summer 2007. (Above, courtesy of Pieter Prall and Jeanie Prall Wing; left, courtesy of the Delaware River Mill Society.)

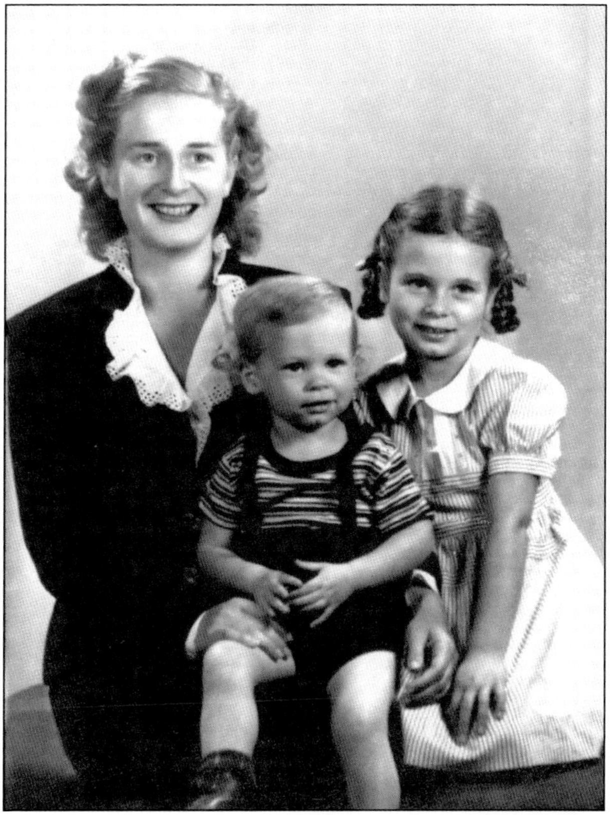

Wife of William, Elsie was born in 1917. She is a descendent of John Drummond, Earl of Perth and a Colonial era governor of East New Jersey. Elsie became a member of the Leonard Bernstein Ladies Auxiliary after World War II. An artist and mother, she is pictured here with two of her children, Jeanie, born in 1939, and Jonathan, born in 1944. In the second photograph, taken by her husband in the late 1930s, she is looking at the portrait of John Prall Jr.'s wife, Amelia Coryell Prall. Elsie died in 1997. (Courtesy of Pieter Prall and Jeanie Prall Wing.)

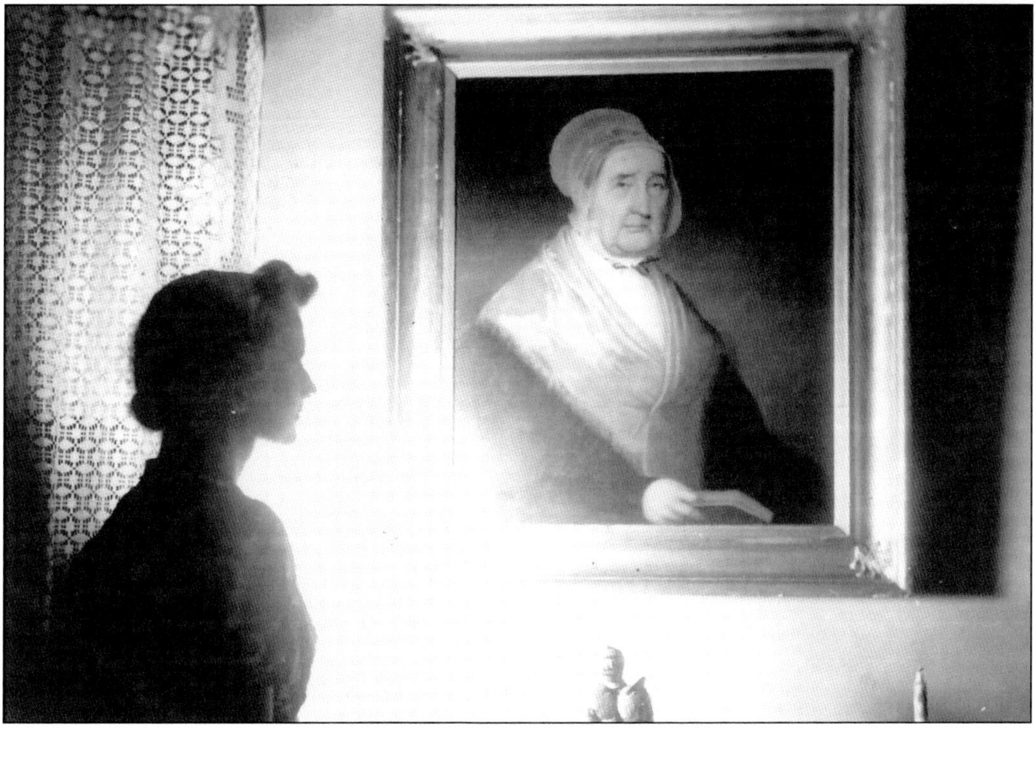

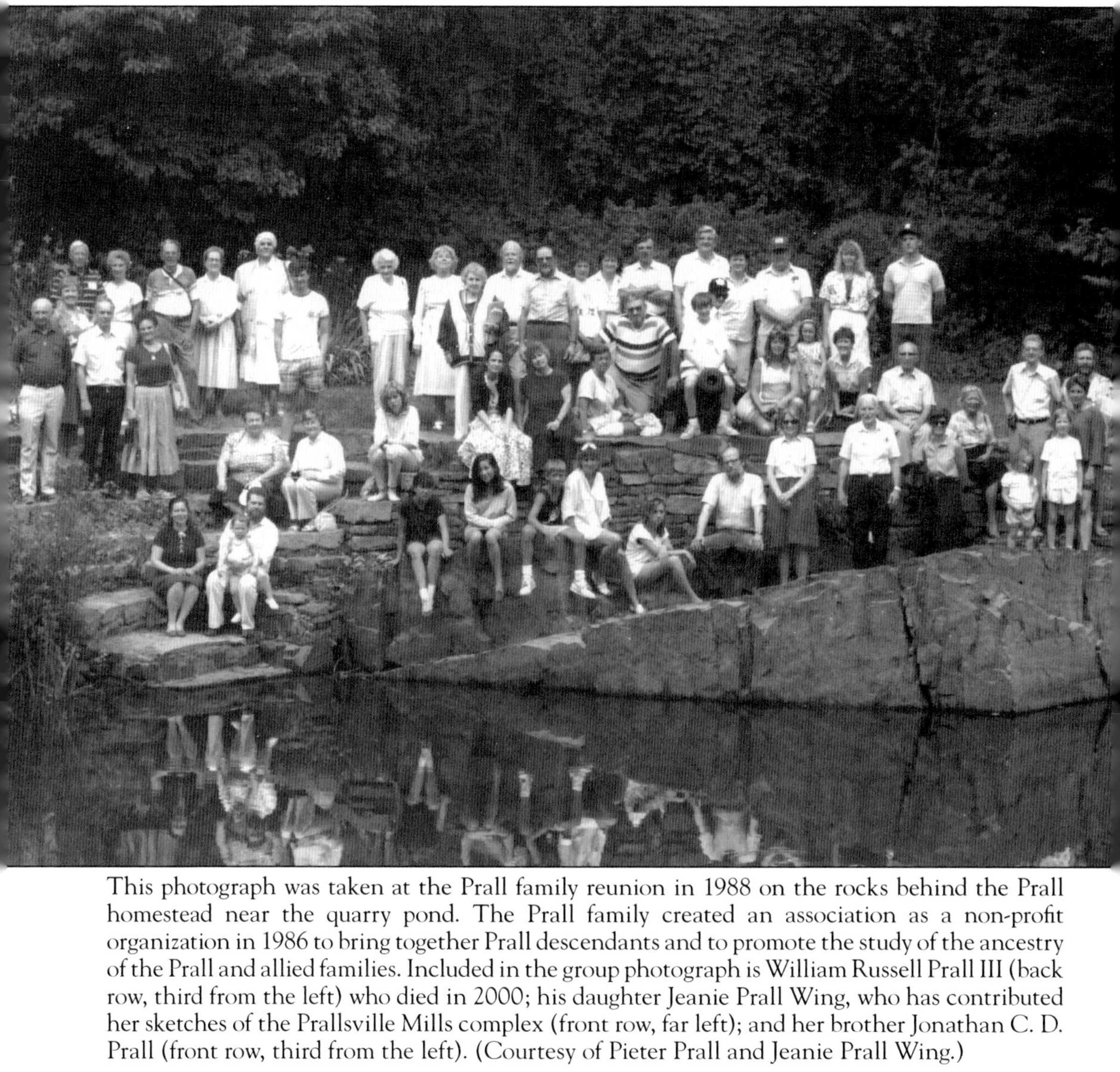

This photograph was taken at the Prall family reunion in 1988 on the rocks behind the Prall homestead near the quarry pond. The Prall family created an association as a non-profit organization in 1986 to bring together Prall descendants and to promote the study of the ancestry of the Prall and allied families. Included in the group photograph is William Russell Prall III (back row, third from the left) who died in 2000; his daughter Jeanie Prall Wing, who has contributed her sketches of the Prallsville Mills complex (front row, far left); and her brother Jonathan C. D. Prall (front row, third from the left). (Courtesy of Pieter Prall and Jeanie Prall Wing.)

Three

Transportation, Industry, and Entrepreneurs

As much as any factor, transportation has played a large role in the development and success of Stockton's industry. The Delaware and Raritan Canal provided a conduit for natural resources and goods into the rich Philadelphia markets and was a source of work for an entire subculture of boatmen and their families. The folklore, music, and history of the region are inextricably tied to these man-made waterways of commerce.

The region was also rich in natural resources. While agriculture's role in the life of Hunterdon County has diminished greatly, Stockton was at one time surrounded by abundant and fertile farmland. The symbiotic relationship between a rural town that supplies goods and services with the farms that supply food and raw materials was vital to Stockton's development. The superb sandstone stored in the hillsides and beneath the earth that was perfect for building houses, bridges, and dams, also supported Stockton's growth.

Living near a river has it benefits, but it also has significant challenges when it overflows its banks. River towns attract resilient, resourceful, and creative people. Stockton has had its fair share of visionaries and entrepreneurs throughout the years; however, all of these factors would count for little if not for the ability to connect to the larger world.

The advent of the railroad eventually rendered the canals irrelevant and pushed the region into a period of expansion and into its modern age. Many of the industries that grew in Stockton did so because of the access to easy transportation. Stockton's final era of industrial output and growth rose and fell with the fortunes of the railroad.

Today the railroad bed turned trail, the canal, river, and the Prallsville Mills complex provide a place of creativity, reflection, and fun for thousands of visitors each year to Stockton and the entire Delaware River region.

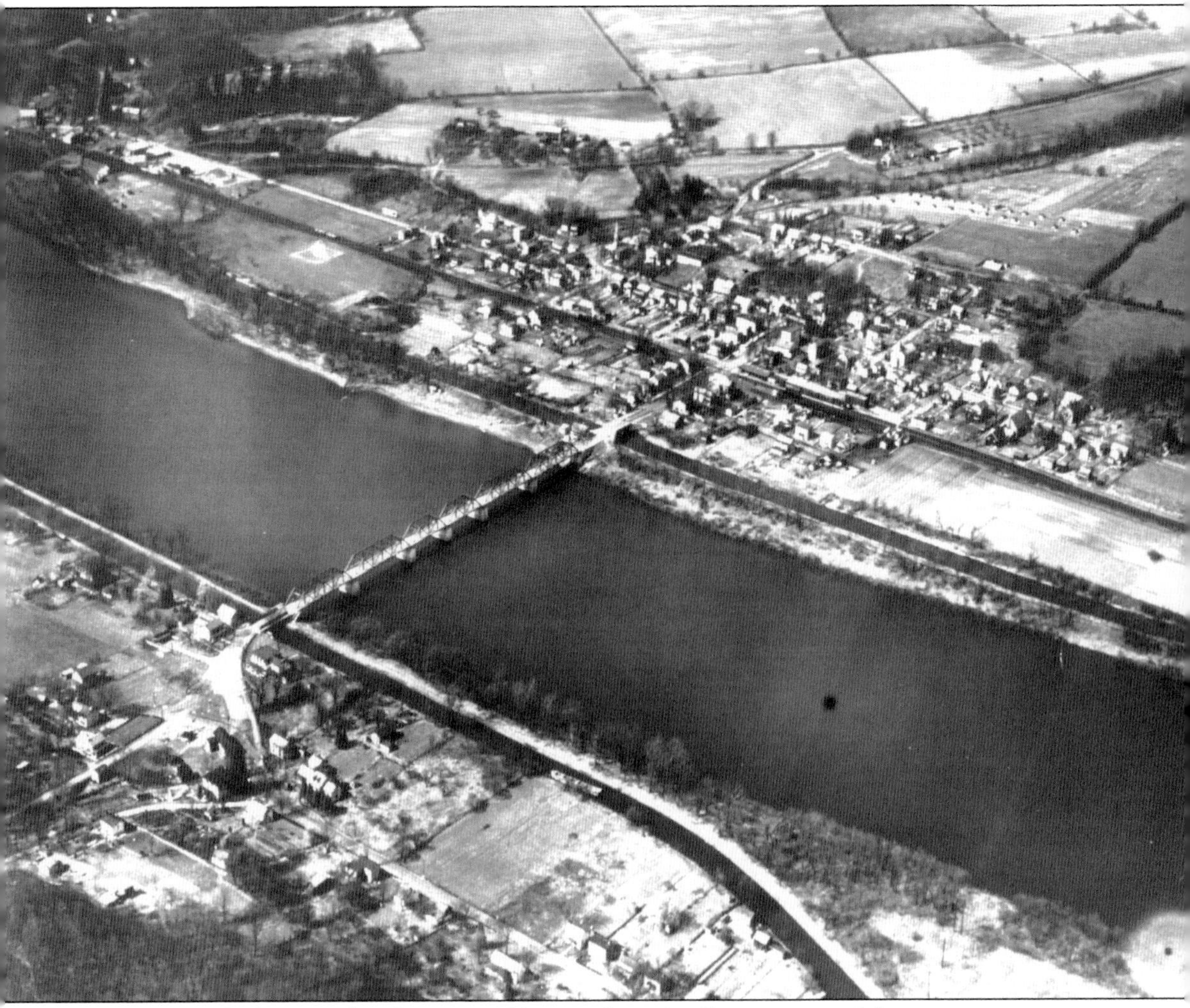

This aerial photograph taken in 1930 provides a bird's-eye view of the various components that contributed to Stockton's commercial success. The most striking landmark is the bridge spanning the Delaware River and connecting Centre Bridge, Pennsylvania (bottom left), and Stockton, New Jersey (upper right). By 1927, the steel bridge that remains in use today had been built and served as a conduit for the businesses on both sides of the river to connect with customers in both states. There are two canals, one on either side of the river, and a canal boat can be seen in the Delaware Canal in Pennsylvania (bottom center). The Prallsville Mills and the old quarries are in the upper left and the railroad runs from there, through Stockton and on to Trenton (upper left to center right). Toward the upper right corner can be seen the rows of chicken houses that make up the famous Pine Tree Chicken Hatchery. Surrounded by lush farmland, Stockton benefited from the farmer's bounty and provided needed services and goods in return. (Courtesy of the Delaware River Mill Society.)

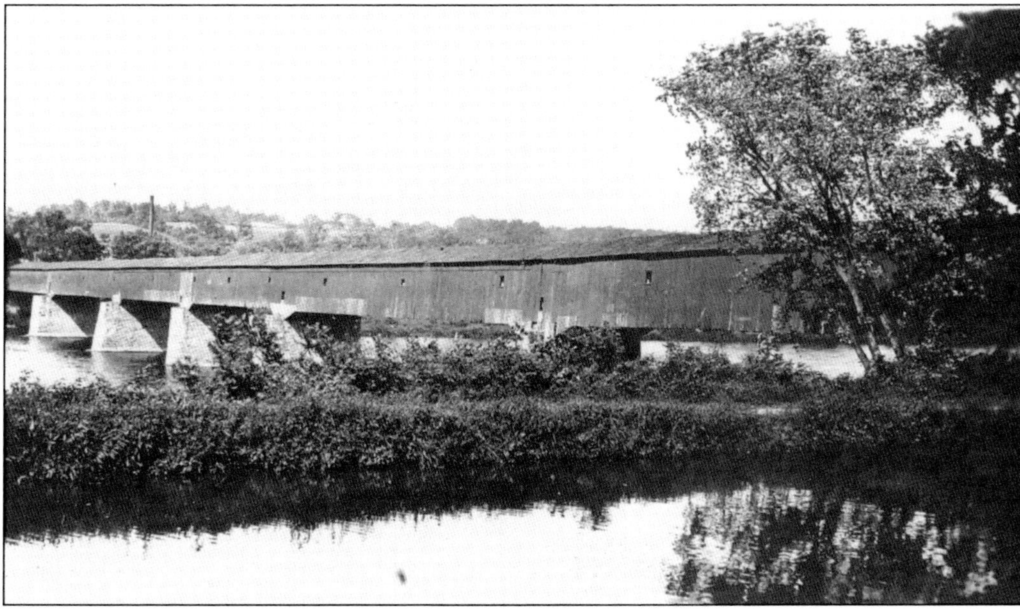

The bridge opened for business in 1814 and was owned and operated by the Centre Bridge Company. In fact, the towns on both sides of the river were known as Centre Bridge until 1851. After that point, the town on the Pennsylvania side remained Centre Bridge and the town on the New Jersey side became Stockton. (Courtesy of the Delaware and Raritan Canal Commission.)

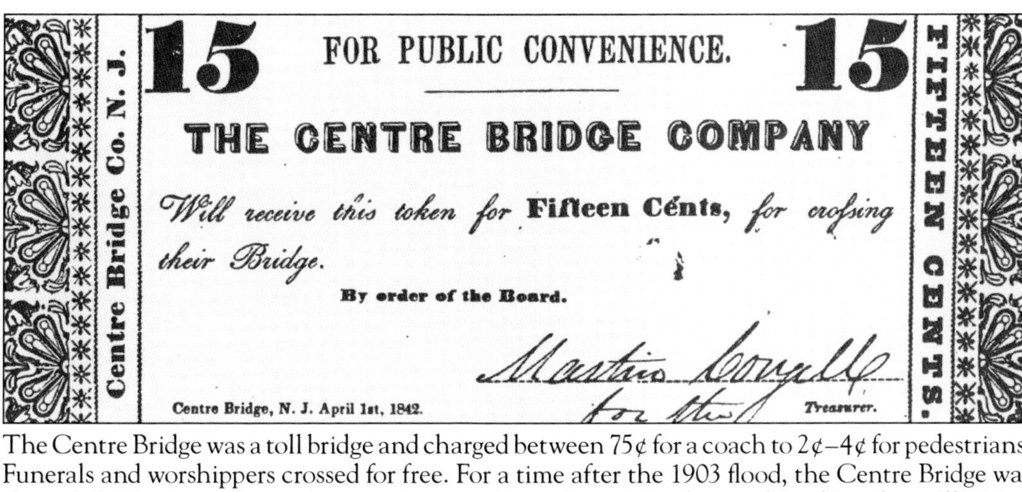

15 FOR PUBLIC CONVENIENCE. 15

THE CENTRE BRIDGE COMPANY

Will receive this token for **Fifteen Cents,** *for crossing their Bridge.*

By order of the Board.

Centre Bridge, N. J. April 1st, 1842. *Treasurer.*

Centre Bridge Co. N. J.

FIFTEEN CENTS.

The Centre Bridge was a toll bridge and charged between 75¢ for a coach to 2¢–4¢ for pedestrians. Funerals and worshippers crossed for free. For a time after the 1903 flood, the Centre Bridge was the only bridge in operation between Easton, Pennsylvania, in the north and Lambertville, New Jersey, in the south. (Courtesy of Carl Cathers.)

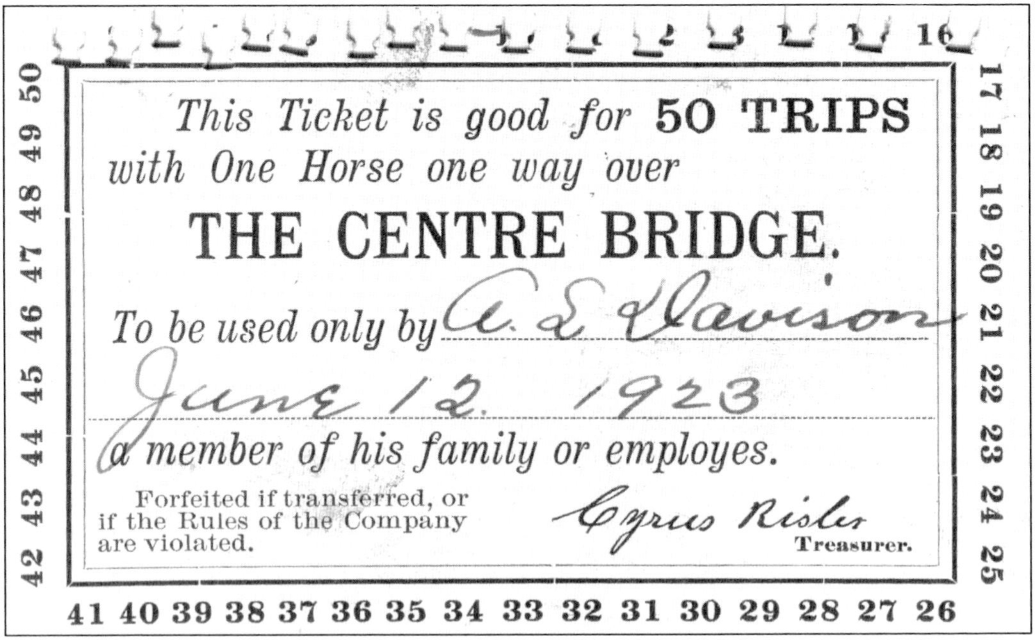

This Ticket is good for **50 TRIPS**
with One Horse one way over

THE CENTRE BRIDGE.

To be used only by A. L. Davison
June 12. 1923
a member of his family or employes.

Forfeited if transferred, or
if the Rules of the Company
are violated.

Cyrus Risler
Treasurer.

This 50-trip ticket belonged to Austin Davison's father. Based on the June 12, 1923, date on the card, it is quite possible that the card never got used completely because of the fire that destroyed the bridge on July 22, 1923. It would be four years before the new steel bridge would be completed in 1927. (Courtesy of Carl Cathers.)

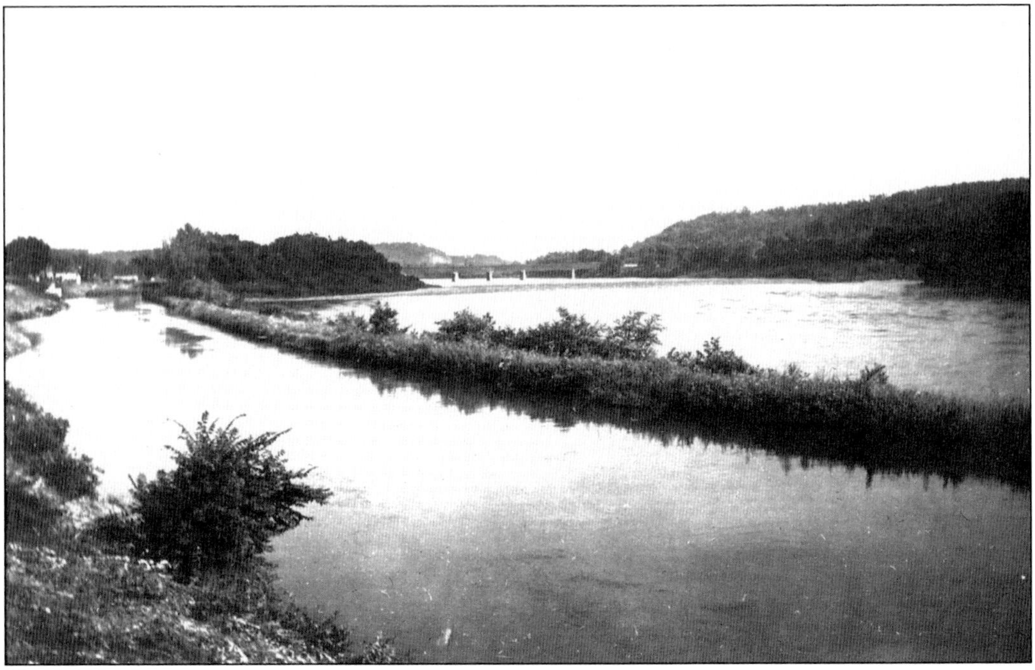

This *c.* 1920 picture is looking south to the Stockton Bridge across the Delaware River. The feeder canal of the Delaware and Raritan Canal flows along the left of the river on the New Jersey side. For the most part 60 feet wide at the top and 6 feet deep, the feeder canal was only navigable by the mule drawn boats. (Courtesy of Carl Cathers.)

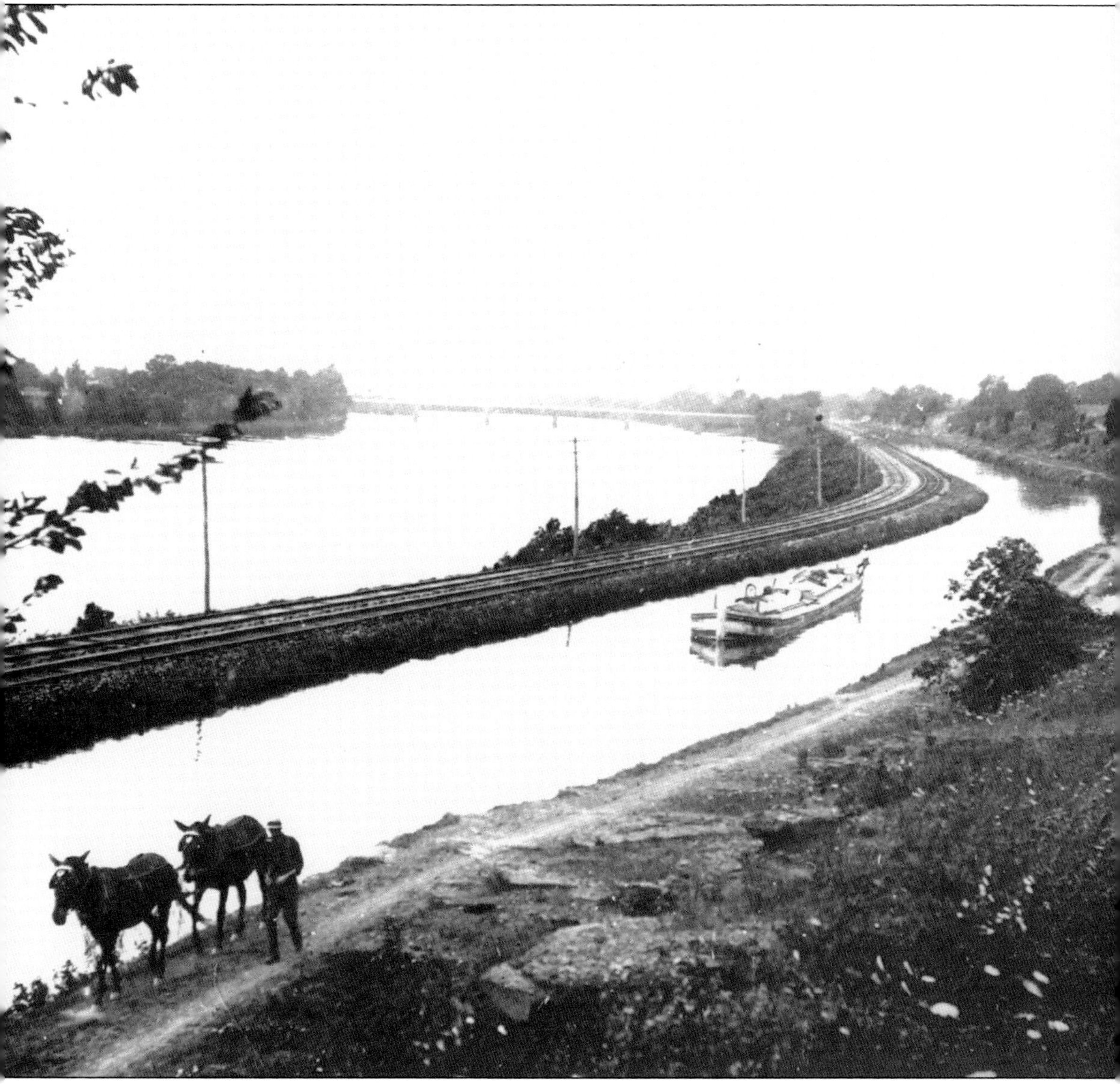

With the Lambertville–New Hope bridge in the distance, mules tow a canal boat heading north in this pre-1903 picture of the feeder canal. Almost 23 miles in length, the feeder canal originated at Bull's Island north of Stockton and continued south all the way to Trenton and supplied water to the Delaware and Raritan Canal. Navigable for the entire distance, the feeder canal was used to transport coal, grain, paper products, and products from the rubber mills in Stockton and Lambertville. The feeder also connected to the Delaware Canal that ran along the Pennsylvania side of the river via outlet locks that allowed the boats to cross the Delaware River at Lambertville and New Hope. Commercial use of the canal started in the 1830s and continued until 1933, when it was abandoned as a commercial waterway. (Courtesy of the Delaware and Raritan Canal Commission.)

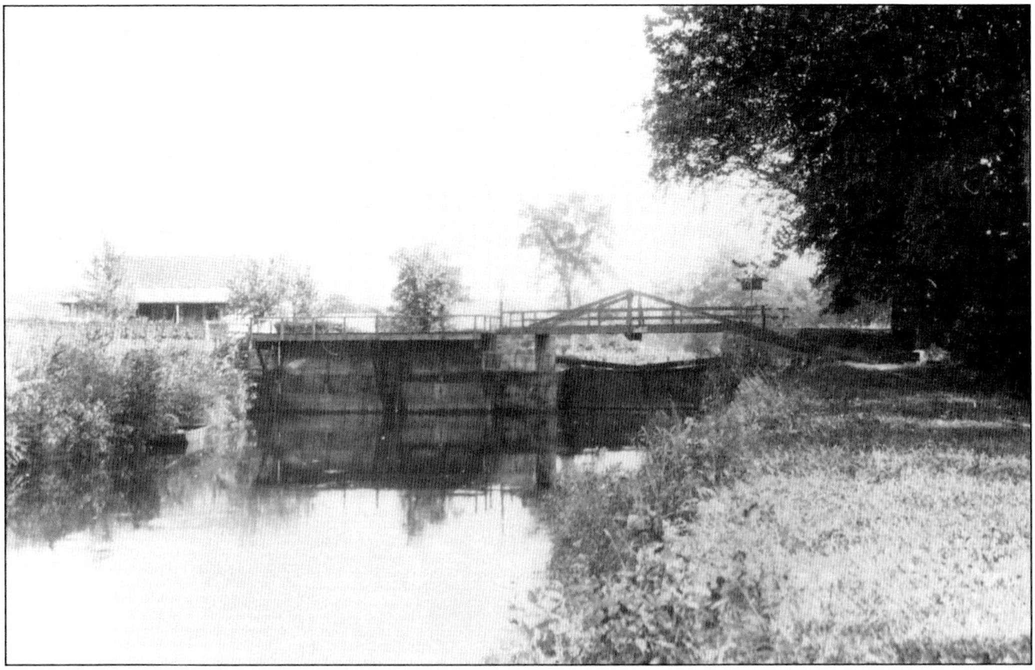

This *c.* 1925 photograph of the Prallsville Lock is looking south toward Stockton. The house to the left was the former quarry office that had been abandoned in 1919. Horace Cathers bought the property for $1,500 in 1920 and converted it into the family homestead. (Courtesy of Carl Cathers.)

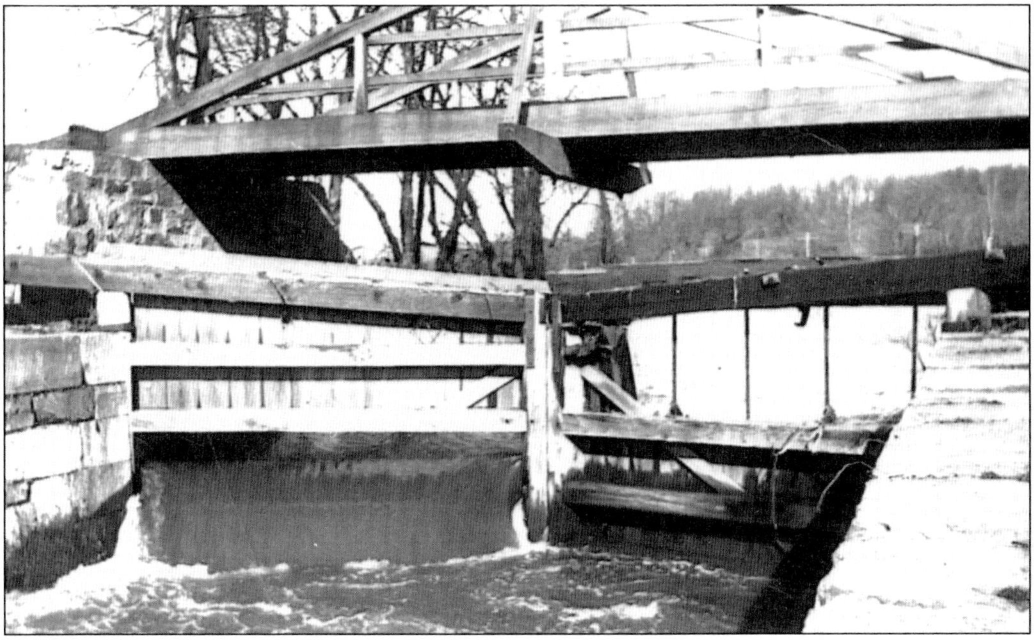

This closer look at the Prallsville Lock shows the damage done to the gates after the 1936 flood. The side of the right gate has been torn off by the floodwaters, leaving the frame behind. The water of the canal on the other side of the lock can be seen through the hole in the gate. (Courtesy of Carl Cathers.)

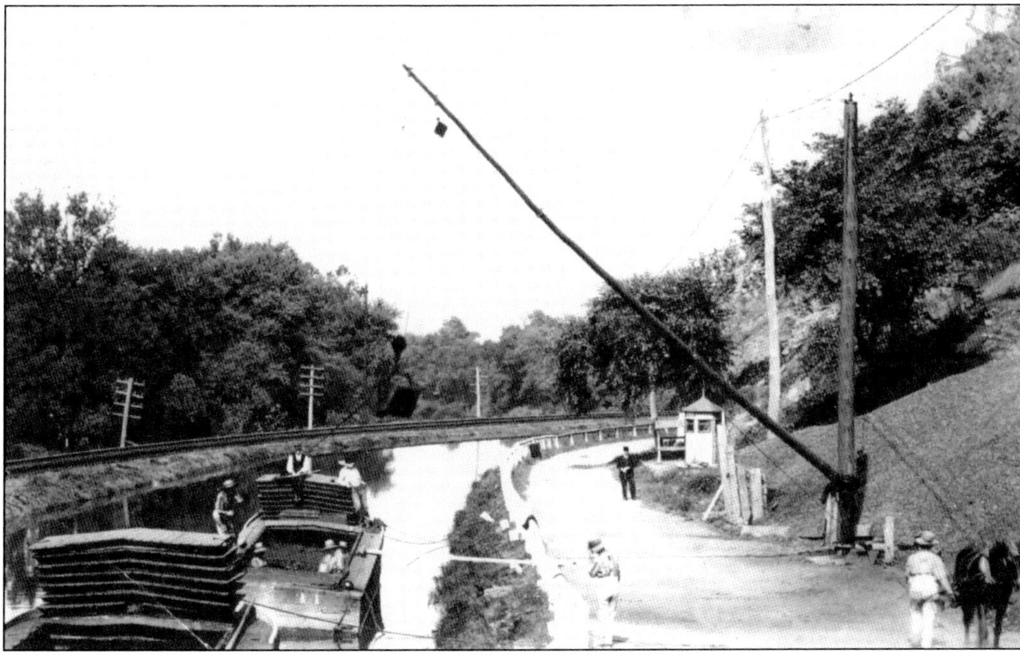

A crew prepares to unload a canal boat north of Hopewell Township. Derricks like these were set up at many places along the canal, and old cable anchors can still be found along Route 29. The mast of the derrick at Prallsville was made of a single 60-foot-long piece of fir that was 12 by 12 inches wide. (Courtesy of the Delaware and Raritan Canal Commission.)

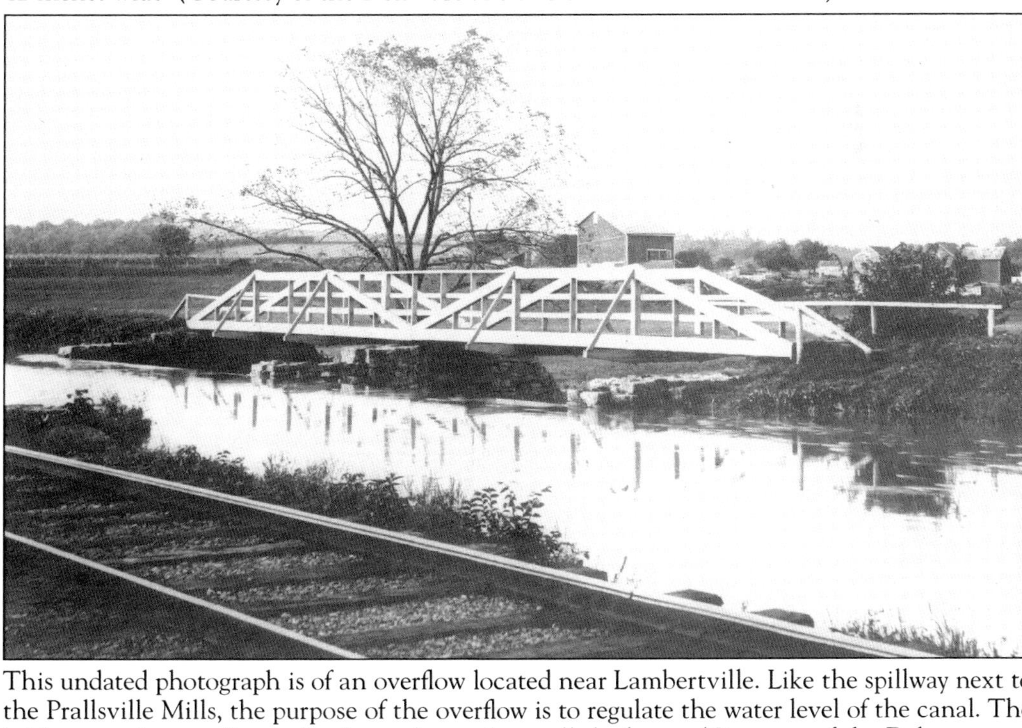

This undated photograph is of an overflow located near Lambertville. Like the spillway next to the Prallsville Mills, the purpose of the overflow is to regulate the water level of the canal. The bridge over the overflow is for the mules as they pull the boats. (Courtesy of the Delaware and Raritan Canal Commission.)

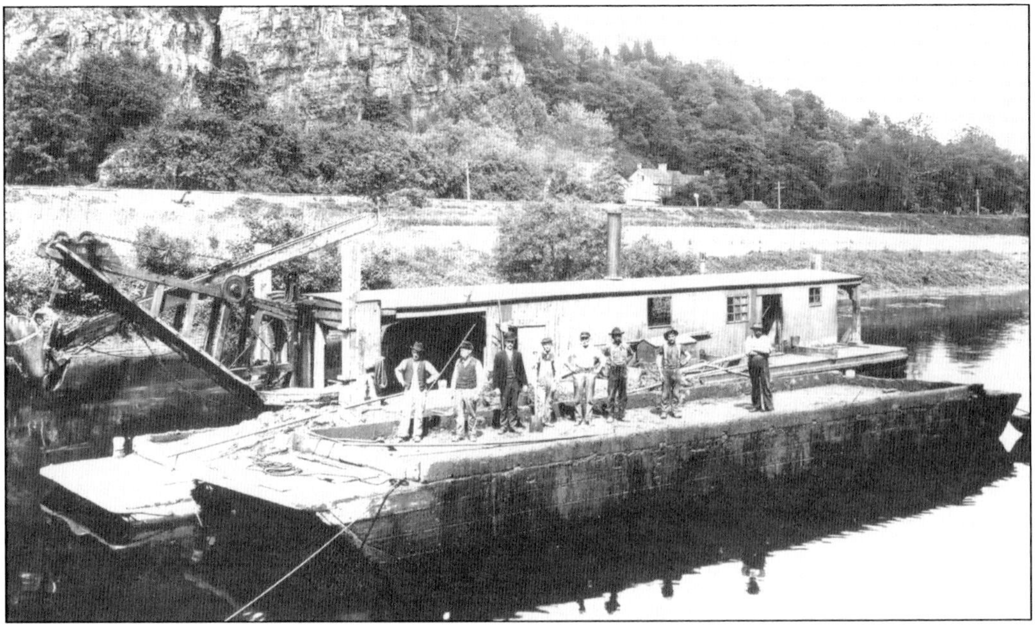

This workboat crew dredged the canal to keep silt from building up, a common problem in the feeder canal. Dory Wilson, who would eventually become the lock tender at the Prallsville Lock, stands at the front of the boat on the left. Wooden timbers were driven into the floor of the canal to stabilize the boat during the dredging operation. (Courtesy of the Delaware and Raritan Canal Commission.)

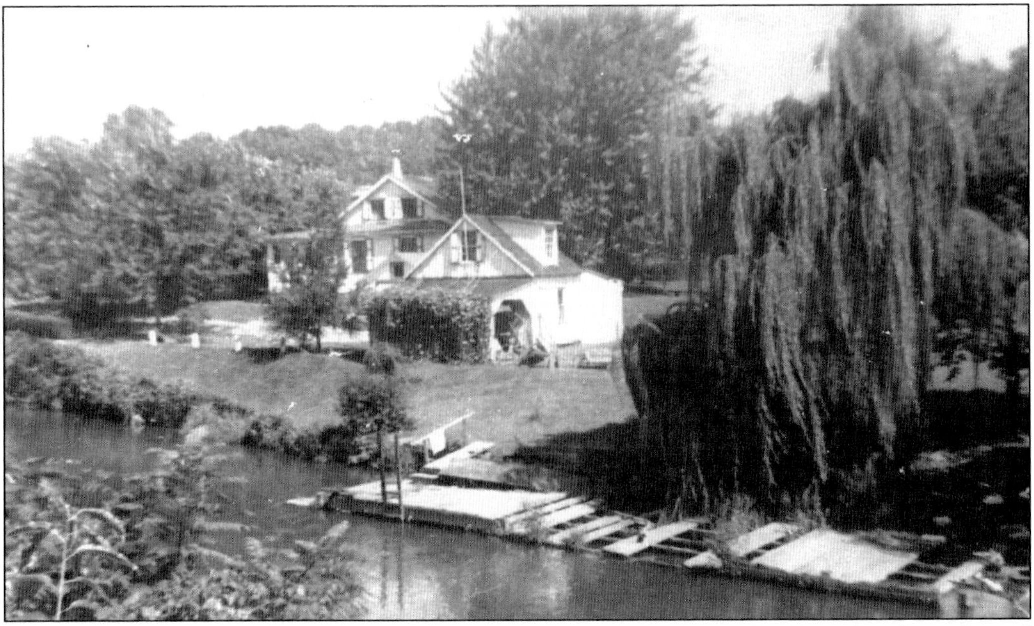

After the canal was abandoned in 1933, the dredging boat was also abandoned and was floated down the canal in order to clear the lock area. In this 1942 picture, the remains of the boat after the deck structure was removed to salvage the wood sit under a weeping willow tree. The boat would remain there until 1955, when it was washed away by the flood caused by Hurricane Diane. (Courtesy of Carl Cathers.)

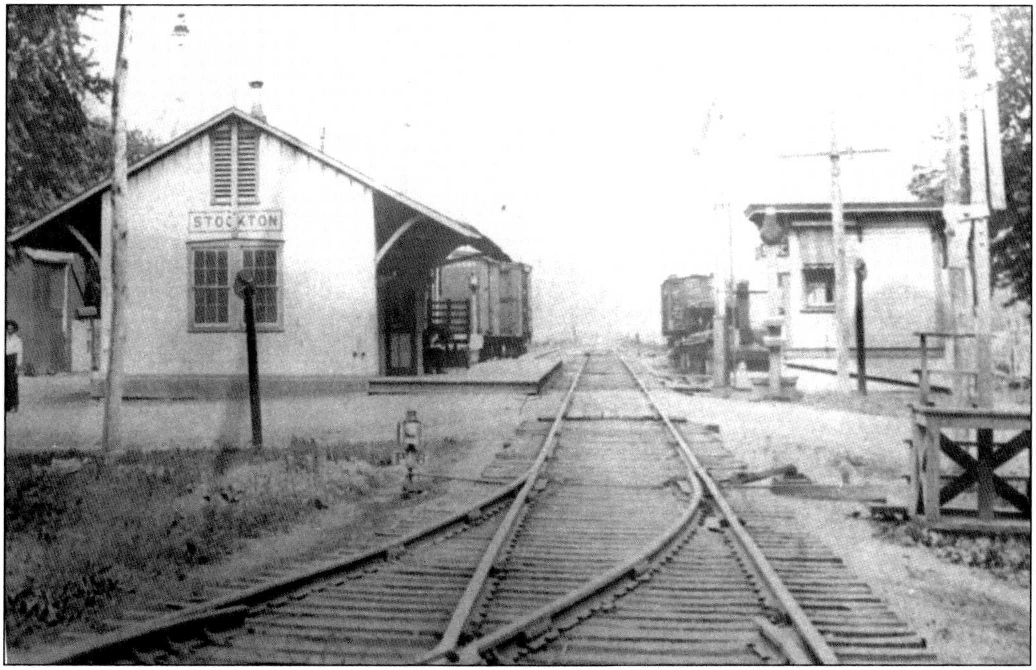

This *c.* 1895 photograph shows the Stockton train station looking south across Bridge Street. The rails that split off to the left are for a siding where the freight trains could wait and let the passenger trains pass by. Today the station building houses a deli and general store. (Courtesy of the Delaware River Mill Society.)

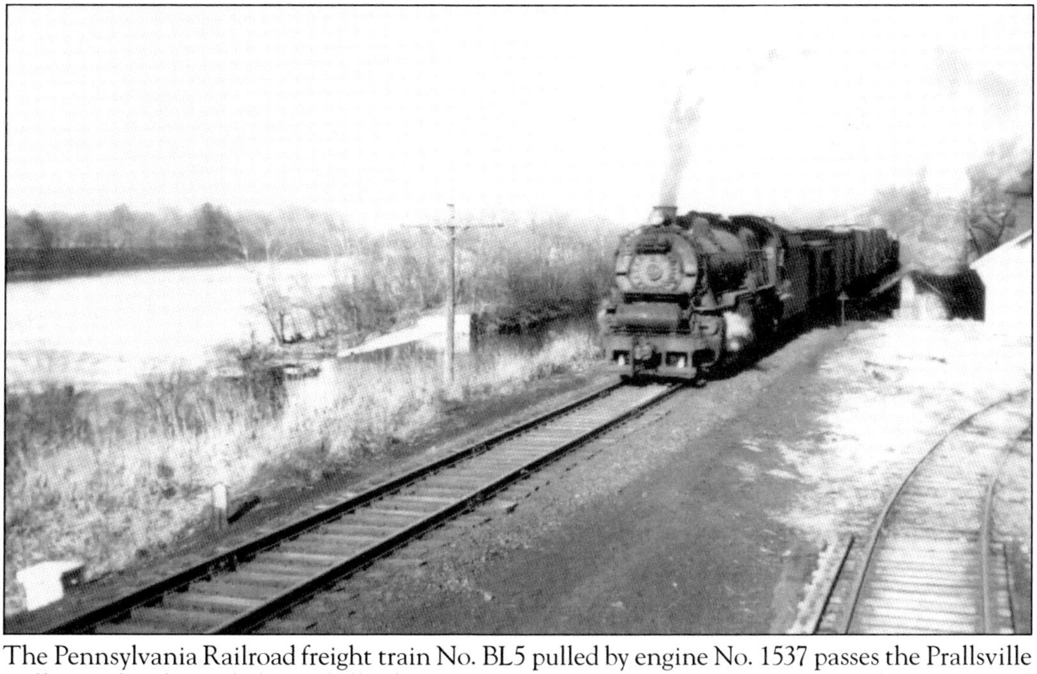

The Pennsylvania Railroad freight train No. BL5 pulled by engine No. 1537 passes the Prallsville Mills as it heads south from Phillipsburg on its way to Wilmington, Delaware. The picture was taken early in 1950 by Frank Barry while he stood on a boxcar that was on the siding by the sawmill. (Photograph by Frank Barry, courtesy of Carl Cathers.)

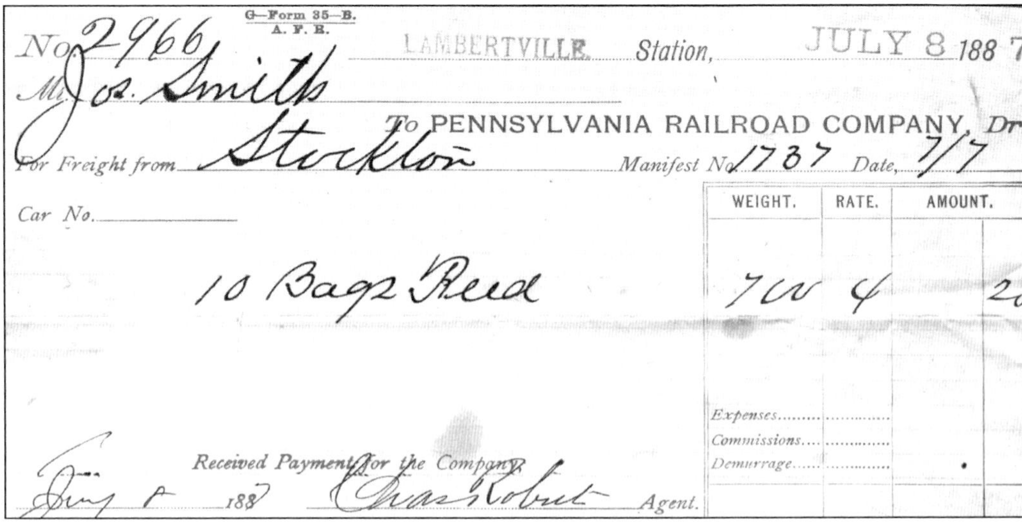

No. 2966 G—Form 35—B. A. F. B.

LAMBERTVILLE Station, JULY 8 1887

Mr. Jos. Smith

To PENNSYLVANIA RAILROAD COMPANY, Dr.

For Freight from Stockton Manifest No. 1737 Date, 7/7

Car No.

	WEIGHT.	RATE.	AMOUNT.
10 Bags Feed	700	4	28
Expenses			
Commissions			
Demurrage			

Received Payment for the Company. Aug 8 1887 Chas Robert Agent.

The businesses of Stockton relied upon the railroad to deliver their products well beyond the borders of the town. This 1887 freight bill is for 10 bags of feed sent from Joseph Smith of the Prallsville Mills in Stockton to the Lambertville Station. It would appear that it cost 28¢ to transport 10 bags of feed from Stockton to Lambertville in 1887. (Courtesy of the Delaware River Mill Society.)

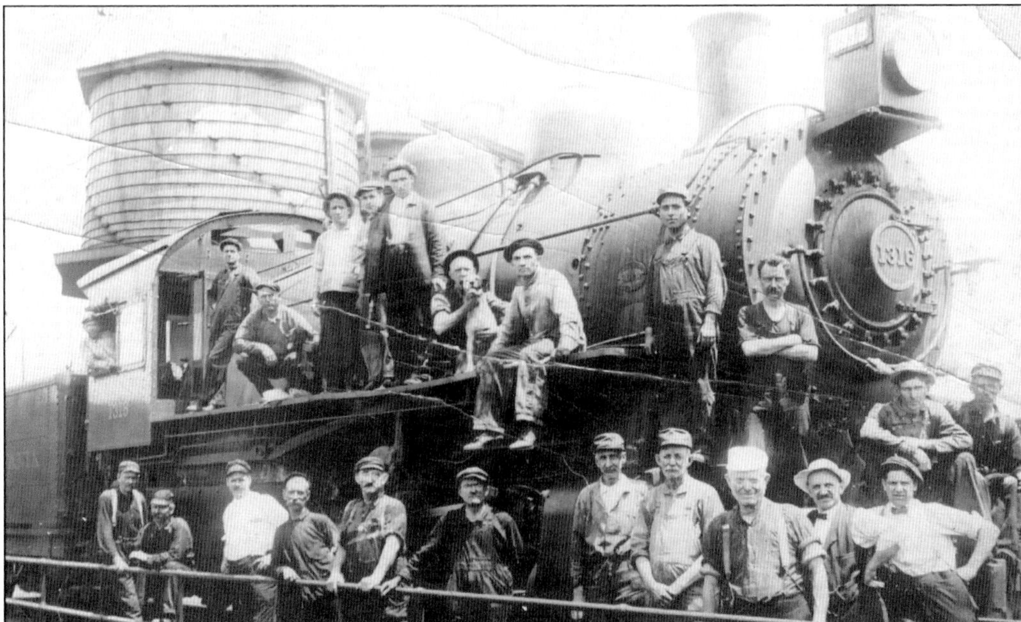

In addition to serving as a transportation conduit for freight and passengers, the railroad provided thousands of jobs. Based on the two water towers in the background, this photograph was taken just north of Stockton in Byram. Life on the railroad was hard, yet the stories of railroad men like John Strunk, the author's grandfather, were highlighted with hobos and other colorful people of folklore. (Courtesy of Carl Cathers.)

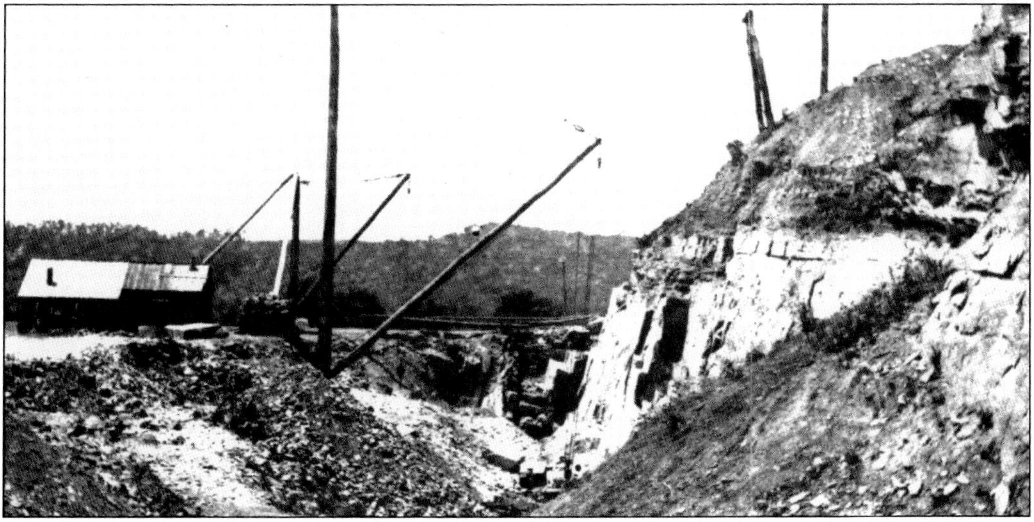

The Prallsville Quarry is seen here in this 1906 photograph. Stockton sandstone, also known as brownstone, was regarded to be the best to be found in the Delaware Valley. Stockton sandstone was used extensively in New York and Philadelphia. Nassau Hall at Princeton University was completed in 1756 and was constructed of Stockton sandstone. (Courtesy of the Delaware River Mill Society.)

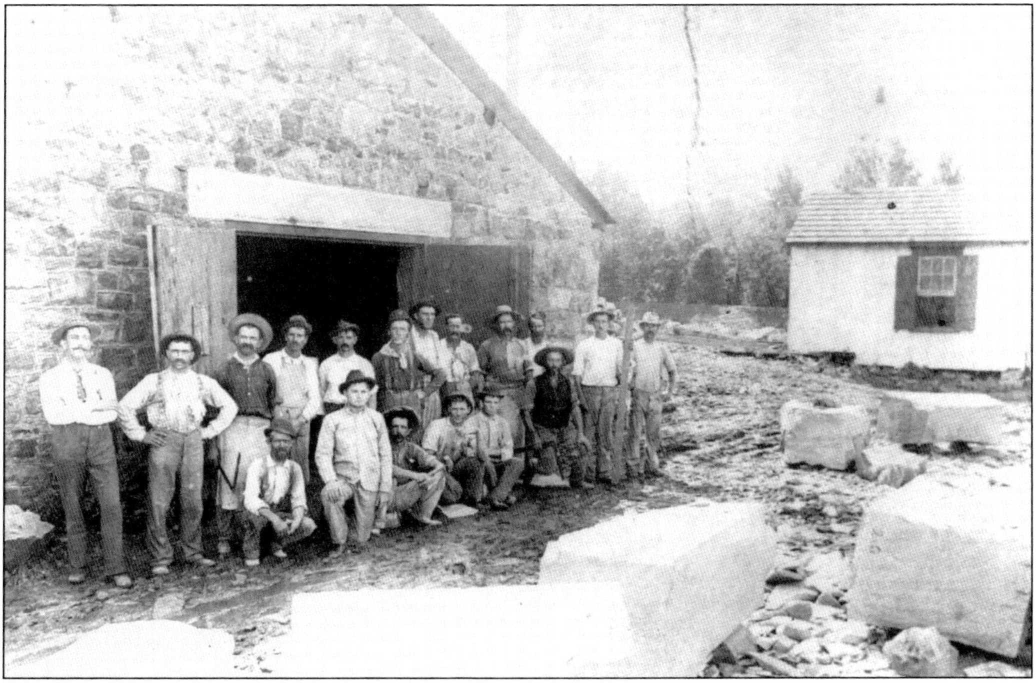

A group of Prallsville Quarry stonecutters posed for this c. 1890 photograph. A highly skilled profession, the stonecutters cut the large rocks that were pulled out of the quarry by hand using "wedges and feathers." The feathers were pieces of metal that were placed in a hole in the rock and into which the wedge was driven, splitting the rock. (Courtesy of the Delaware River Mill Society.)

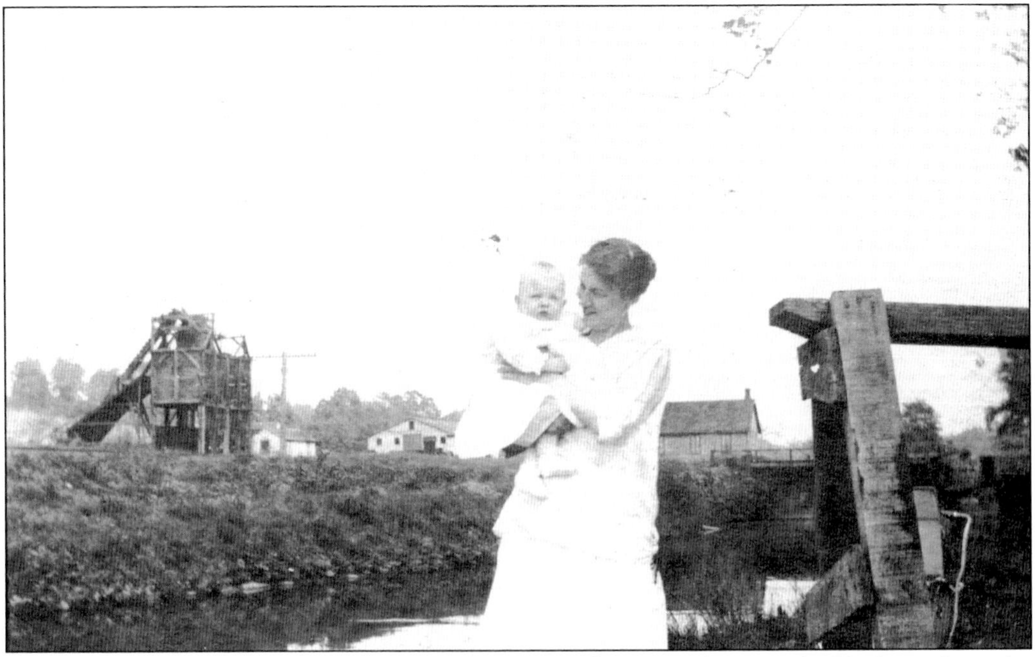

Eleanor Cathers holds her son Horace Cathers Jr. in this 1919 photograph. To the right is the abandoned quarry office. The tall structure on the left is a stone crusher designed to crush stone into ballast for the railroad track bed. The structure did not remain for long as the stone from the Prallsville Quarry was too soft to serve as effective ballast. (Courtesy of Carl Cathers.)

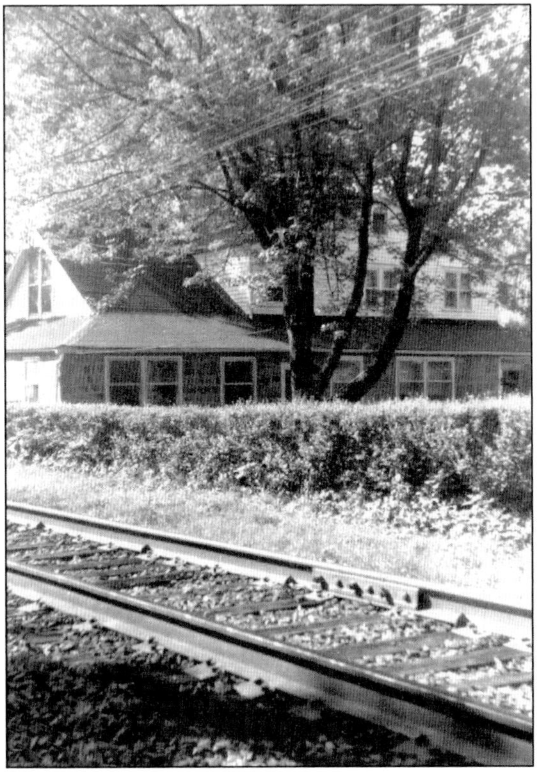

Seen here is the abandoned quarry office, as it looked many years later after being converted into a home. When the quarry was in operation, the men would come to this office to be paid. A small window in the stone wall through which the men were handed their money was one of the few visible remnants left of the building's former function. (Courtesy of Carl Cathers.)

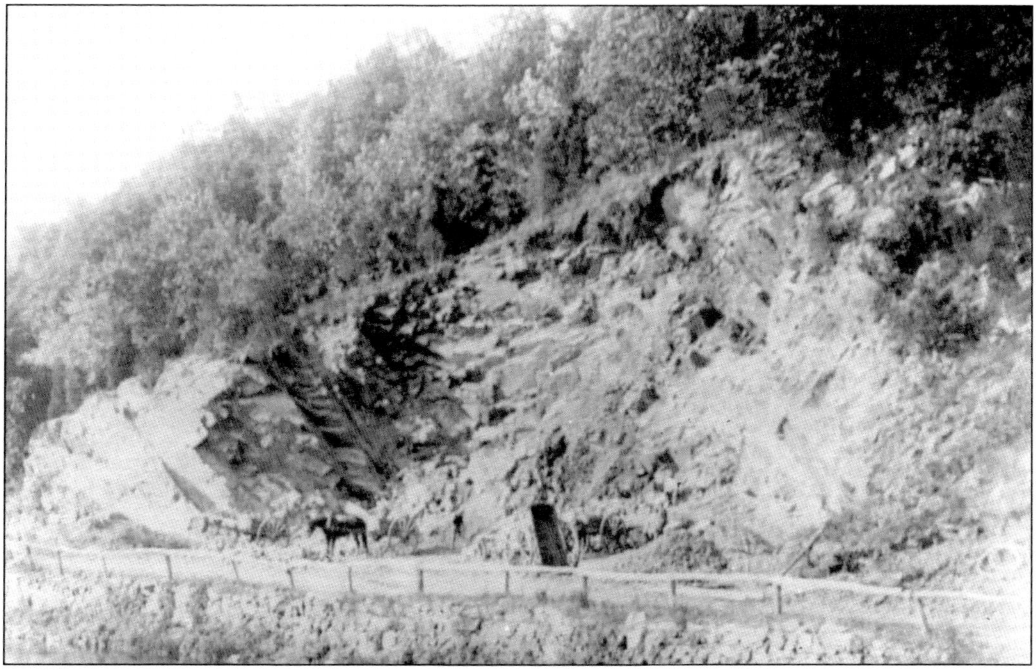

Unlike the Prallsville Quarry, this quarry located just south of Brookville, had stone hard enough to serve as ballast or "trap rock" for the railroad track beds. This late-1800s photograph shows a mule hitched to a wagon waiting patiently for the man in the middle of the picture to fill the wagon. (Courtesy of the Delaware and Raritan Canal Commission.)

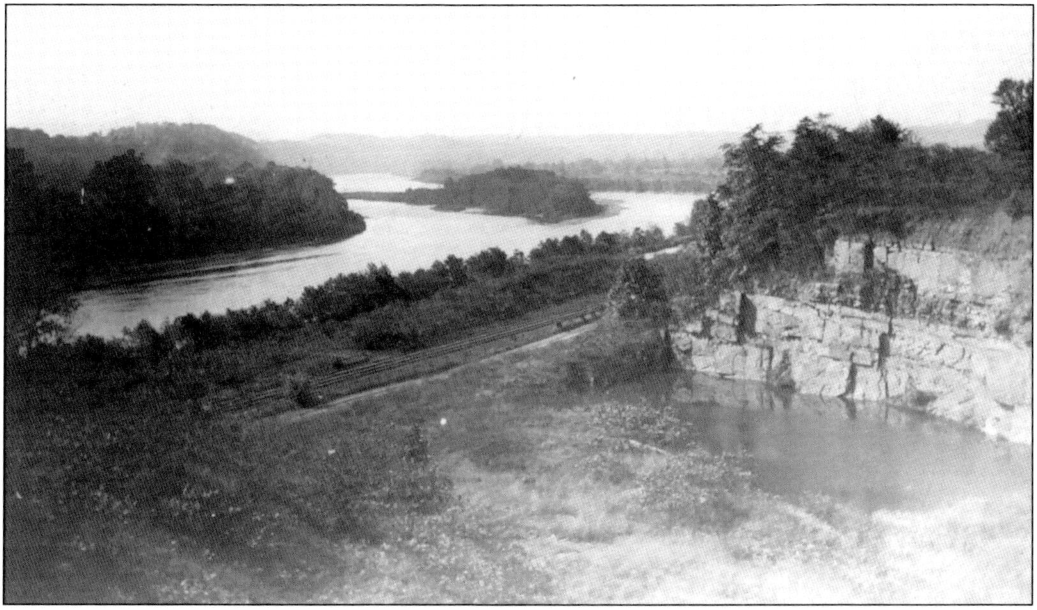

This early-1930s photograph shows the last quarry operation to close, located north of Stockton on Route 29. The quarry lake has been filled in; however, the carved stone wall looking like an abstract Mount Rushmore is still clearly evident from the road. Hendricks Island is at the left and Eagle Island sits in the middle of the Delaware River in the middle of the picture. (Courtesy of Carl Cathers.)

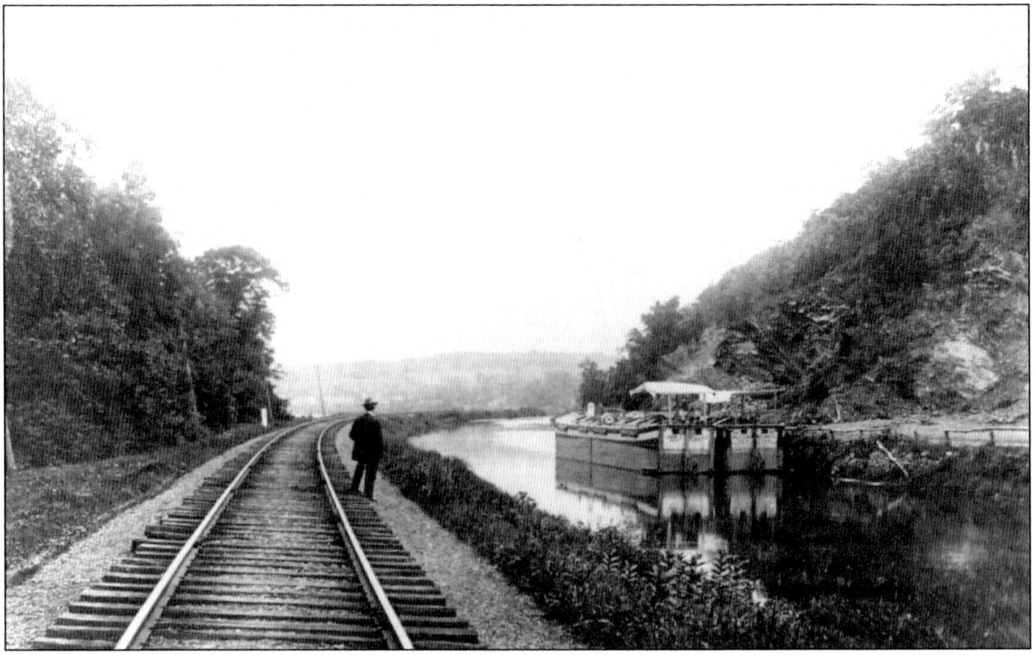

Waiting to be loaded at a quarry near Lambertville, it is clear that the boats are empty because of how high they are riding in the water. The languid feel of the picture is in keeping with the slower mode of transportation that the canal represented. The man on the tracks seems to be watching the past from the vantage point of the future. (Courtesy of Carl Cathers.)

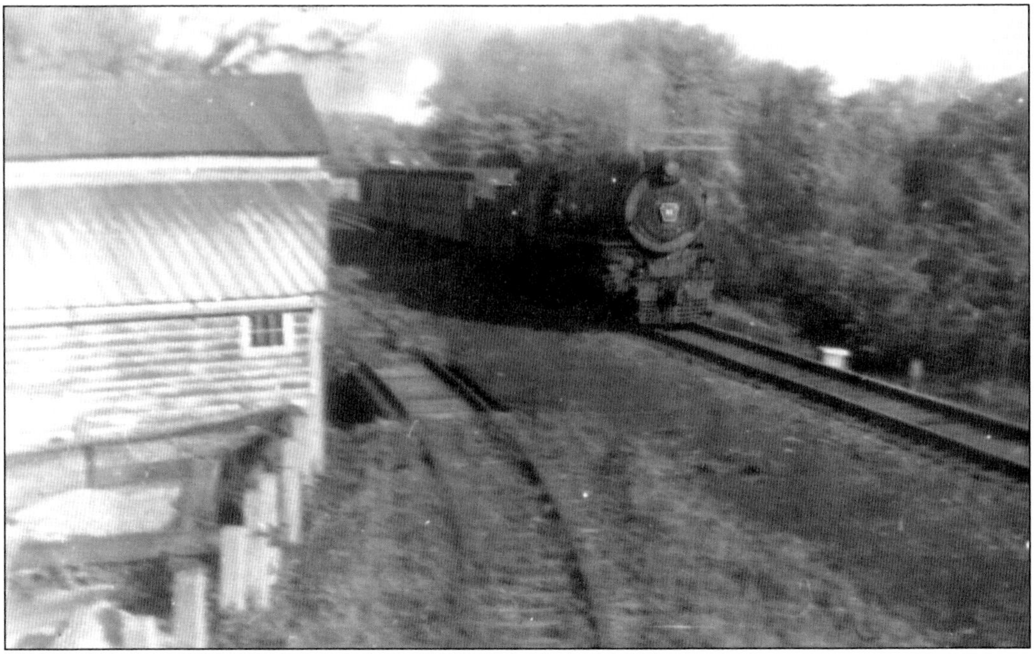

The trains could carry far more freight per trip and complete the trip far faster than the canal boats. Trains like this one barreling north past the Prallsville Mills complex would soon seal the fate of the canals, making them quaint relics of a slower time. (Photograph by Frank Barry, courtesy of Carl Cathers.)

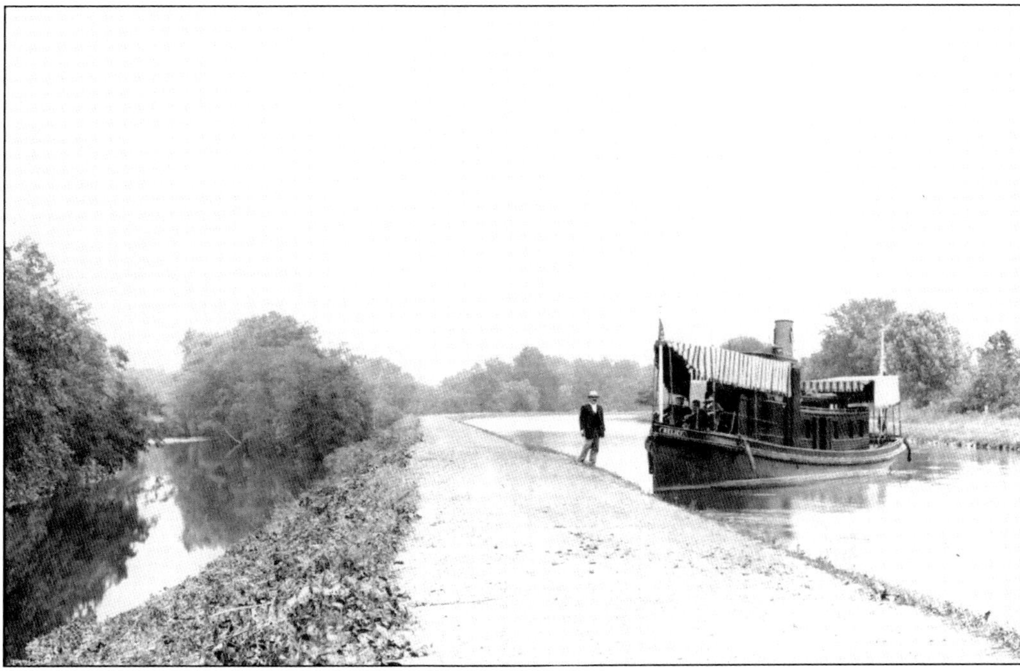

George Holcombe, paymaster for the Delaware and Raritan Canal, chats with the crew of the *Relief*, which served to break up ice that formed on the canal as the weather got colder. Eventually the canal would be partially drained for the winter, providing opportunities for winter recreation but not much transportation. (Courtesy of the Delaware and Raritan Canal Commission.)

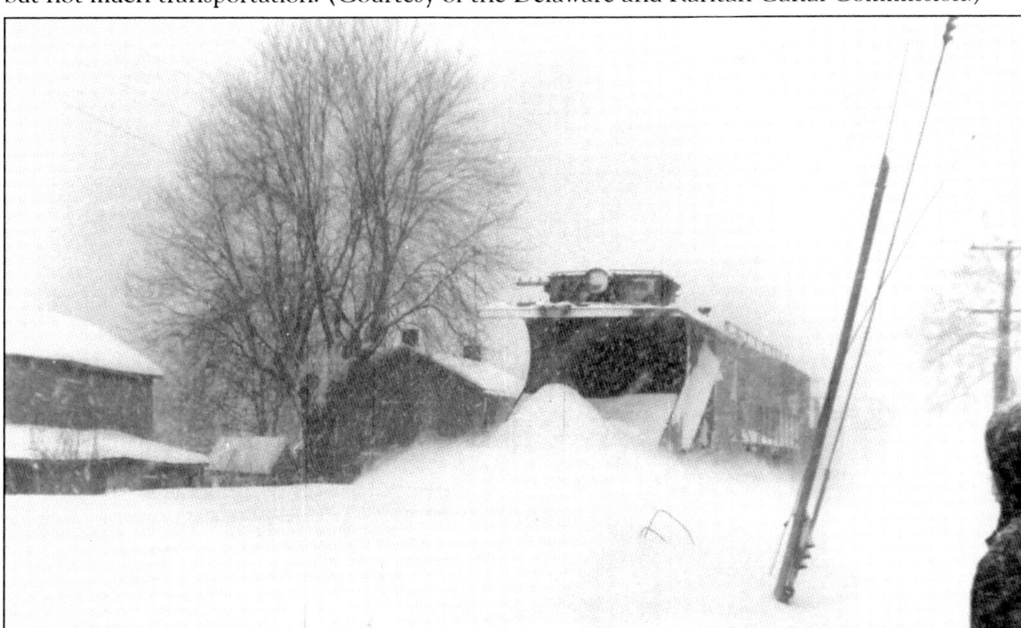

In contrast, a youngster watches as the Pennsylvania Railroad snowplow passes through Stockton clearing the tracks through a very heavy snowstorm. The specially built plow in this undated photograph was pushed through the drifts by a steam locomotive. Even in the dead of winter, freight moved by train. (Courtesy of the Delaware River Mill Society.)

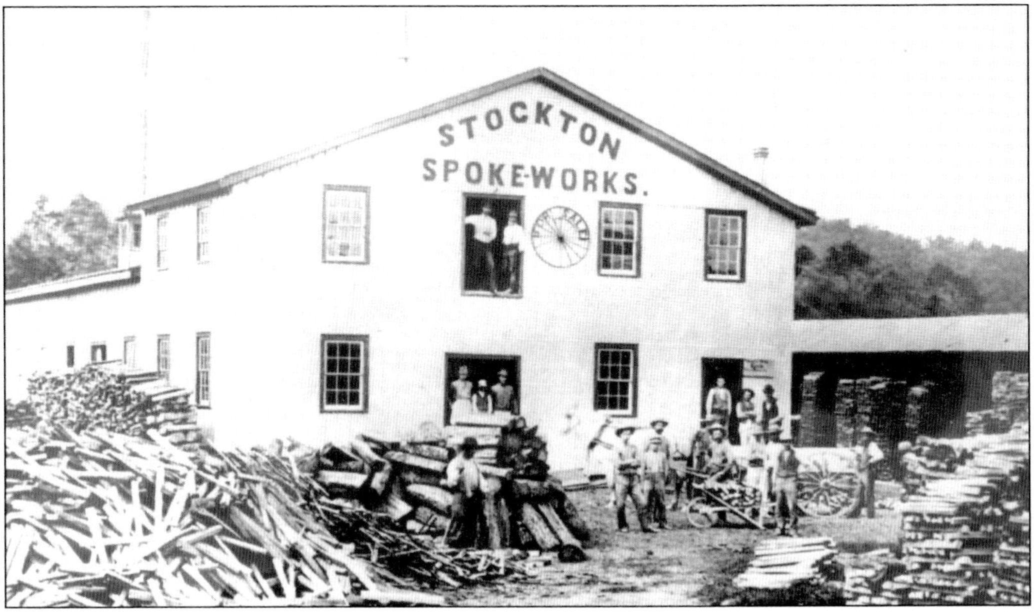

A number of businesses flourished due to the easy access to transportation that both the canal and railroad provided. Located on the canal north of Bridge Street was the Stockton Spoke Works. It is clear in this late-1800s photograph that there were far more spokes being produced than was needed in Stockton alone. Eventually torn down, the little house that was the office is all that stands today. (Courtesy of Carl Cathers.)

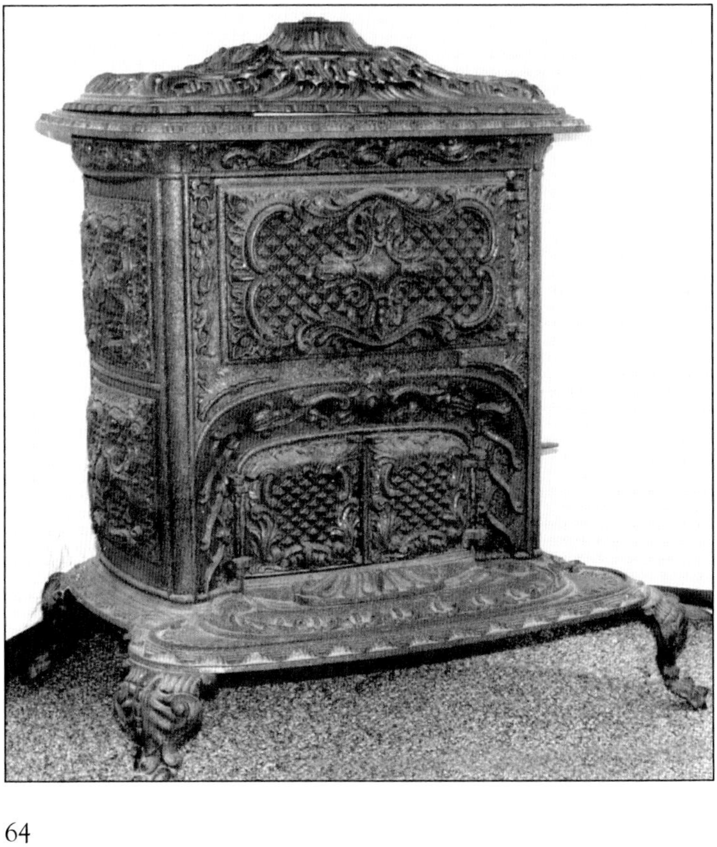

The Deats Stove was produced at the H. Deats and Company foundry located in Brookville south of Stockton. The foundry manufactured plows as well as the decorative and practical Deats Stove. The popular side-feeder stove, easily delivered by train, soon became a popular item across the United States during the 1850s through the 1870s. (Courtesy of the Delaware River Mill Society.)

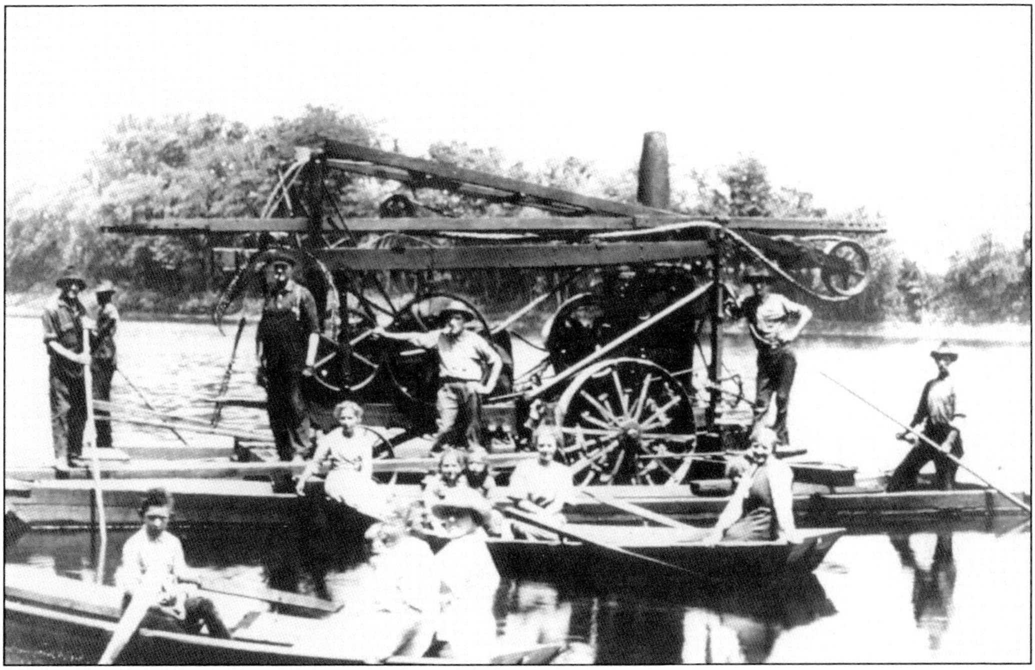

Mayor Theodore S. Moore, who served as Stockton's first mayor, owned a well-drilling business. In this photograph, taken after the bridge had been destroyed by fire on July 22, 1923, the drilling rig is being transported across the river by boat. Moore is standing on the rig, third from the left. (Courtesy of Carl Cathers.)

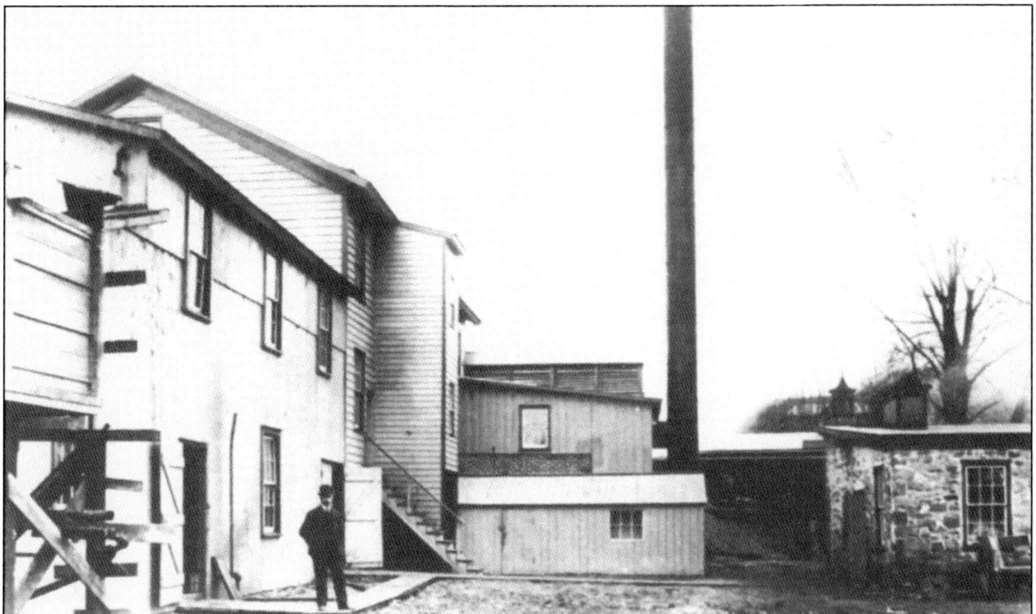

A man stands at the back of the rubber mill, which was located on the site of the former bicycle factory. The rubber mill burned down in a spectacular blaze in the 1920s. The only remnant of the building is a large cement structure, the purpose of which no one can seem to remember, that sits near the old train station building. (Courtesy of Carl Cathers.)

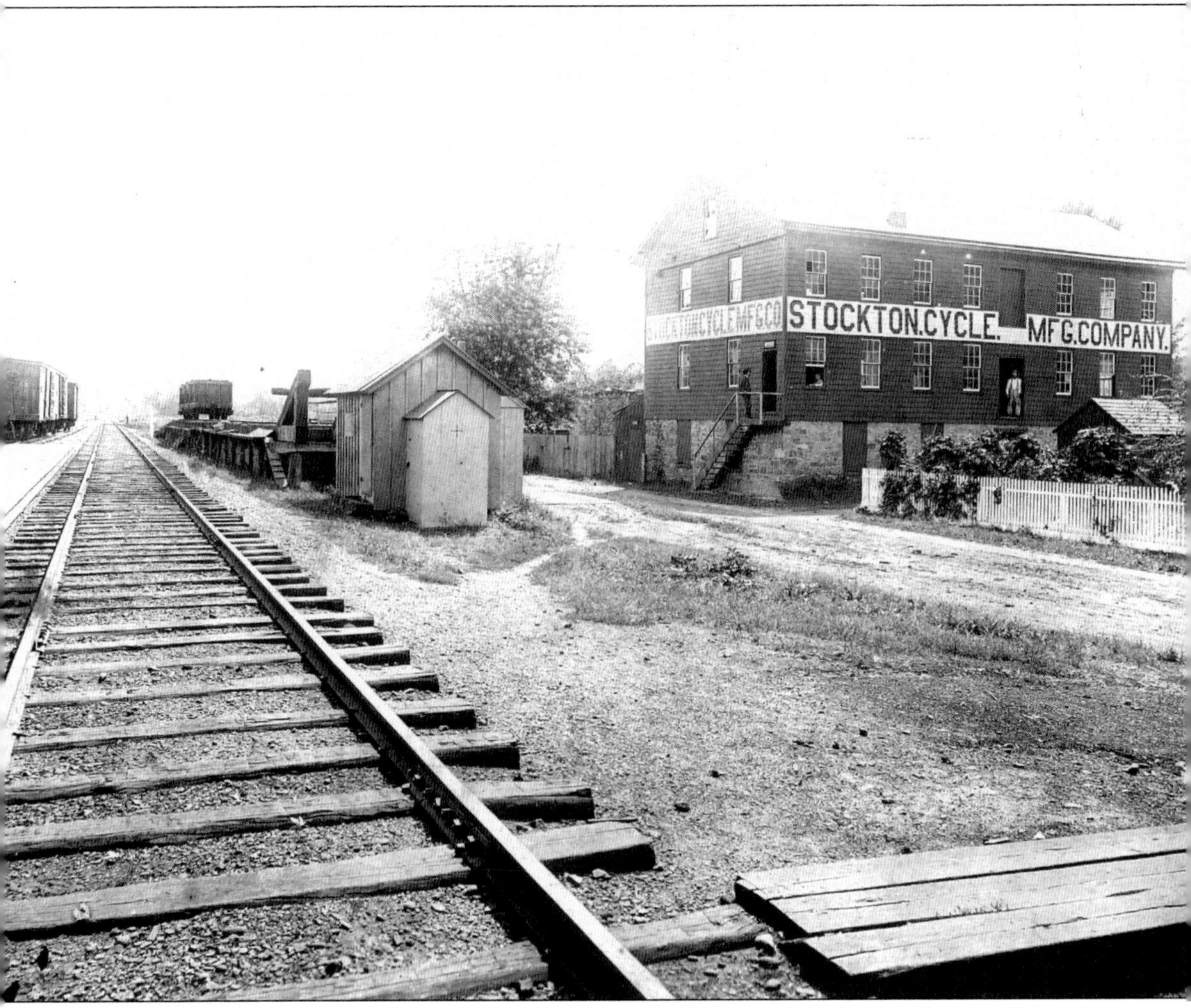

The proximity of the Stockton Cycle Manufacturing Company to the Stockton railroad depot had a direct impact on its business. In the days of this c. 1900 photograph, it was not unusual for bicyclists to ride very long distances. People would arrive by train from as far as Trenton, some 19 miles away, to buy their bicycle directly from the Stockton Bike Factory and then ride their new bike home. The train yard held other attractions, especially for the kids. Aside from the universal train activity of putting pennies on the tracks for the locomotive to flatten, the old coal bin on the left of the photograph behind the small shed could support hours of activity. The boys would burst out of school and run down Skeeter's Alley to the train yard and leap into the empty bins to play. (Courtesy of Carl Cathers.)

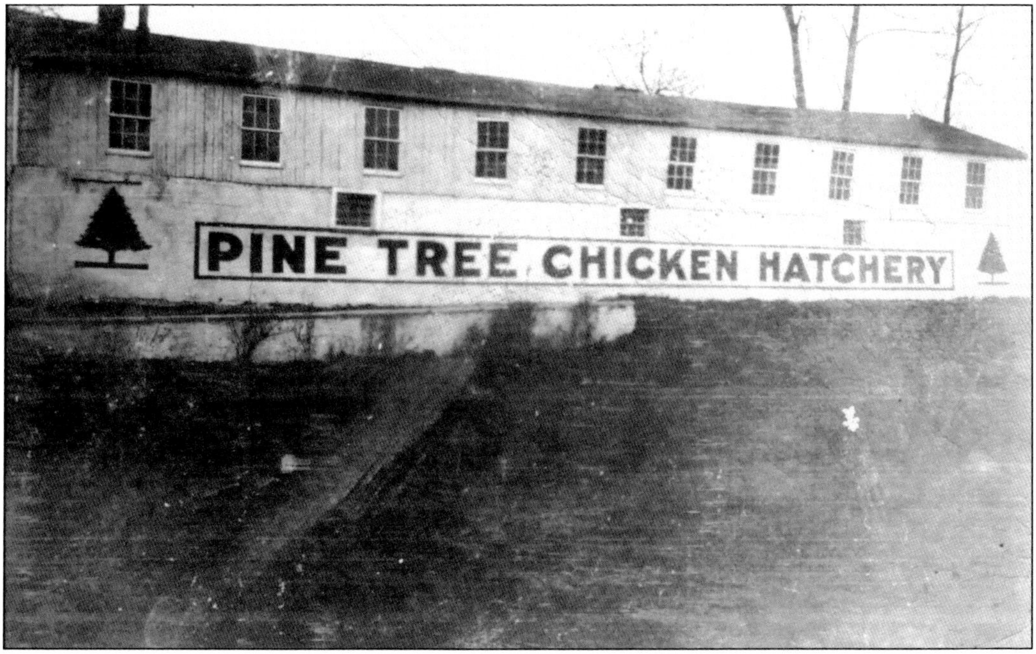

The Pine Tree Chicken Hatchery is the result of Joseph Wilson's groundbreaking discovery about shipping newly hatched chicks. In fact, Wilson, or "Chicky Joe" as he was known to the locals, created a new industry with nationwide impact from this spot behind his home on Main Street in Stockton. (Courtesy of Edith McCloughan.)

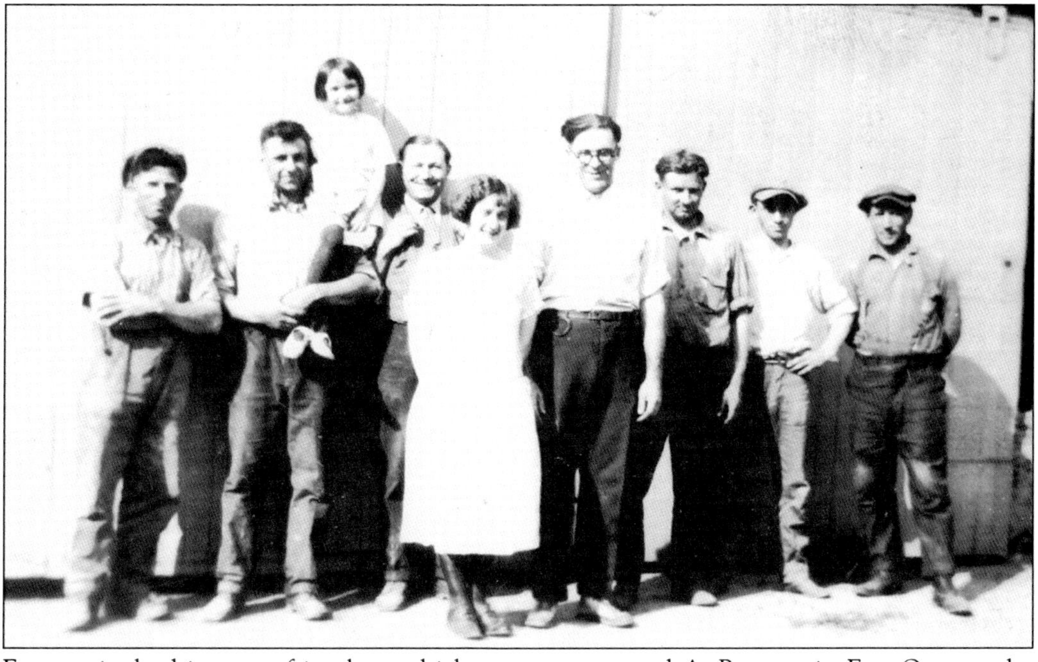

From a single shipment of just-born chicks to a man named A. Runyun in East Orange, the business grew to a 150,000 egg plant when Wilson handed down his business to his son, Emmert. Sitting atop a hatchery worker's shoulders is young Edith Wilson (now McCloughan) with her father, Emmert to her left. (Courtesy of Edith McCloughan.)

Pine Tree Hatchery
Stockton, New Jersey

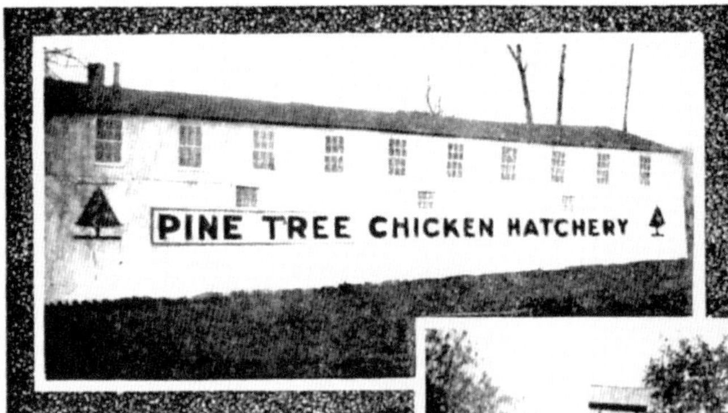

ONE WING OF OUR BIG HATCHERY

Pine Tree Hatchery is located on a knoll, high and dry. Concrete walls protect the incubators from sudden temperature changes.

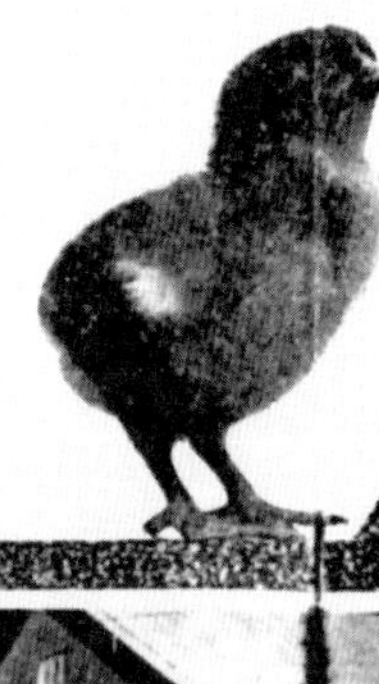

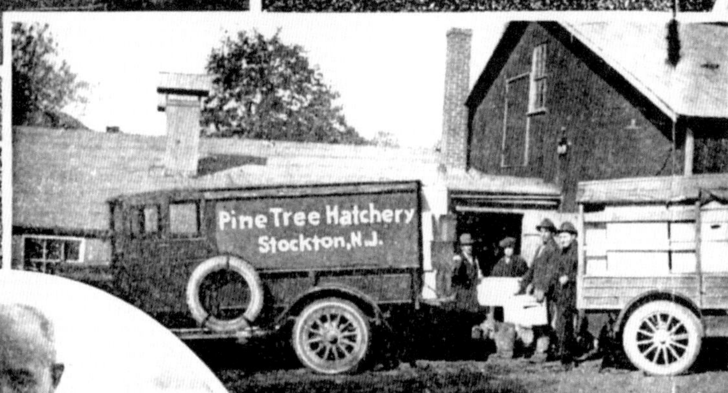

Hatching Eggs from Pine Tree Breeders

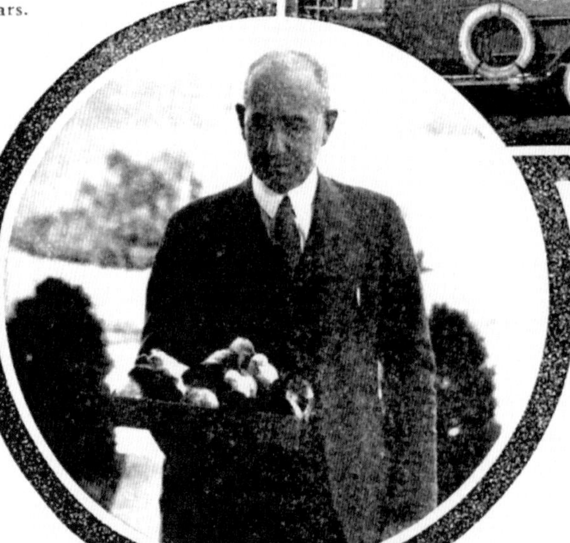

Jos. D. Wilson, Founder and Owner of Pine Tree Hatchery, with chicks from a recent hatch. Mr. Wilson has been actively interested in artificial incubation for 45 years.

MEMBER NEW JERSEY BABY CHICK ASSOCIATION

ONE OF THE ORIGINAL PINE TREE INCUBATORS

This Incubator shown at the right was built by Jos. D. Wilson in 1890. It has a capacity of 420 eggs and proved to be an excellent hatcher. We have preserved this crude but very satisfactory hatcher.

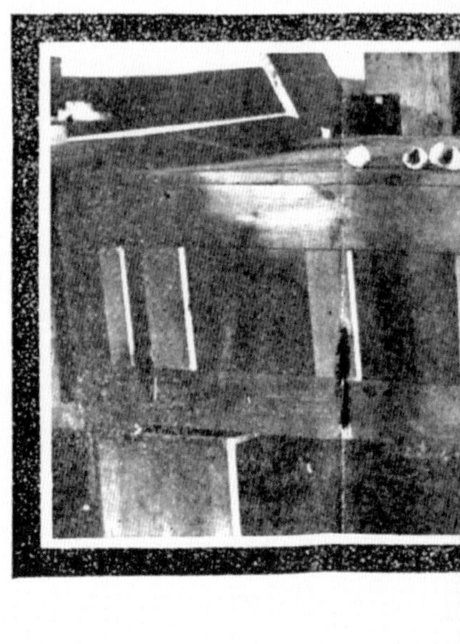

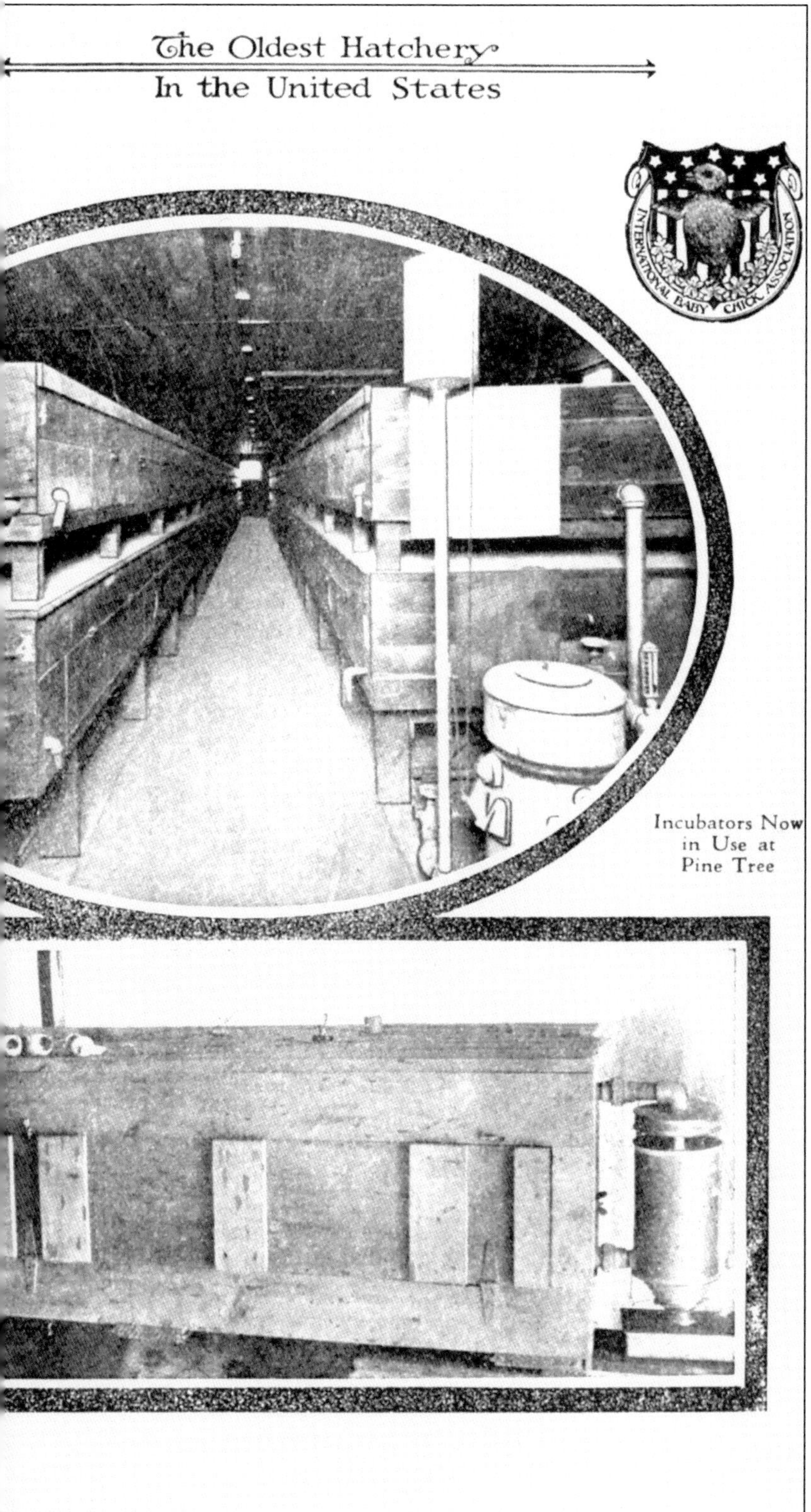

Each year the Pine Tree Chicken Hatchery sent out a brochure with the offerings for the season. This picture is the middle page spread of the 1933 brochure, which also offered tips on raising chicks. It all started when Joseph Wilson took the common-known fact that newborn chicks do not eat for the first 40 hours after hatching and used it to launch the live chick shipping industry. After spending several years perfecting his incubators to hatch strong, healthy chicks, Wilson put an advertisement in *American Poultry Advocate*, offering to ship live chicks for 8¢ apiece. Although his first successful shipment went to East Orange, his second order for 500 chicks to be sent to a Chicago suburb was the real test. The chicks arrived healthy, safe, and clamoring to be fed. (Courtesy of Edith McCloughan.)

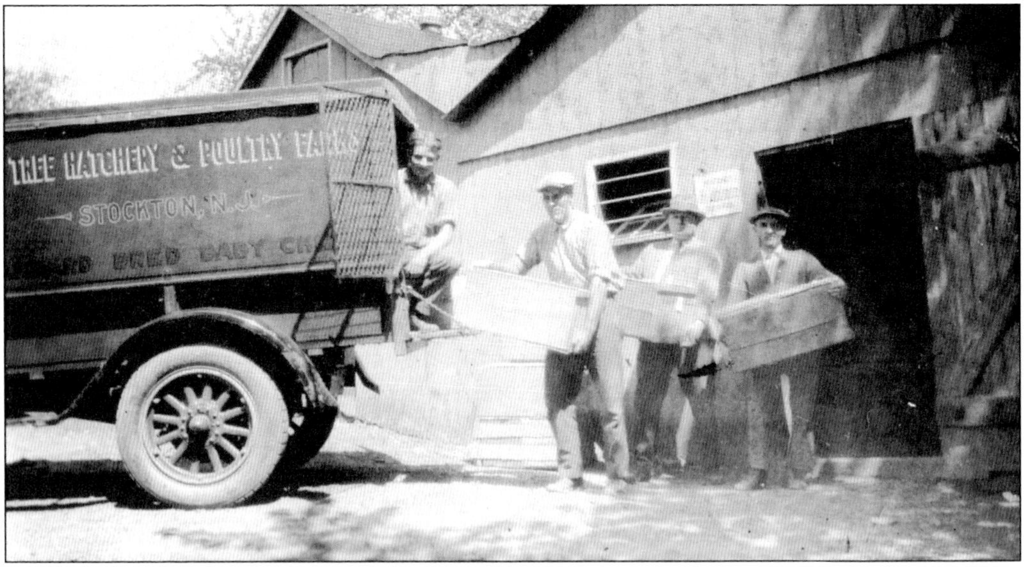

After the first shipments in 1892, Joseph Wilson was visited by a dubious postal inspector that, after the inspector was convinced there was no fraud at play, ended with the inspector staying for dinner. This 1930s-era picture shows the men loading the truck with chicks to take to the train station. Emmert Wilson is second from the right. (Courtesy of Edith McCloughan.)

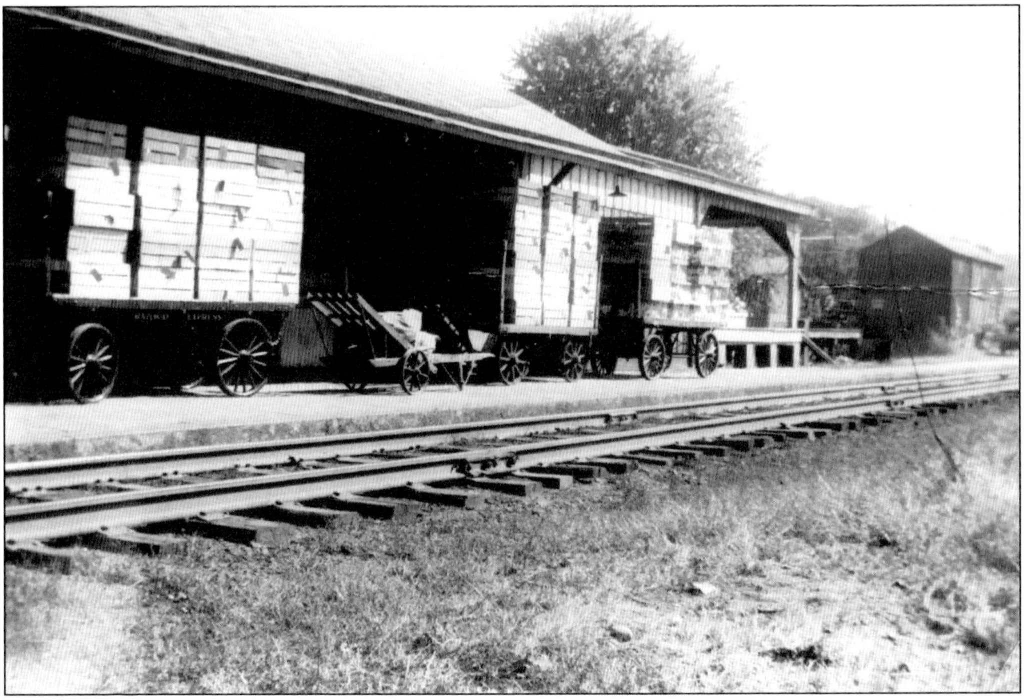

These three carts in this *c.* 1930s photograph are loaded with boxes of chicks to be sent all across the country. It would usually take at least 15 minutes to load the boxes, which many times held up the train, much to the chagrin of the conductor. Chirping chicks waiting to be loaded was a familiar sound at the station. (Courtesy of Edith McCloughan.)

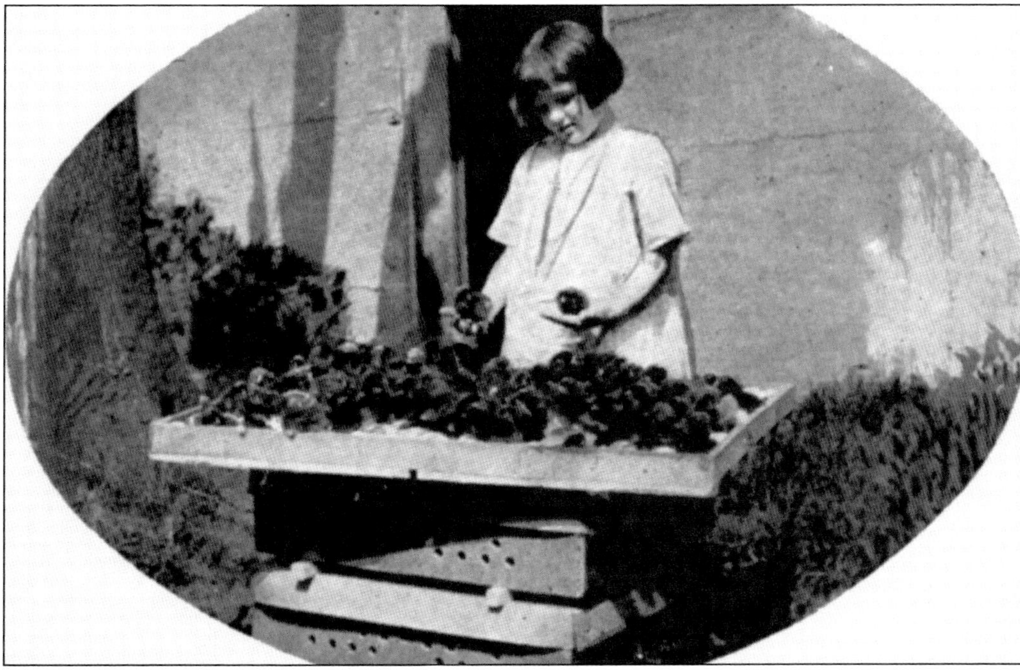

The 1928 Pine Tree Chicken Hatchery brochure featured Joseph Wilson's nine-year-old granddaughter Edith Wilson in front of a brood of chicks and holding two of the chicks in her hands. The boxes with the holes in the sides on which the chicks are sitting were used to ship the chicks. They were insulated so the chicks would survive extremes in temperature. (Courtesy of Edith McCloughan.)

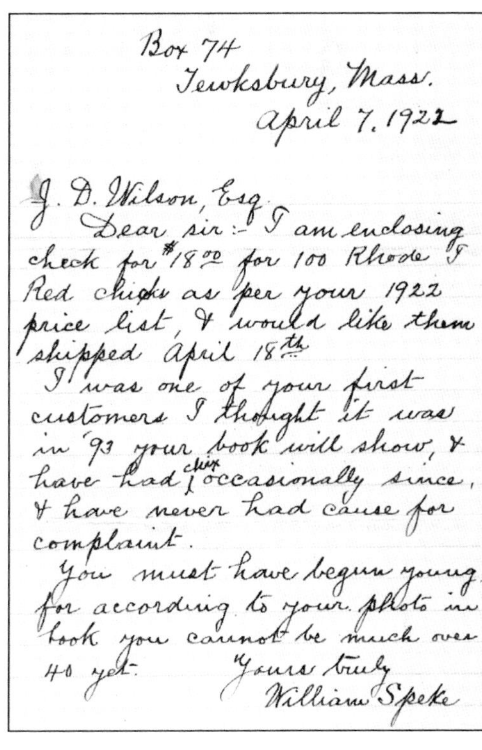

Box 74
Tewksbury, Mass.
April 7. 1922

J. D. Wilson, Esq.
Dear sir:- I am enclosing check for $18.00 for 100 Rhode I Red chicks as per your 1922 price list, & would like them shipped April 18th.
I was one of your first customers I thought it was in '93 your book will show, & have had chix occasionally since, & have never had cause for complaint.
You must have begun young, for according to your photo in book you cannot be much over 40 yet.
Yours truly
William Speke

Only half of 1 percent of the chicks that Pine Tree Chicken Hatchery shipped died in transit, which was compensated by always adding a few more chicks than were requested to the order. This kind of attention to detail led to over $450,000 in sales by 1955. The Pine Tree Chicken Hatchery customers were appreciative and loyal, as this 1922 customer's letter to Wilson shows. (Courtesy of Edith McCloughan.)

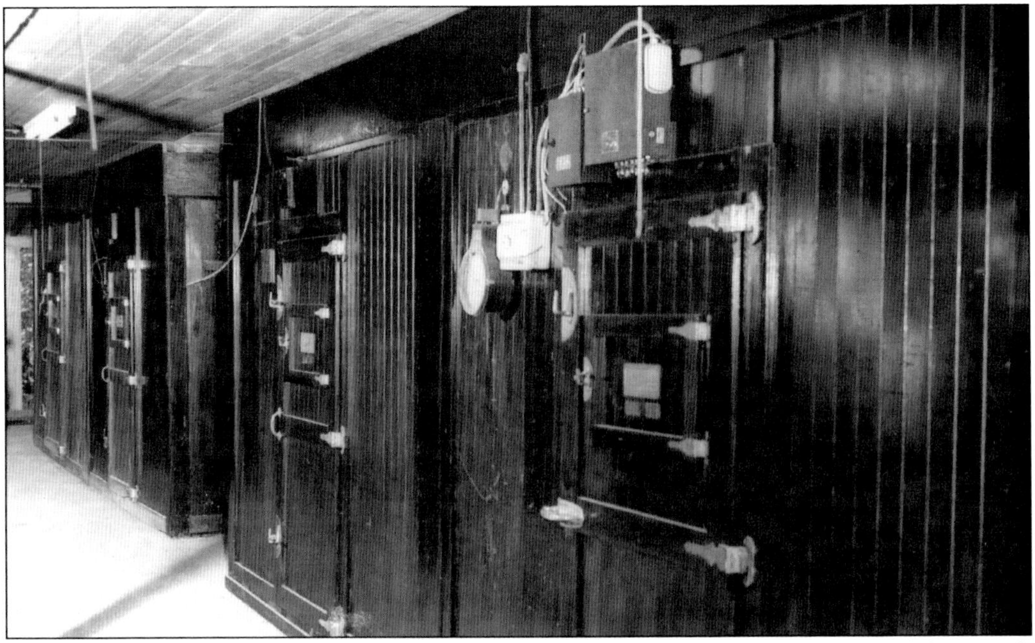

By the 1940s, the hatchery had moved well beyond the first pine wood incubator built by Joseph Wilson. These modern incubators featured automatic egg turners, automatic heat control, lights, and alarms so that the hatching process could be monitored at all times. The healthy chicks that Pine Tree Chicken Hatchery produced kept the hatchery competitive in an ever-growing market for day-old chicks. (Courtesy of Edith McCloughan.)

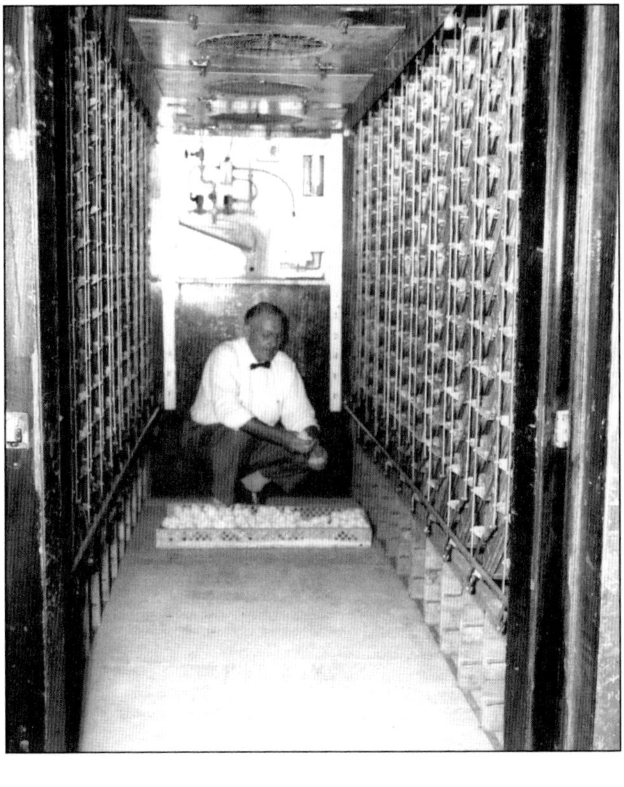

Just after World War II, Wilson retired and handed down the hatchery business to his son Emmert. As was the custom in Stockton, a father's nickname often followed from father to son. Although the family called Emmert "ER," the locals knew him as "Chicky Joe." (Courtesy of Edith McCloughan.)

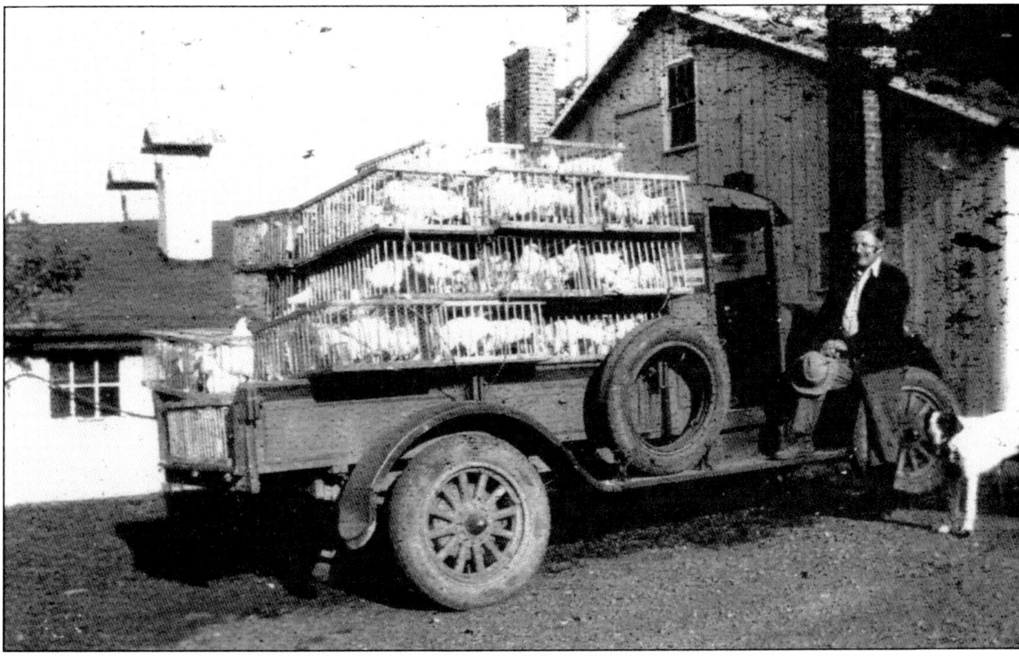

Emmert is seen in this 1940s-era photograph with his dog Pointer. This was taken during the time that he was selling young hens or pullets as well as baby chicks. Remembering the name of the dog was easy. An avid hunter, Emmert owned many dogs over the years, and they were always named Pointer. (Courtesy of Edith McCloughan.)

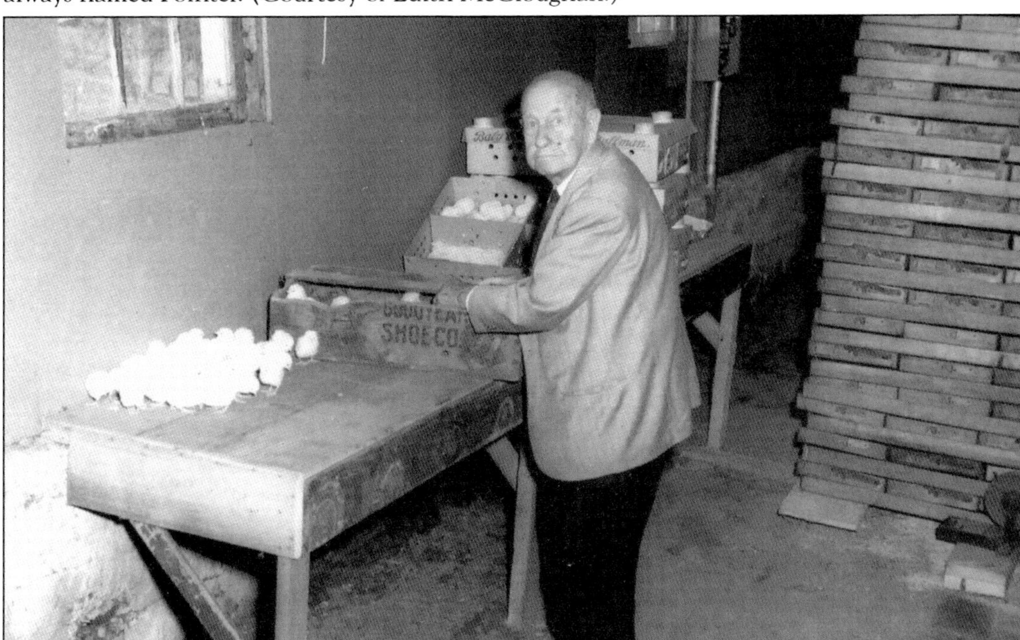

Joseph is pictured here at age 94 shortly before his death in 1961. Joseph's self-confessed passion for raising poultry and his unique innovation revolutionized the poultry business in this country and led the way for Hunterdon County to become the leading chick producer in the nation through the 1970s. (Courtesy of Edith McCloughan.)

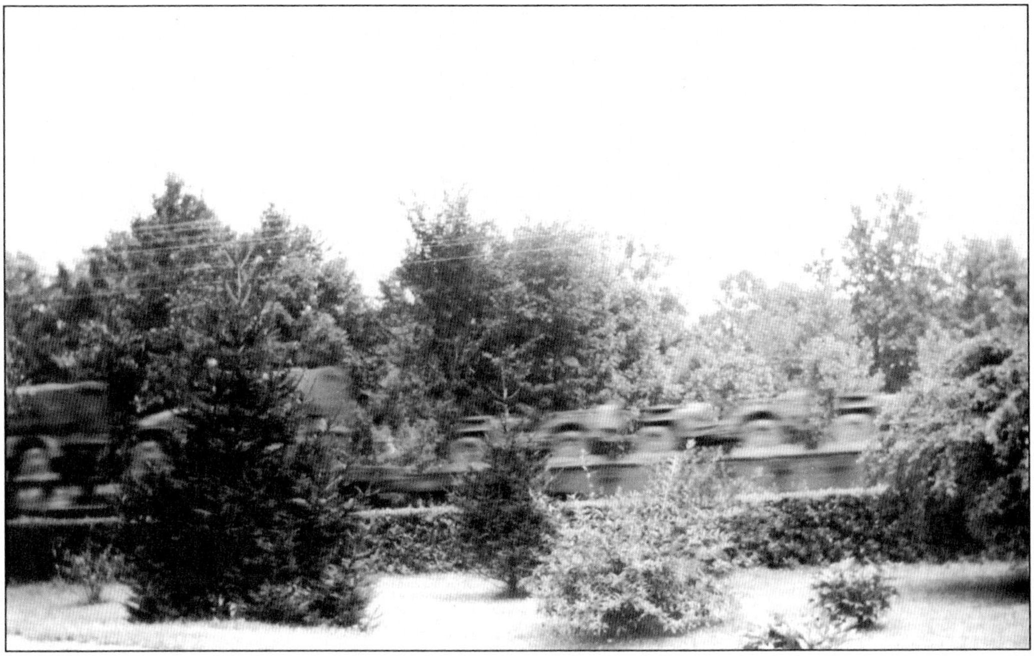

During World War II, the Pennsylvania Railroad, like other freight and passenger carriers of the time, focused their resources on the efficient movement of troops and supplies. Coordinated through the Office of Defense Transportation (ODT), the railroad's advertisements reinforced the idea that the railroad's primary job was not just moving troops but moving all they required as well. The railroad pointed out that each soldier going overseas required an average of eight tons of freight including ammunition, equipment, food, and supplies. In this 1942 photograph, army trucks, strapped two to a flat car with wood chocking around their wheels, are transported through Stockton. (Courtesy of Carl Cathers.)

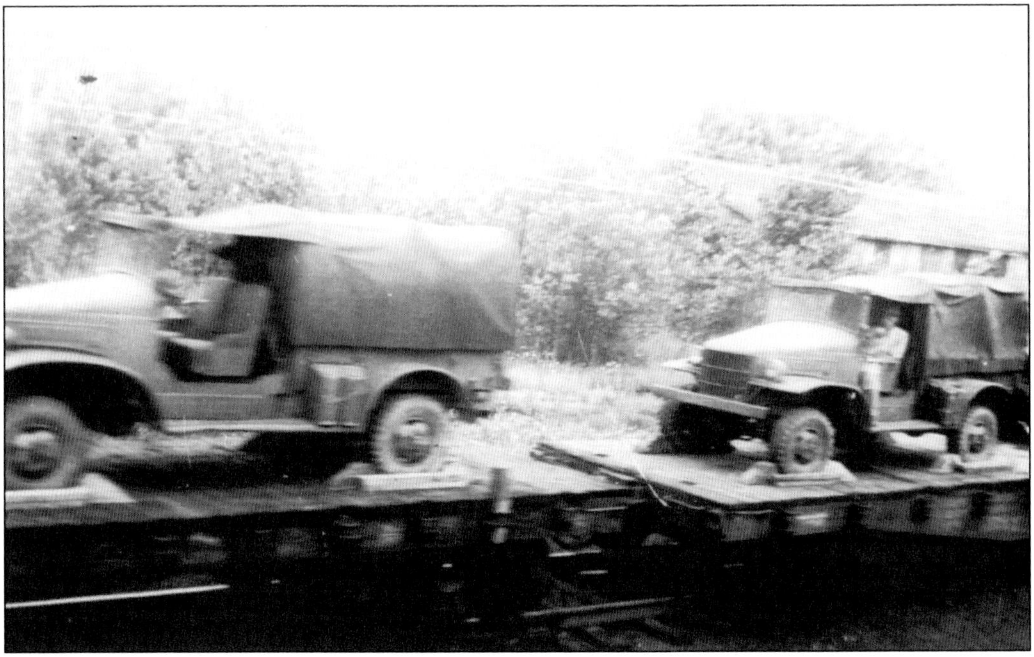

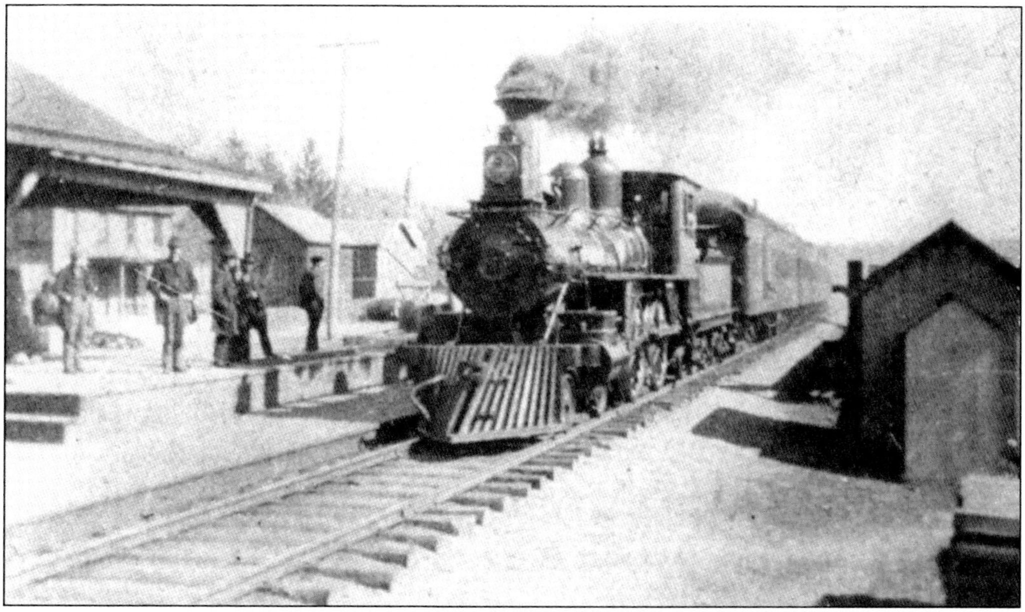

The northbound Belvidere Delaware (Bel-Del) train arrives at the Stockton station in this c. 1890s photograph. Locomotive No. 239 was an American type 4-4-0, class D-14A engine built in Altoona, Pennsylvania, in the 1890s. Chartered March 2, 1836, the Bel-Del operated as part of the Pennsylvania Railroad system. (From the collection of Wesley Hendricks, courtesy of Carl Cathers.)

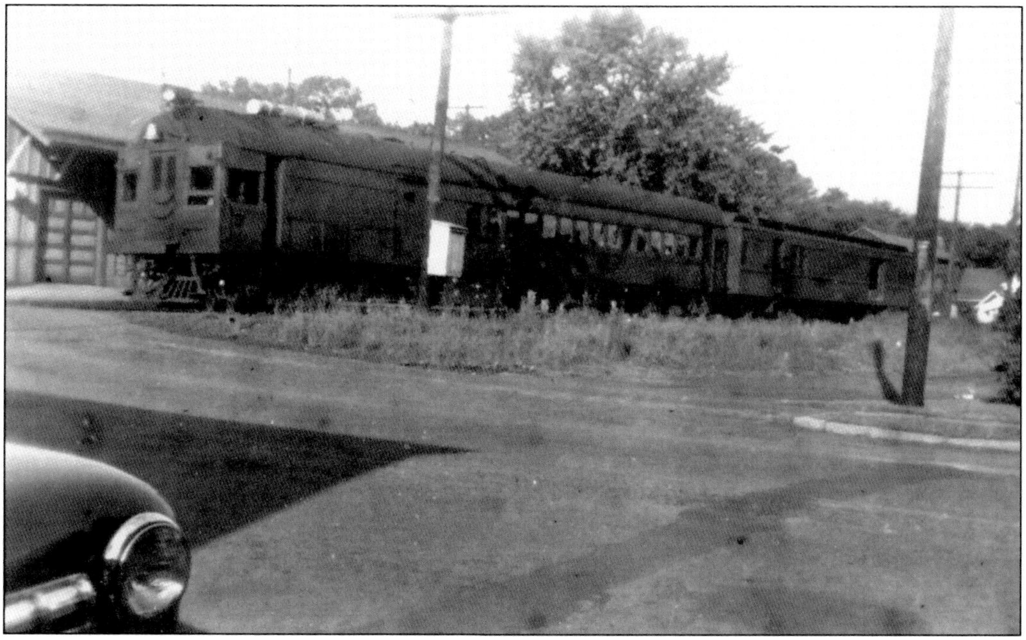

Doodlebugs had replaced the steam locomotive for passenger travel 50 years later. In this 1950s photograph, Doodlebug 4669, with a baggage car attached, arrives at Stockton station to pick up northbound passengers. The origin of the name is unclear; however, it may have been taken from the phrase "doodling through town." The last passenger train passed through Stockton on October 24, 1960. (Photograph by Frank Barry, courtesy of Carl Cathers.)

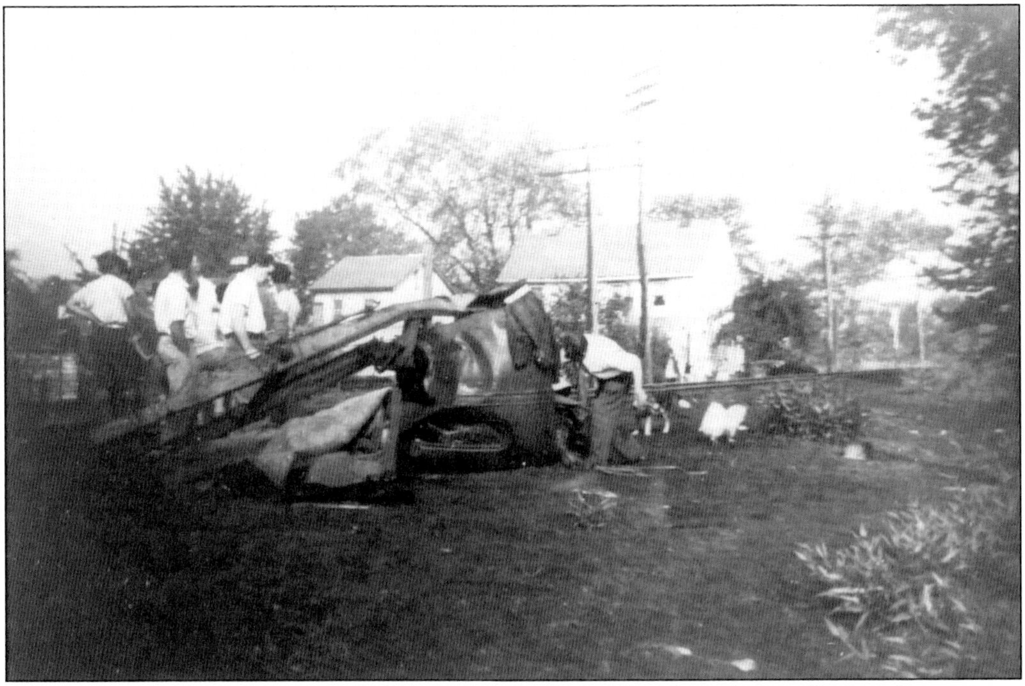

On a summer day in 1941, a truck delivering a canoe to a local resident stalled on the tracks at the Prallsville crossing. The driver was unable to restart the truck, and it was struck by a passing train, destroying the truck and killing the driver. (Courtesy of Carl Cathers.)

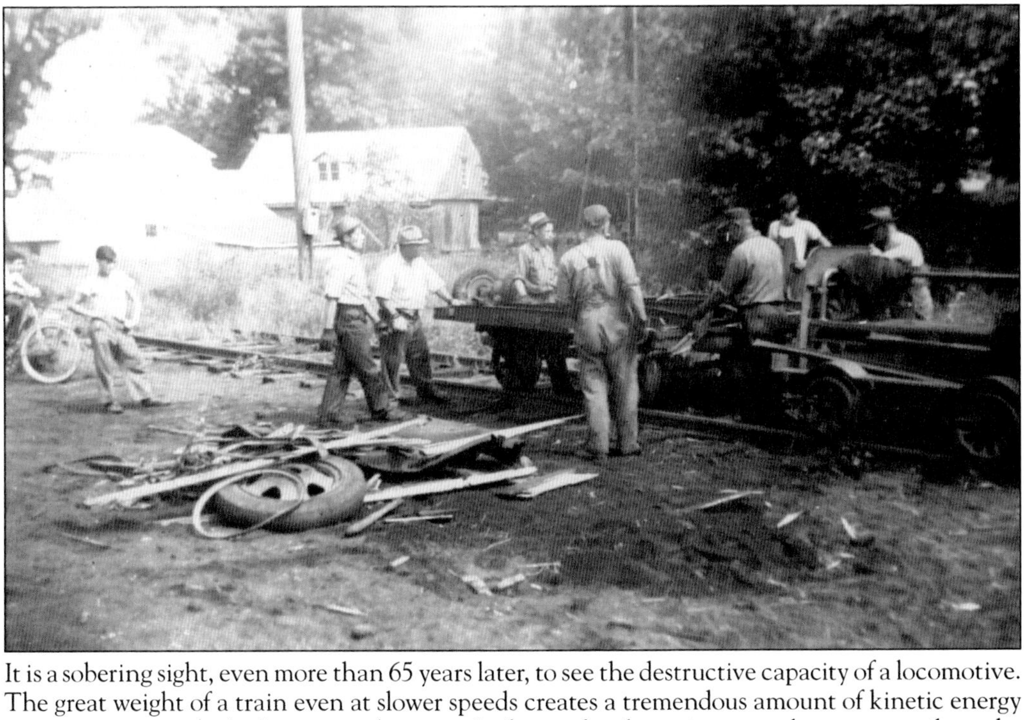

It is a sobering sight, even more than 65 years later, to see the destructive capacity of a locomotive. The great weight of a train even at slower speeds creates a tremendous amount of kinetic energy requiring a great deal of stopping distance. In fact, a freight train may take up to a mile and a half to come to a stop. (Courtesy of Carl Cathers.)

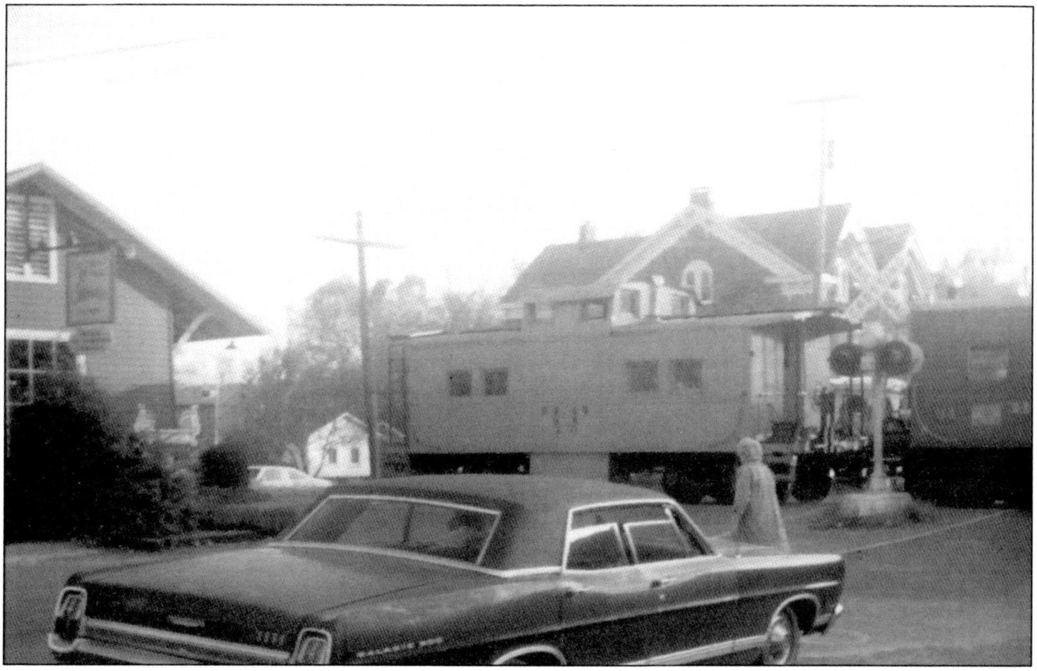

Just as the era of the canal came to a close in 1933, the era of the railroad ended in Stockton on November 12, 1978. In this photograph, Anne Matthews, who, while playing Stella Dallas, saw the passing of the radio age, watches as the last train to roll through Stockton crosses Bridge Street past the old station, which by then had become a retail space. (Courtesy of Carl Cathers.)

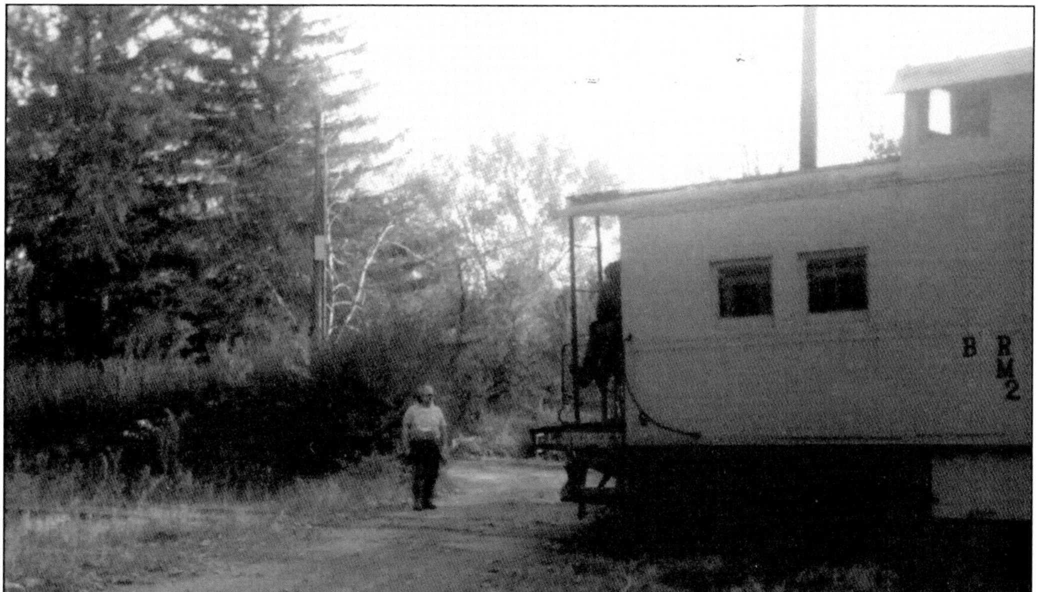

A member of the train crew sits perched at the back of the caboose, watching the towns and people disappear into the distance. After providing transportation for passengers and a means for moving products to the wider world for more than 100 years, the last train passes over the Prallsville crossing and into history. (Courtesy of Carl Cathers.)

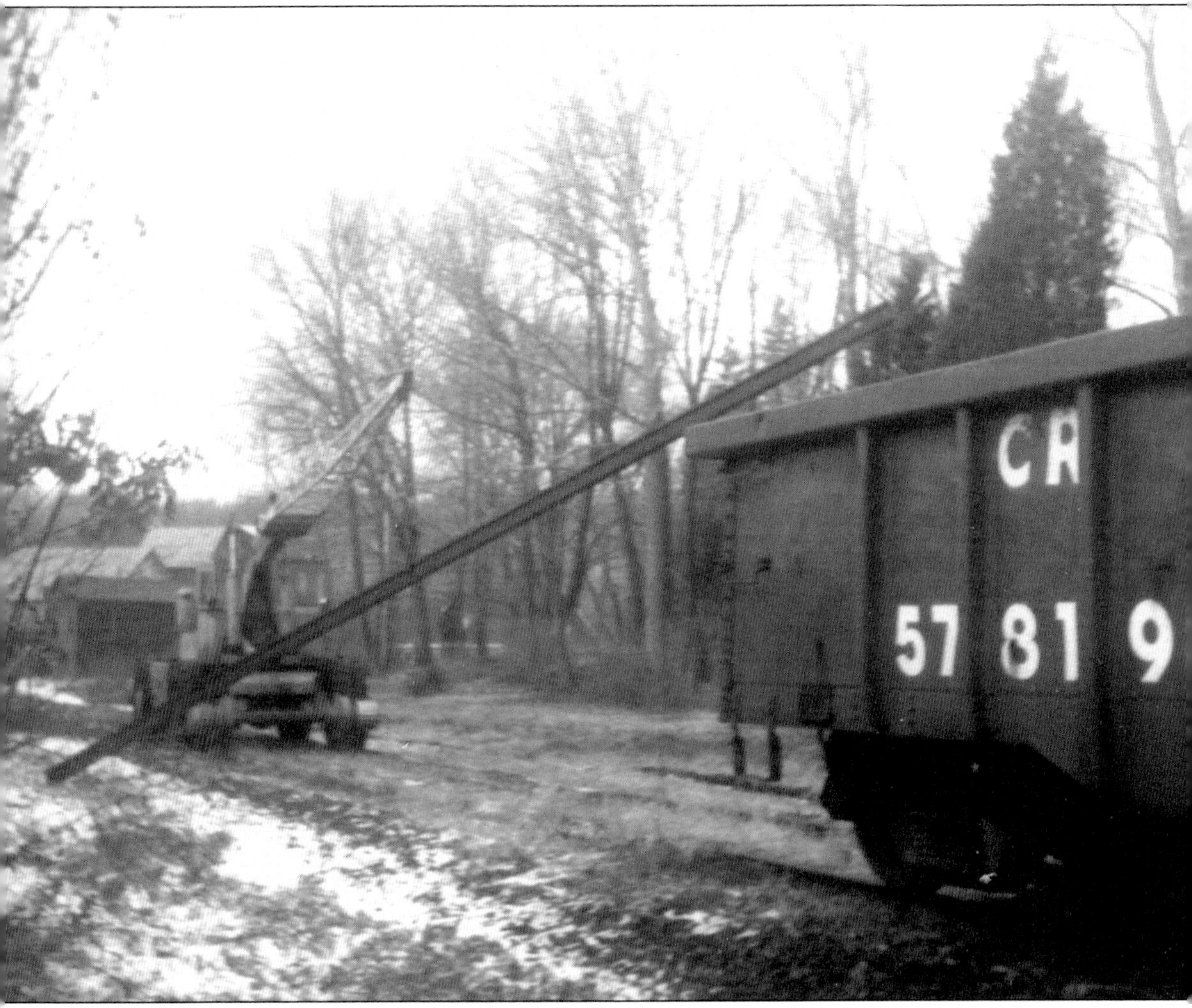

On January 9, 1980, the rails of the old Bel-Del were removed to make way for the Rails to Trails program. Almost 30 years later, the course of the former rail line now provides a "rail trail" along the Delaware River that stretches more than 31 miles from Frenchtown to Trenton. On a trip along the 16-mile stretch from Frenchtown to Lambertville, bicyclists and hikers can enjoy Bull's Island with a footbridge to Lumberville, Pennsylvania; Prallsville Mills; Stockton; the Holcombe-Jimison farmstead; Lambertville; and New Hope, Pennsylvania. Location and accessibility provided by the river, canal, and railroad were in large part responsible for the manufacturing era of Stockton in the 18th, 19th, and 20th centuries. It is again Stockton's location along the river, canal, and railroad, now turned to trail, that gives it a solid place in the tourism industry of the 21st century and beyond. (Courtesy of Carl Cathers.)

Four

LIFE IN STOCKTON

The region along the Delaware River and the surrounding towns of Stockton, Lambertville, and Sergeantsville, on the New Jersey side, and New Hope, Pipersville, and Doylestown, on the Pennsylvania side, have for generations been known as a haven for artists, writers, and actors. Home to "the small hotel with the wishing well" from the Richard Rodgers song, the area was labeled the "Genius Belt" many years ago, as it played host to George S. Kaufman, Dorothy Parker, Lorenz Hart, Paul Whiteman, and artists of all types. The area still possesses a creative energy that can be seen and felt in the many cultural and artistic events throughout the region.

Located a few miles north of where George Washington crossed the Delaware River in the Battle of Trenton, the area is rich in history dating back to the revolution. From the many covered bridges, to the quiet towpath along the Delaware and Raritan Canal, to the limekilns imbedded in the side of a hillside in Uhlerstown that supplied gunpowder for the Colonial army, one can touch the history of the area around virtually every corner.

Through it all wends the Delaware River, providing the boundary between Pennsylvania and New Jersey. Floating in a tube or paddling in a canoe brings one into close and wonderful contact with a landscape that has been painted, drawn, and photographed by thousands of artists over the years. Adding to the beauty are the deer, fox, beavers, eagles, and hawks that can be spotted everywhere.

The beauty of Stockton in the midst of this extraordinary area is that it is a town that is unimpressed with its own credentials and unpretentious in its demeanor. The people are friendly and welcoming, and the pace is a bit saner than that of the larger world.

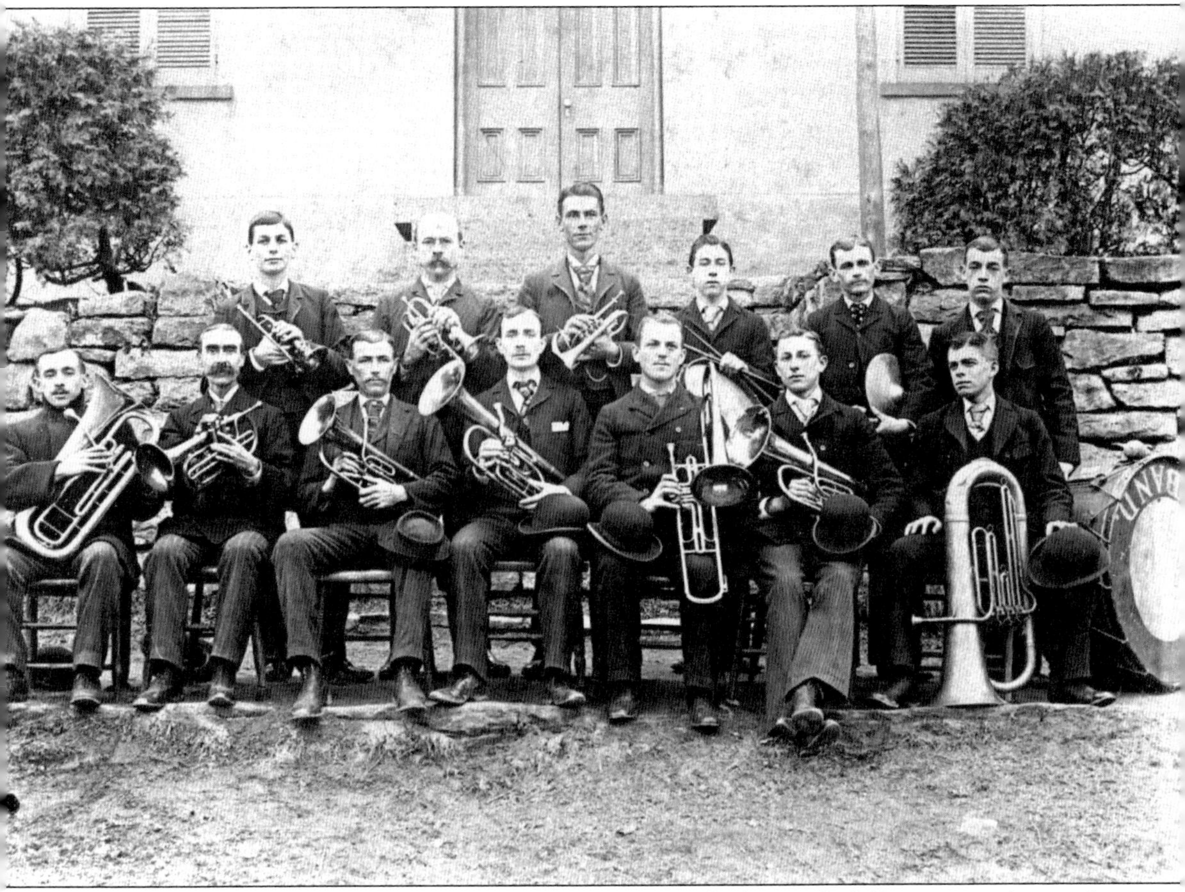

Life in Stockton at the beginning of the 20th century had a much different pace than it does today. Yet even in today's frantic world, Stockton beckons a visitor to relax and stay a bit. Many years ago, Emmert "Chicky Joe" Wilson wrote down his recollections of Stockton. The Stockton that was home to the 1893 Stockton Cornet Band pictured here can be found in Wilson's memories. He writes, "A. L. Davidson maintained a general livery stable and many salesmen would arrive by train and hire a rig to dispense of his wares throughout the rural community. Saturday evening was a particularly busy time for the younger gentry to have a rig to spark the lady of his love." The members of the 1893 Stockton Cornet Band include, from left to right, (first row) George Hoffman, Charles Robinson, Harvey Holcombe, George B. Horner, Willis Wall, Smith Cottrell, and Howard Hunt; (second row) D. Wilson, Dory Everett, Fred Dilts, Sam Diamond, John Shivery, and David Holcombe. (Courtesy of the Delaware River Mill Society.)

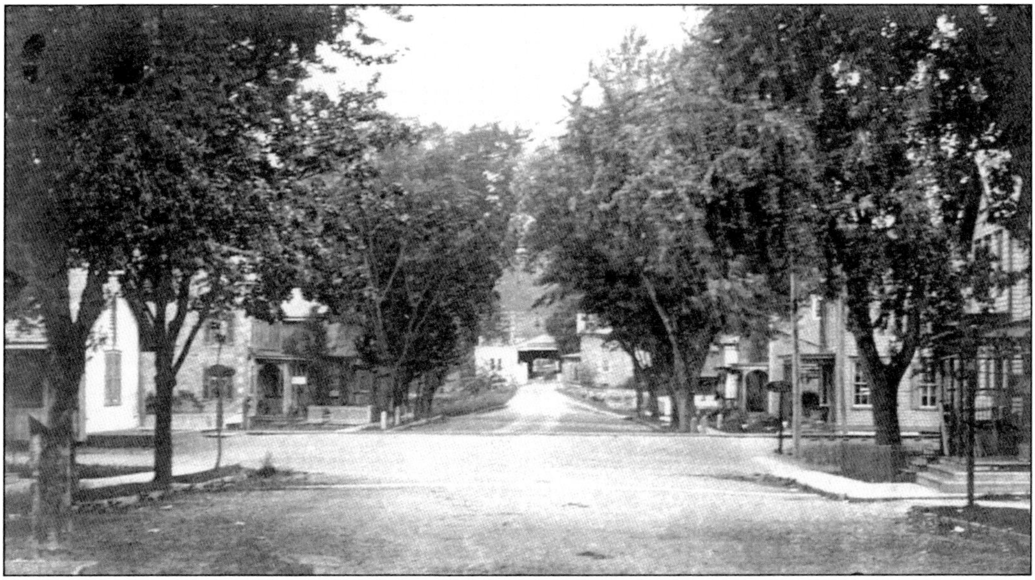

This 1920s view of Bridge Street looks west toward the bridge to Pennsylvania. At some places along the street, there can be seen stone hitching posts at the curb. Any home with a stone hitching post belonged to a stonecutter from one of the quarries. (Courtesy of Carl Cathers.)

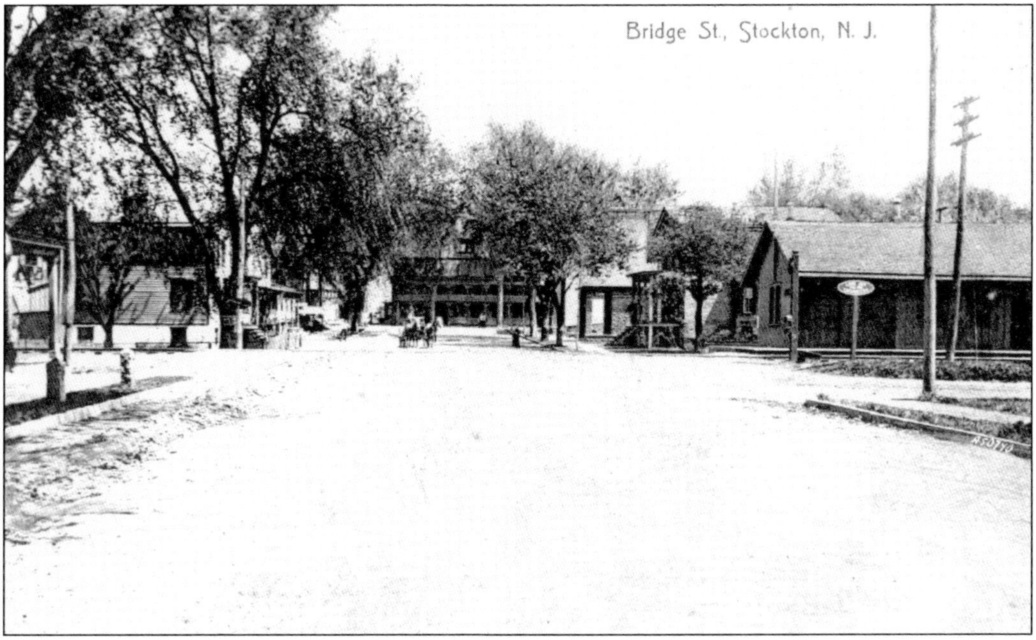

This is Bridge Street looking east toward the Stockton Inn from around 1900. Regarding the streets, Wilson wrote, "During this period the streets were dirt and MUD. During the annual spring thaw, (March–April) the horse drawn rigs encountered hub deep mud in some sections. Not until 1913 did some crushed stone prevail where the streets were really bad." (Courtesy of Carl Cathers.)

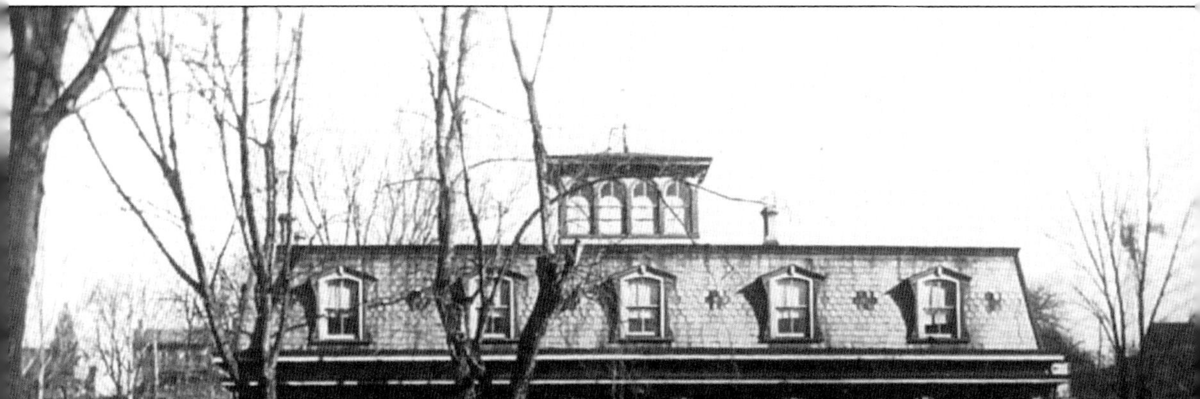

This is the famous Stockton Inn immortalized as "the small hotel with the wishing well," in the Lorenz Hart and Richard Rodgers song "There's a Small Hotel" from their 1936 Broadway hit musical *On Your Toes*. Evident in this c. 1890s photograph are the improvements made to the inn by John S. Hockenbury in 1878 that included a third story with a French roof and an observatory on top. Elizabeth Weiss acquired the inn in 1922 and married Joe Colligan, who was an artist and part-time bartender. Colligan's Stockton Inn became a destination for artists, actors, and writers, including Dorothy Parker, Robert Benchley, and Rodgers and Hart. During the early horse-and-buggy days, the Stockton Inn was a bar only and did not serve food. An old gentleman named Sank Farley was the official hostler who did not tolerate rowdiness on the premises. Emmert Wilson noted of Farley that, "he could out box and outsmart any quarrelsome individual in his day. His favorite stunt was to kick the hat off an average man's head accurately and quickly." (Courtesy of Carl Cathers.)

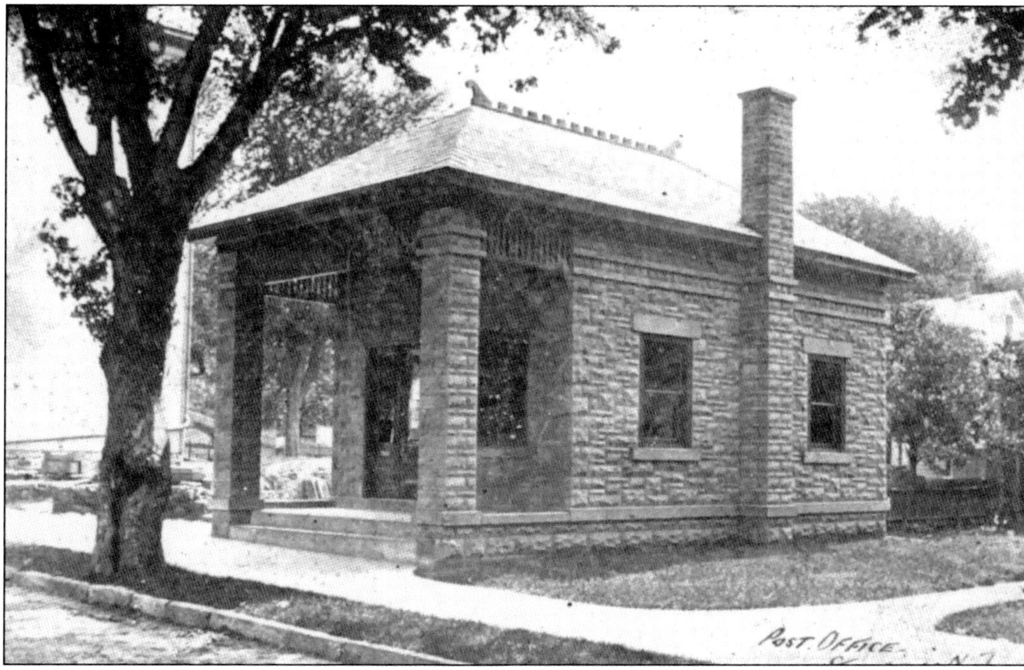

The Stockton Post Office was built by the first mayor of Stockton, Theodore Moore in the early 1900s. Built of cement blocks, it was, in its day, a center of activity for the town. The building was razed in the 1950s when the post office moved to a new, larger facility. (Courtesy of Edith McCloughan.)

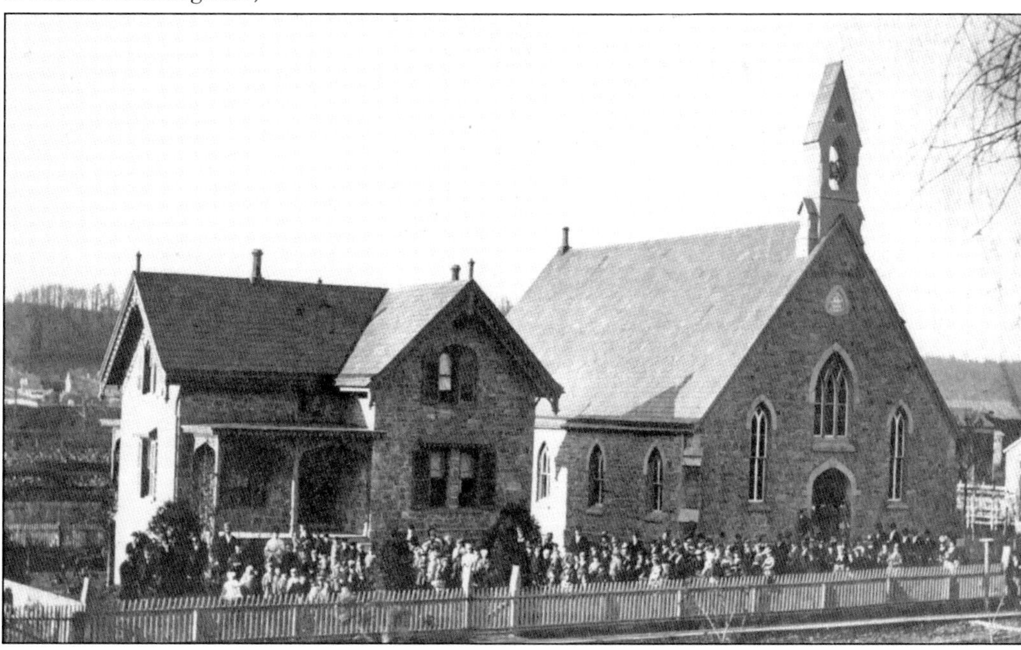

This photograph of the Presbyterian Sunday school and church property was taken on November 9, 1872. The church and the minister's house next to it were both constructed of Stockton sandstone. Although there is much more built around the church, it still looks much the same today as it did in the late 1800s. (Courtesy of the Delaware River Mill Society.)

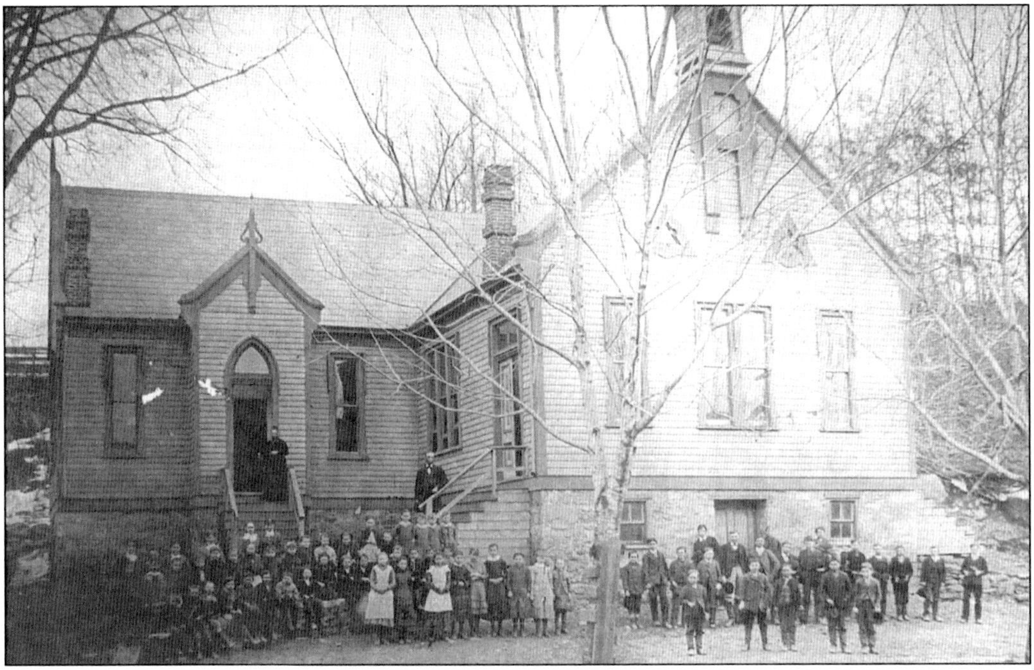

This group photograph of the students taken in front of the Stockton School was taken prior to 1884. The school looks much the same as it did then; however, the bell tower is no longer on the roof. The bell itself is currently on top of the town hall with plans to move it back to the schoolhouse after the next renovation. (Courtesy of Carl Cathers.)

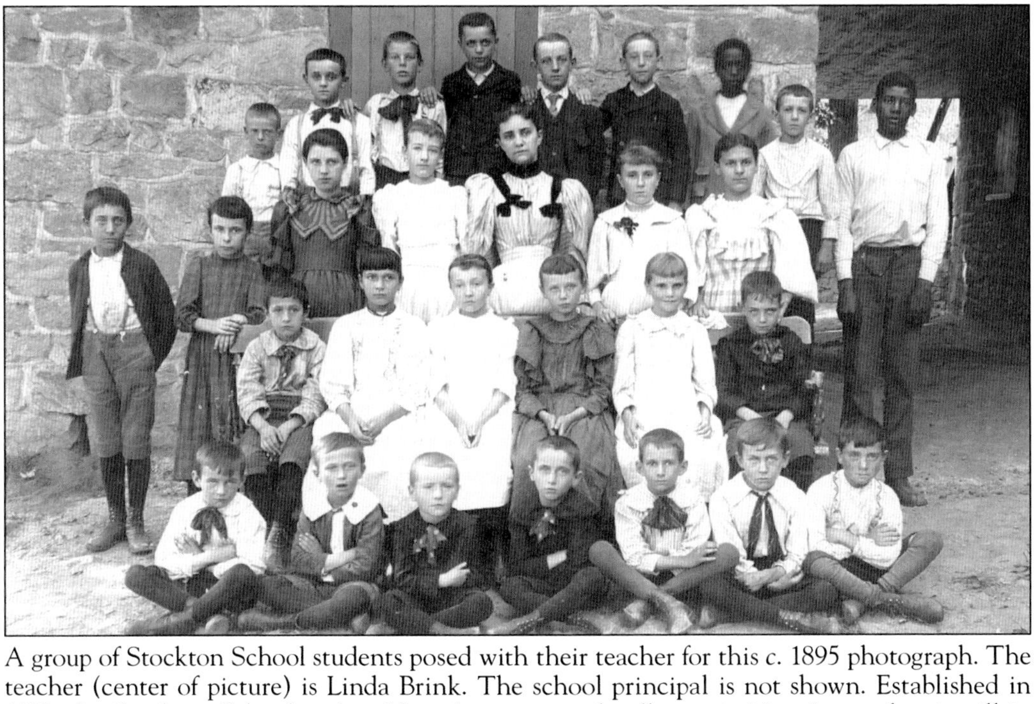

A group of Stockton School students posed with their teacher for this c. 1895 photograph. The teacher (center of picture) is Linda Brink. The school principal is not shown. Established in 1872, the Stockton School is the oldest three-room schoolhouse in New Jersey that is still in operation. (From the Ada Reading collection, courtesy of Carl Cathers.)

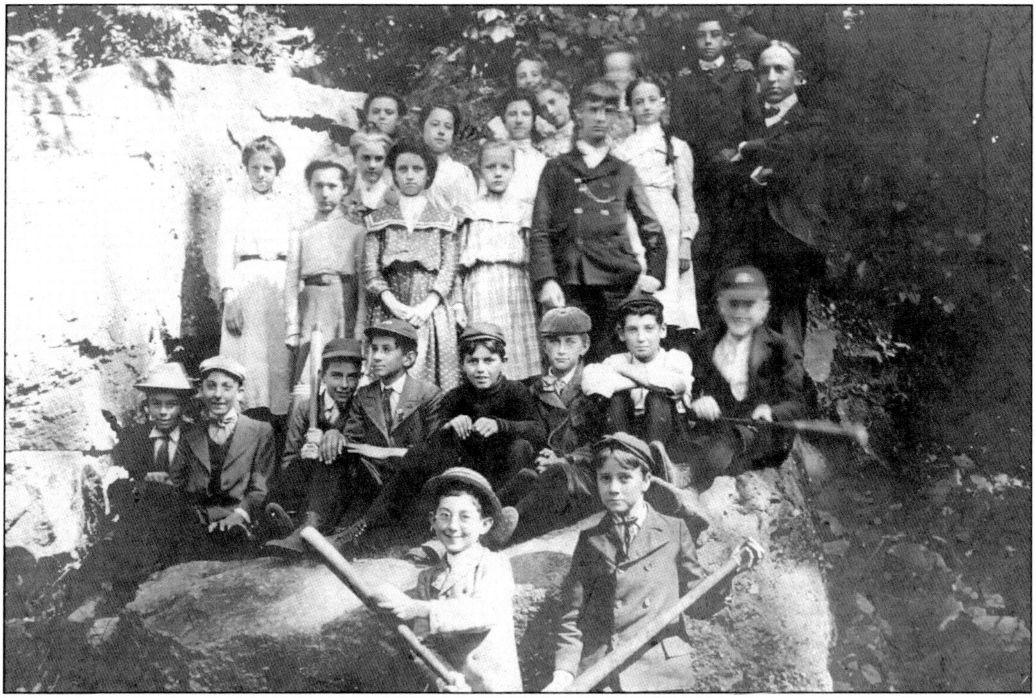

This group of Stockton School students posed on the rock at the back of the school around 1908. Among the students are Eleanor Sillery (third from right, standing), Thomas Errico (second from right, seated), and Raymond Mason (right foreground). The dark mark on the rock to the left of the students is due to the daily burning of the paper trash in that spot. (Courtesy of Carl Cathers.)

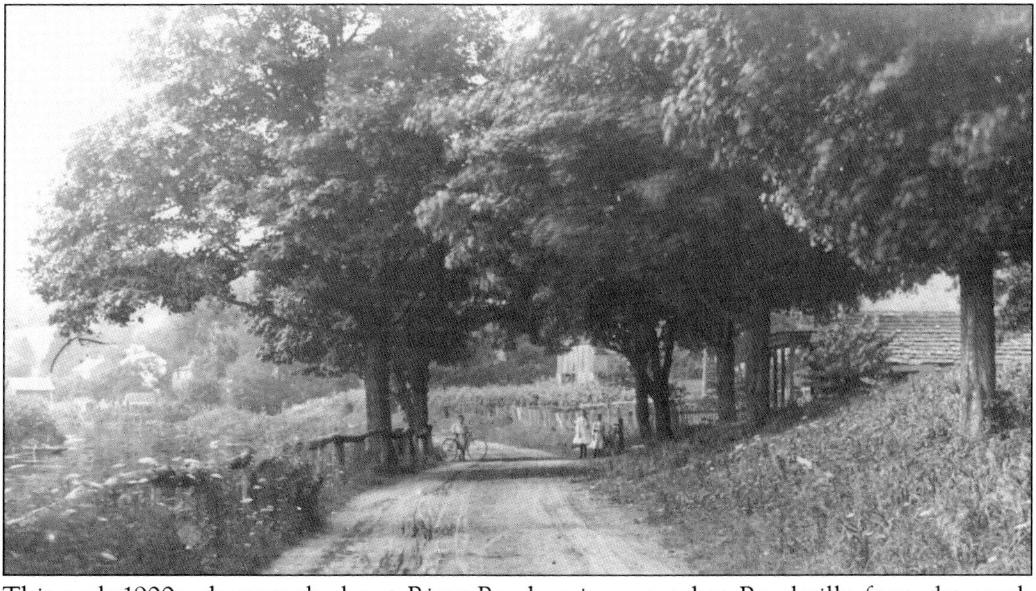

This early-1900s photograph shows River Road as it approaches Brookville from the south heading north toward Stockton. The girls have paused under the shade of the trees to rest from their ride. The area is rich in wildlife, dotted with historical points of interest, and features more than a few covered bridges, which make it a favorite for bicyclists to this day. (Courtesy of the Delaware River Mill Society.)

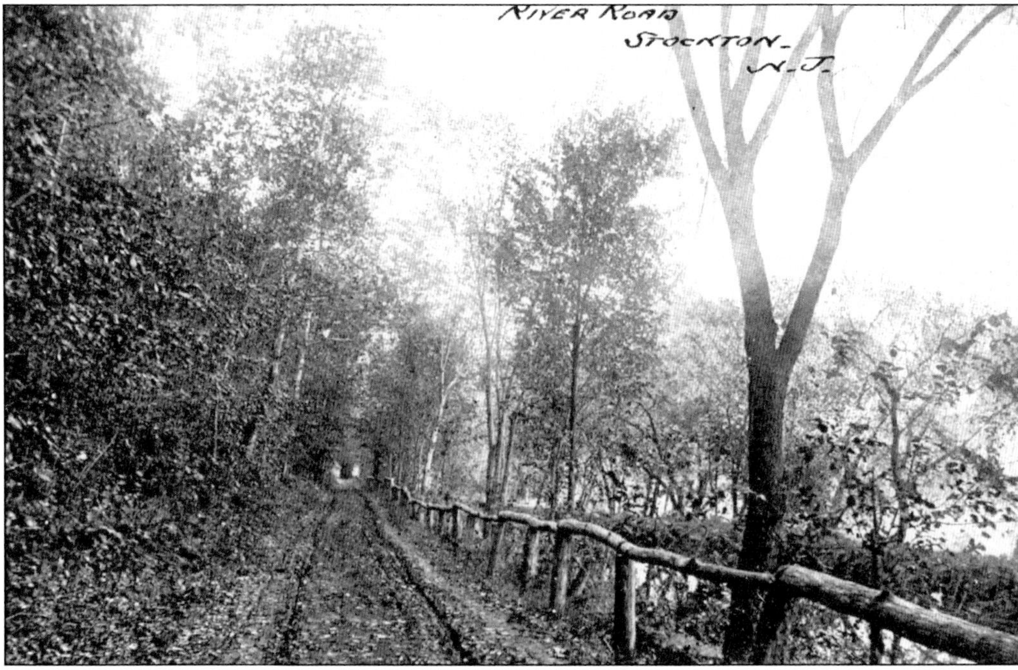

This very early view of River Road is from the north looking south toward Prallsville and Stockton. During this time, River Road's course took it over old Prallsville Bridge at the Wickecheoke Creek and directly through the Prallsville Mills complex. The two small white squares off in the distance are the mill buildings. (Courtesy of Edith McCloughan.)

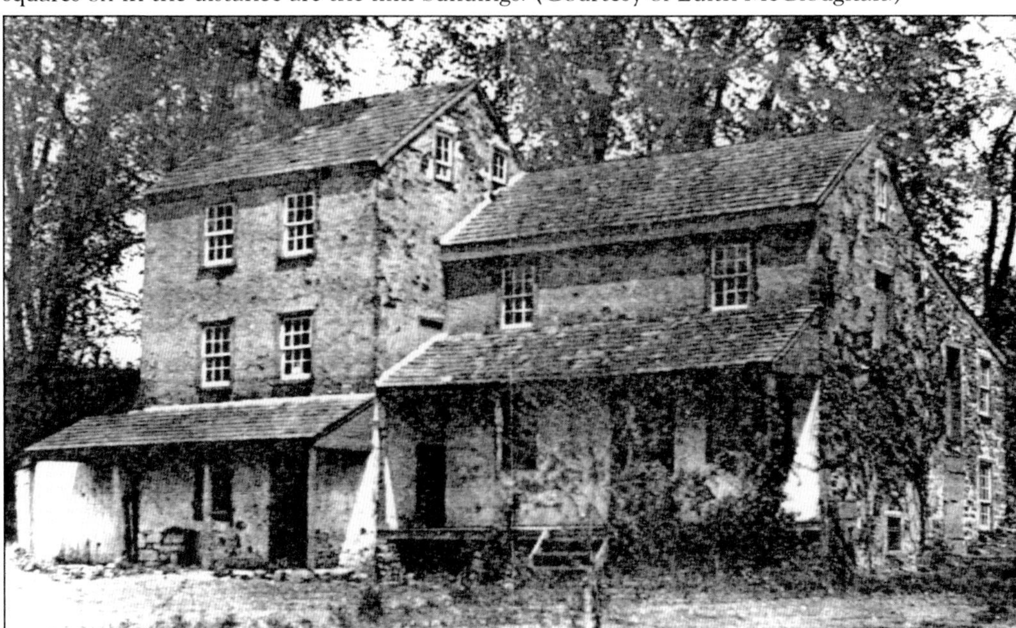

This undated photograph is of the building that was once the Sharp and Lambert store, which was the first store in Stockton. Now a private residence, it sits on Old Prallsville Road behind the building that was Schuck's Garage. The Lambert family was connected to the Prall family through the marriage of Jacob Lambert to John Prall Jr.'s daughter Letitia. (Courtesy of Carl Cathers.)

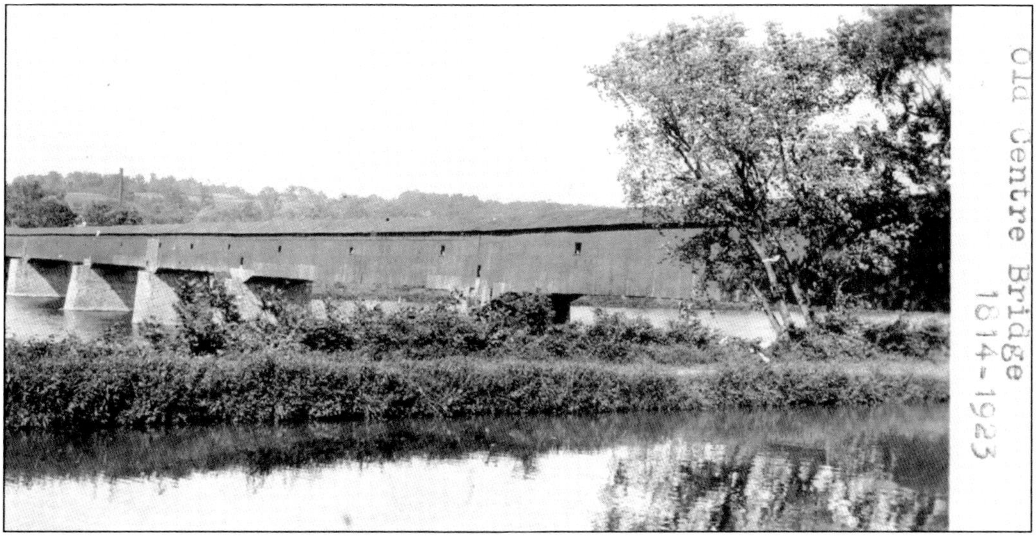

Postcards were very popular during the early part of the 20th century in Stockton. There were of course some features of the area that were favorite subjects such as the canal, the river, and the old covered Centre Bridge, which was among the longest covered bridge spans ever built. This postcard has been notated by Austin L. Davison Jr., who collected and catalogued many postcards. (Courtesy of Carl Cathers.)

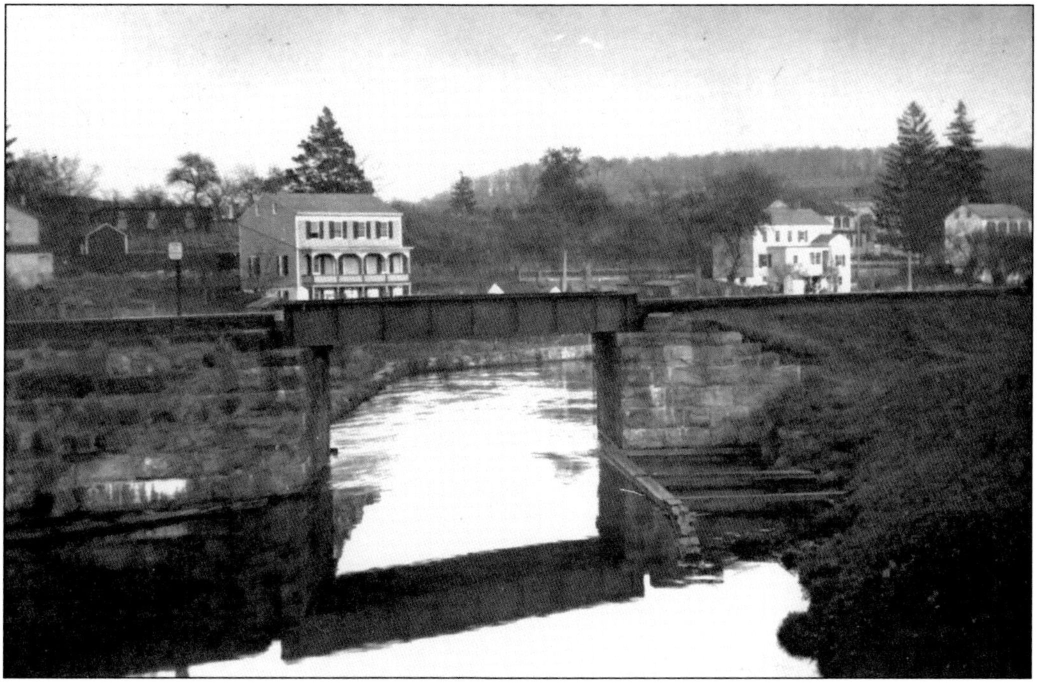

This is Brookville around 1910. In his 1929 essay about Brookville, Egbert T. Bush describes Horne's Creek "rippling sweetly over its stony bed" as it flows toward the Delaware River, an old mill remembered only by the "old people," and a wagon cut perfectly in half in an ownership dispute and leaned "against the corncrib that all might look and wonder." (Courtesy of the Delaware and Raritan Canal Commission.)

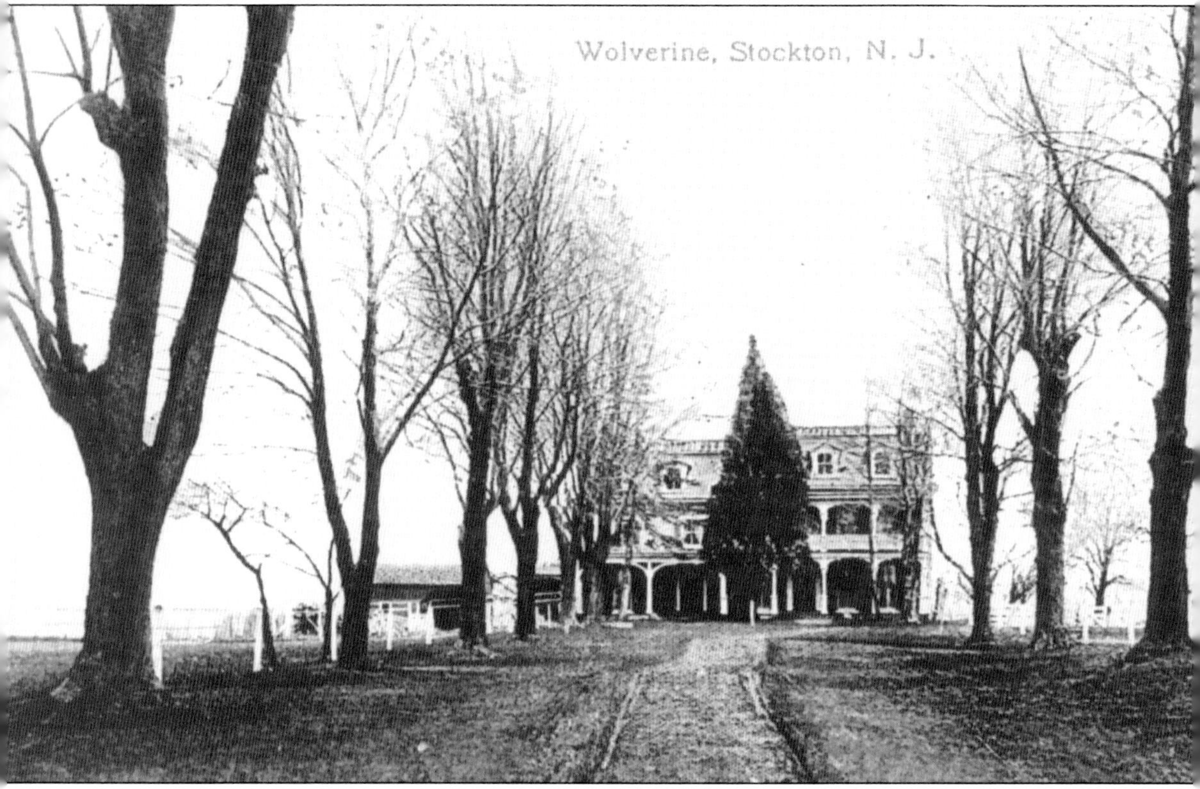

This postcard of the plantation house is noted as being "Wolverine, Stockton, N.J." as it was known at one time. In 1731, Charles Woolverton acquired a plantation on the hill above Stockton, which included the property on which the inn was built. John Prall Jr. acquired the property 61 years later in 1792 and built the plantation house in 1793. In his memoirs, John Parker Prall described the house as such: "All the work my grandfather did was of the same solid style. The kitchen fireplace was of the same pattern as the [manor] house, with heavy lug pole up the chimney from which hung two long iron trammels for hanging the boilers and kettles, with room for several chairs under the chimney where we could hug the fire on the cold winter nights." Maurice Woolverton bought the plantation house in 1850, which now serves as a bed-and-breakfast and carries the family name as the Woolverton Inn. (Courtesy of Carl Cathers.)

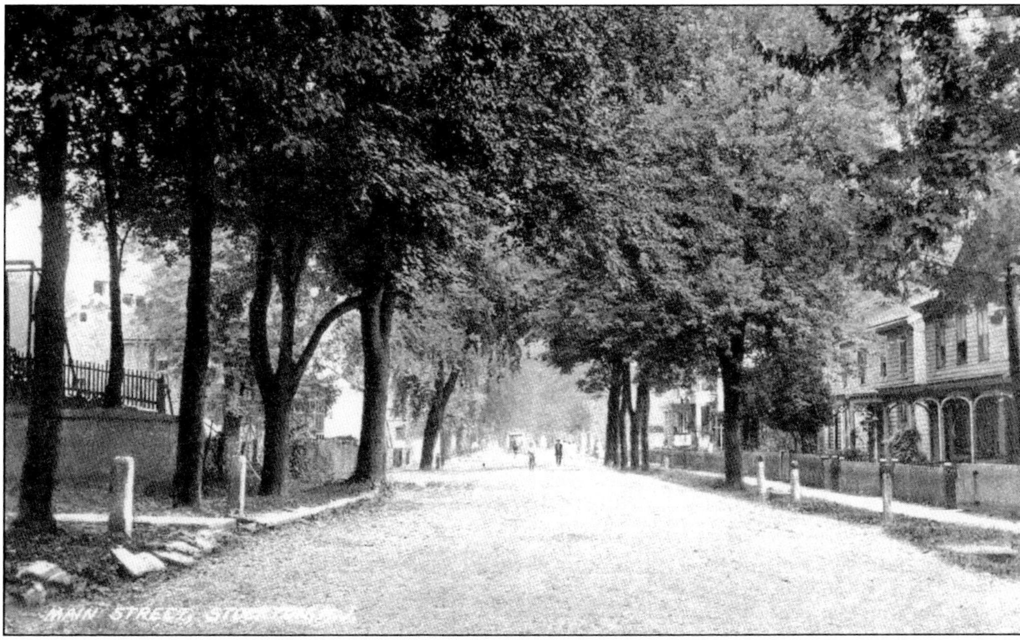

Lighting 1900s Main Street is described here by Emmert Wilson: "The street lights were oil burning pole units . . . George Farley was custodian of lighting. His duties were to light in the evening and to extinguish in the morning daily. During the great flood of 1903, Mr. Farley used a row boat down Bridge Street to complete his activities. He never failed a day of duty." (Courtesy of Edith McCloughan.)

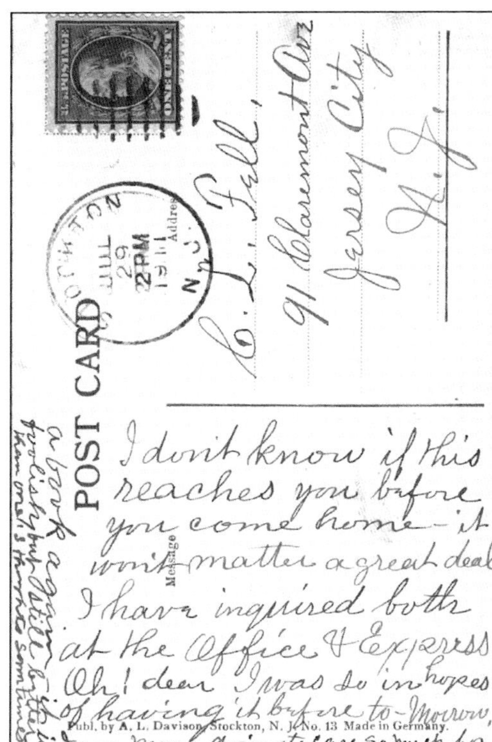

The back of this 1911 postcard reads, "I don't know if this reaches you before you come home—it won't matter a great deal. I have inquired both at the Office and Express. Oh! dear I was in hopes of having it before to-morrow. I am never going to care so much for a book again—it is foolish but still better than one's own thoughts sometimes." (Courtesy of Carl Cathers.)

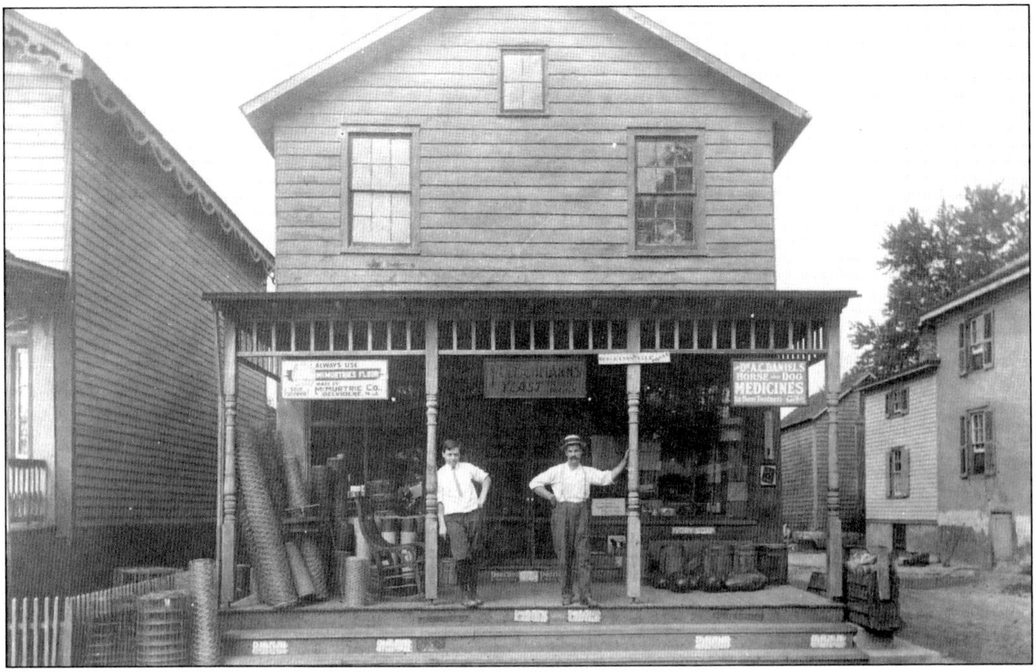

Lewis Wilson (right) and his son Charlie (left) pose on the front porch of Wilson's Store, which sold everything from salt mackerel to overcoats and featured a "Sergeantsville Phone." If one wanted to reach someone in Sergeantsville, one could call to the general store in Sergeantsville, and they would find the desired party and bring them to the phone. (Courtesy of Carl Cathers.)

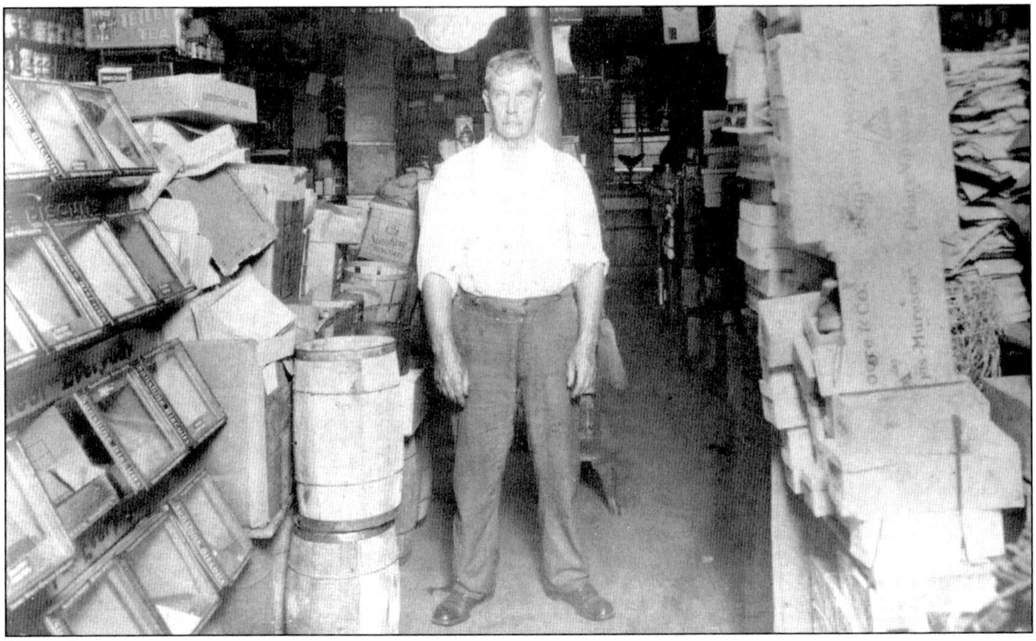

This c. 1920 photograph shows Lewis inside his store. Dry goods were to the right and the bins (left) held crackers and other food stuffs. The kegs held nails and served as seats that the men would pull up to the potbellied stove in the evenings to, in Emmert Wilson's words, "engage in the rural pastime of discussing politics, religion and general gossip." (Courtesy of Carl Cathers.)

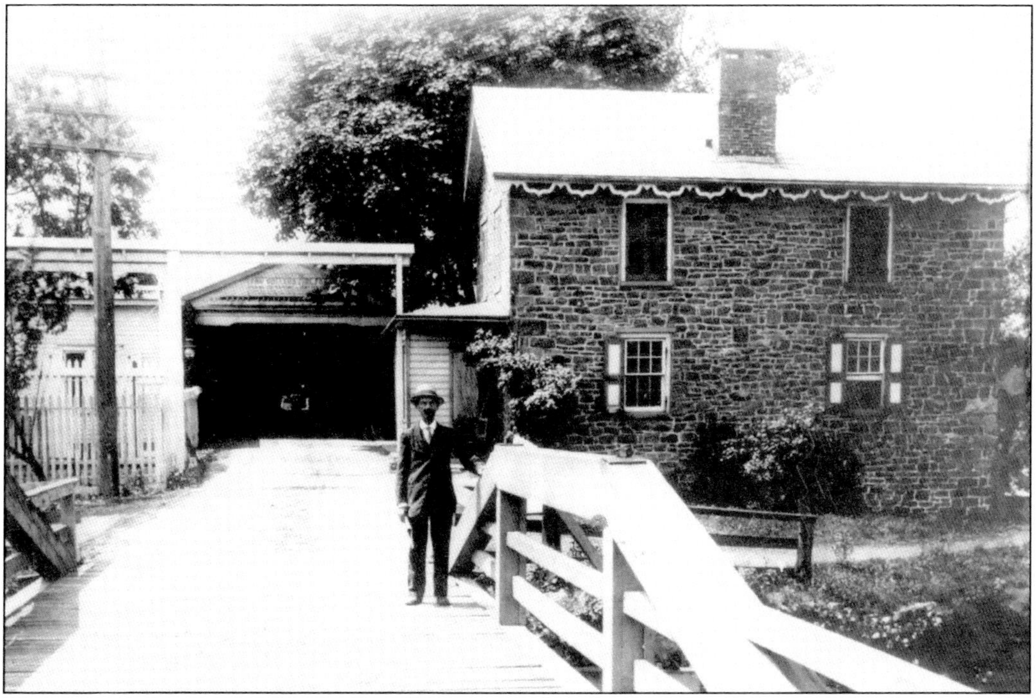

This 1920s photograph shows bridge tender Reading Dilts standing on the canal bridge on the Stockton side of the Centre Bridge. The bridge tender was on duty 24 hours a day, and he lived in the stone house seen behind him with his family. Sylvester Ledger was the last "bridge cop" to live in the house, which was torn down in 1952. (Courtesy of Carl Cathers.)

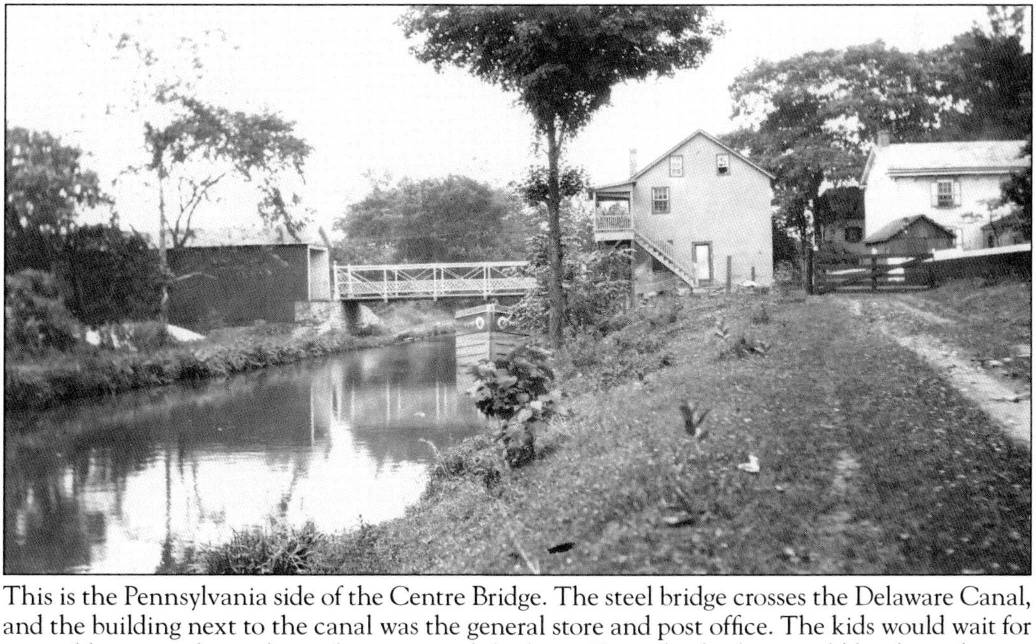

This is the Pennsylvania side of the Centre Bridge. The steel bridge crosses the Delaware Canal, and the building next to the canal was the general store and post office. The kids would wait for a canal boat to ride on the mule as it towed the boat. To get back, they would hitch a ride on a mule pulling a boat back toward home. (Courtesy of Carl Cathers.)

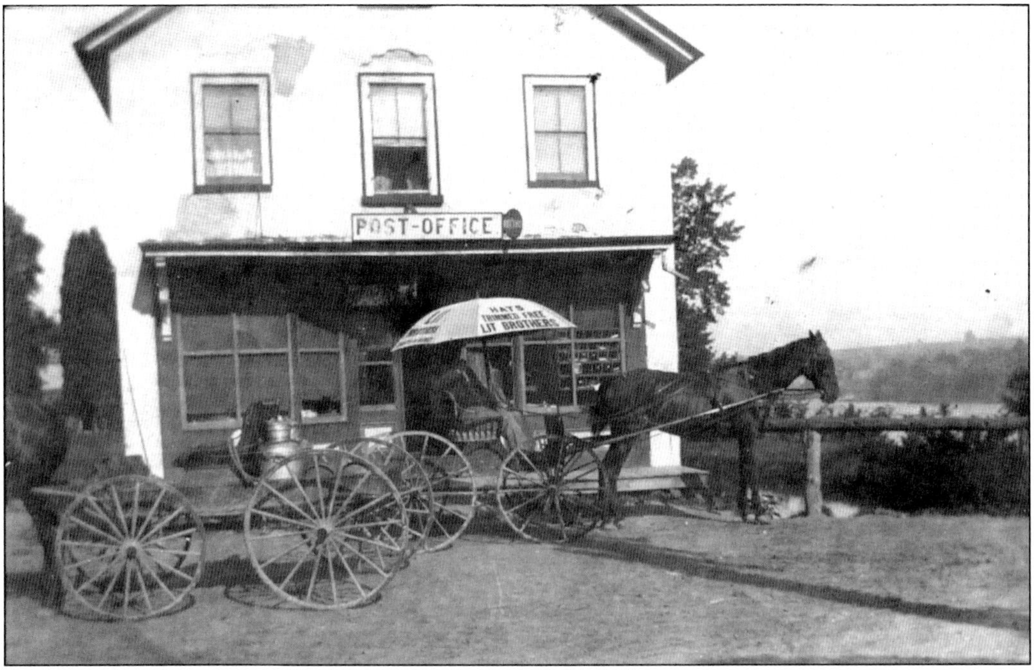

Two carriages wait outside the Centre Bridge Post Office around 1890. Mary Bowlby was the post mistress from 1891 to 1925. The inscription on the back of the photograph reads, "Mr. Reading's horse and wagon—right. He hauled mail from Stockton to Centre Bridge. Solebury [Pennsylvania] mail was resorted at Center Bridge and taken to Solebury." (Courtesy of Carl Cathers.)

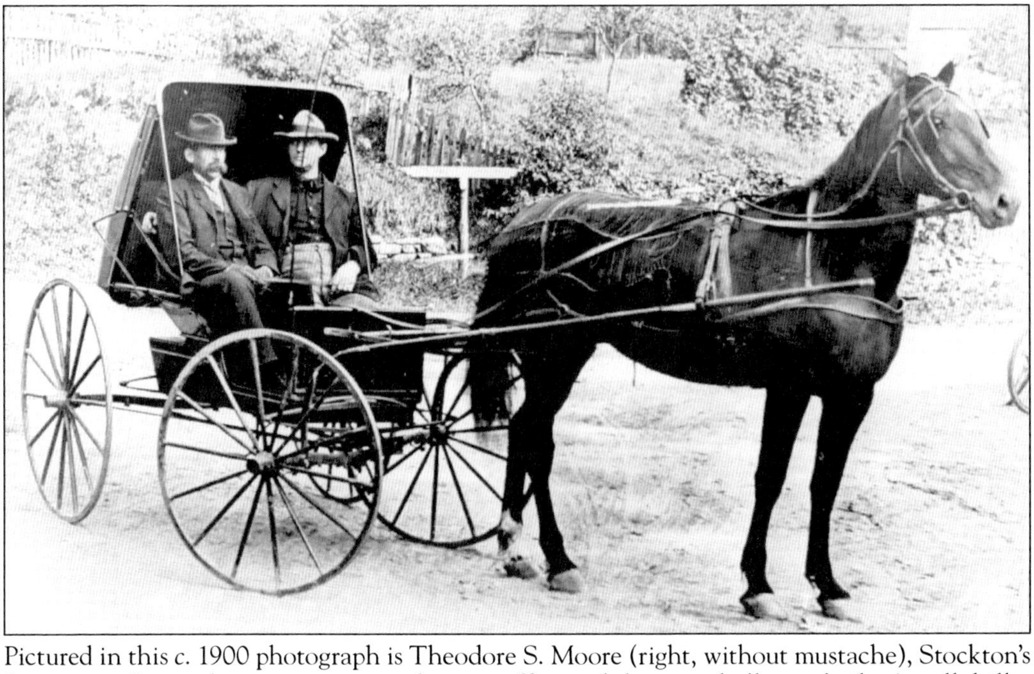

Pictured in this *c.* 1900 photograph is Theodore S. Moore (right, without mustache), Stockton's first mayor. During his time as mayor, the post office and the town hall were built. A well driller by trade, he was also responsible for installing the Stockton water system. (Courtesy of the Delaware River Mill Society.)

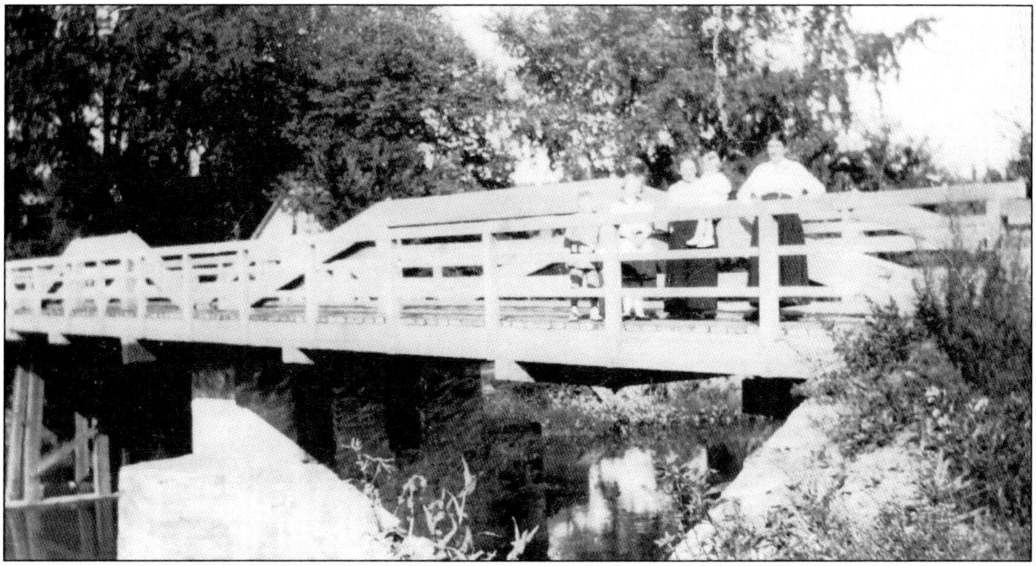

This group enjoys a stroll across the canal bridge in Stockton. Elizabeth Kelley Sillery (second from right) holds her young grandson Horace Cathers Jr. in her arms, which places the photograph at about 1920. The roof peak seen through the trees at the left belonged to a creamery. It is currently the location of the Stockton Post Office. (Courtesy of Carl Cathers.)

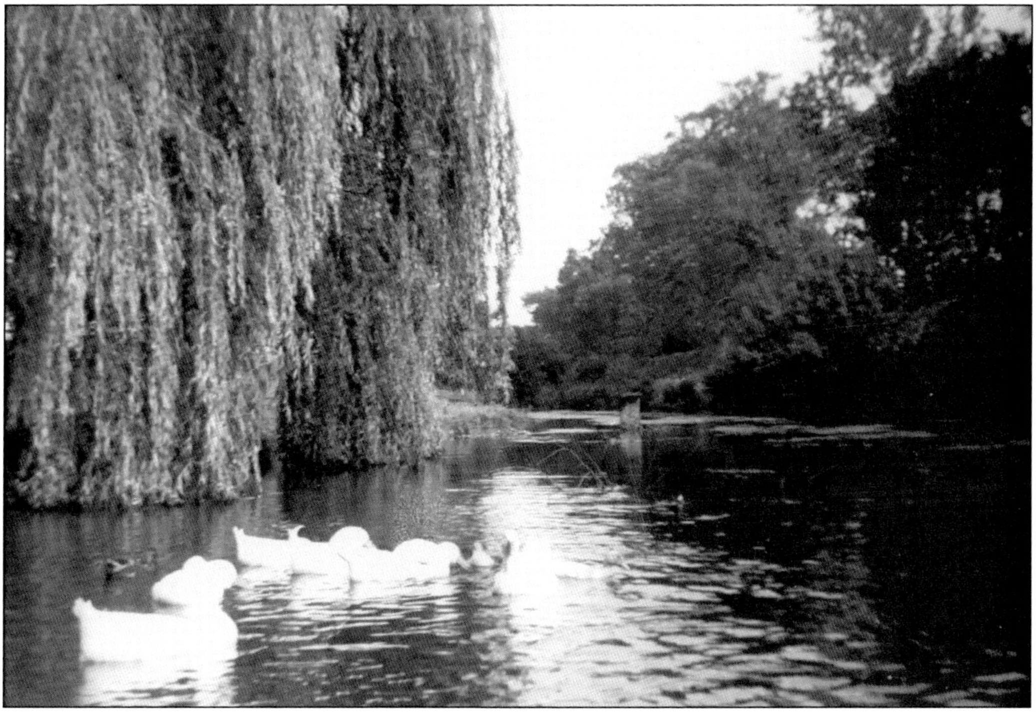

This 1940 photograph features a gaggle of ducks floating along the canal. According to the New Jersey Conservation Foundation, the wildlife that lives in and along the Wickecheoke Creek, which flows into the Delaware and Raritan Canal, includes beavers, hawks, herons, and long-tailed salamanders. In addition, over 400 species of native plants flourish within the environs of the creek. (Courtesy of Carl Cathers.)

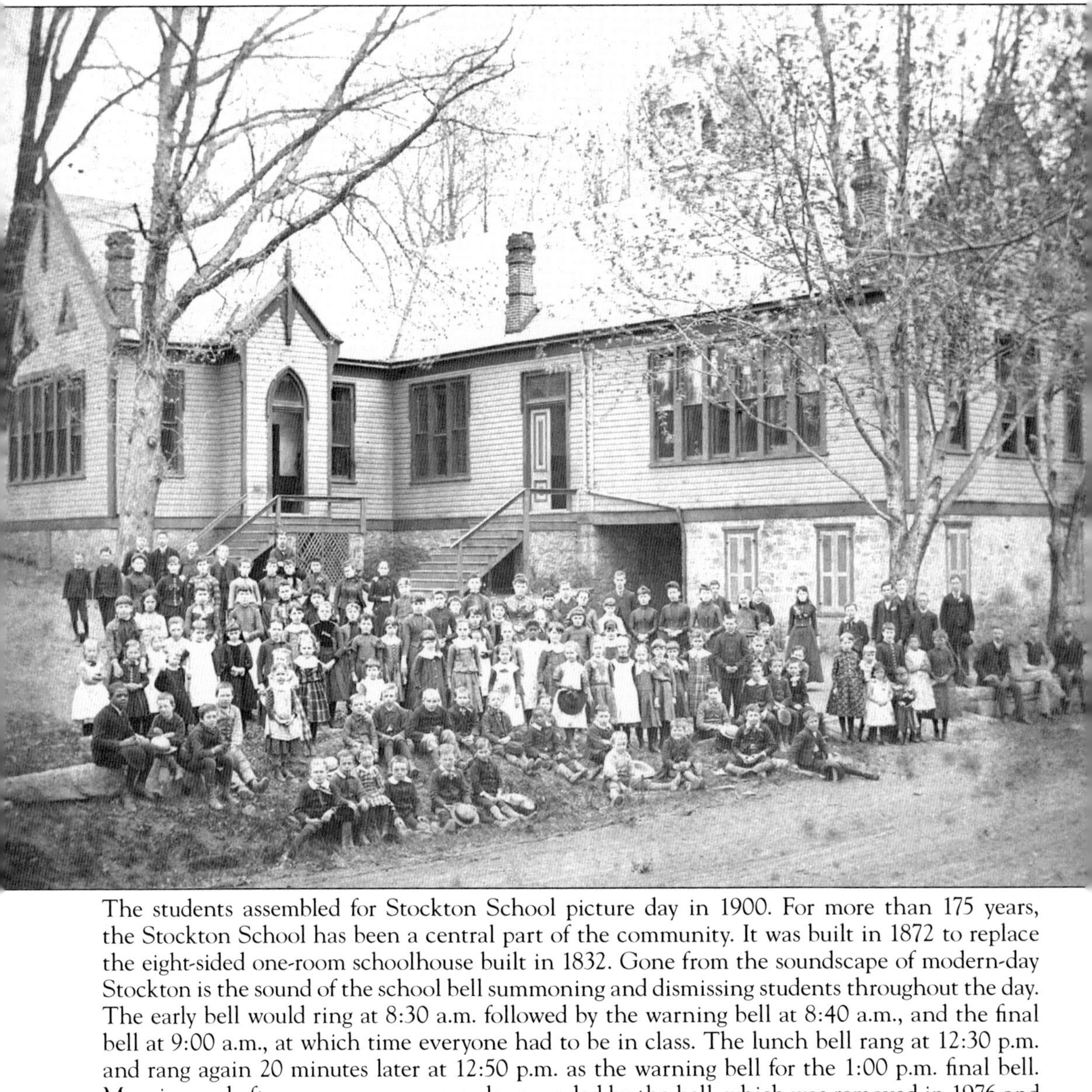

The students assembled for Stockton School picture day in 1900. For more than 175 years, the Stockton School has been a central part of the community. It was built in 1872 to replace the eight-sided one-room schoolhouse built in 1832. Gone from the soundscape of modern-day Stockton is the sound of the school bell summoning and dismissing students throughout the day. The early bell would ring at 8:30 a.m. followed by the warning bell at 8:40 a.m., and the final bell at 9:00 a.m., at which time everyone had to be in class. The lunch bell rang at 12:30 p.m. and rang again 20 minutes later at 12:50 p.m. as the warning bell for the 1:00 p.m. final bell. Morning and afternoon recesses were also sounded by the bell, which was removed in 1976 and placed on borough hall. The school was placed on the state historic register in 2005. (Courtesy of Carl Cathers.)

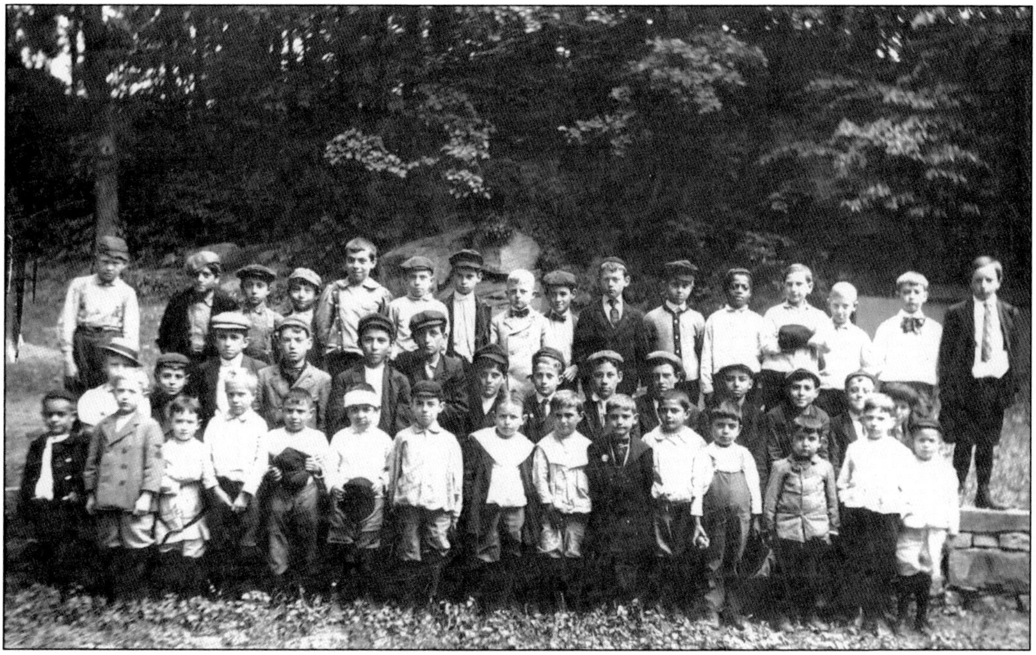

Egbert T. Bush was a teacher and principal at the Stockton School when this photograph was taken around 1909. Emmert Wilson, a student during Bush's tenure, described him as a "stern but thorough and scholarly teacher." Bush's writings on the history of the area are informative and gracefully written with sensitivity to the human side of history. (From the collection of Wesley Hendricks, courtesy of Carl Cathers.)

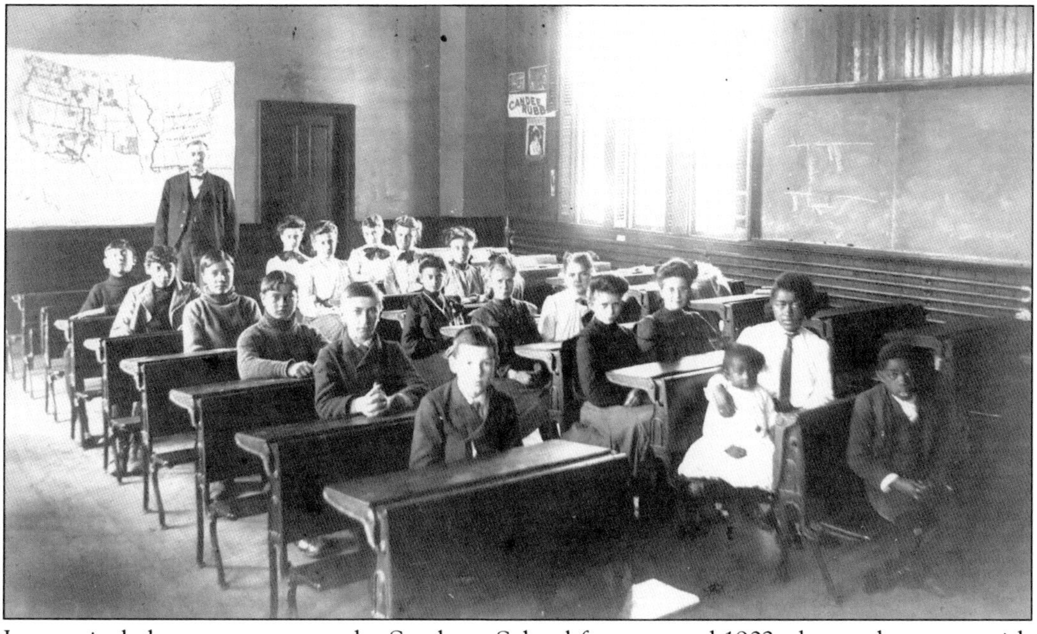

In a typical classroom scene at the Stockton School from around 1902, the teacher poses with his class. Seated in the last seat of the middle row is Eleanor Sillery. Thomas Errico is in the first row on the left, second from the back. The door in the back of the classroom leads to the outside. (Courtesy of Carl Cathers.)

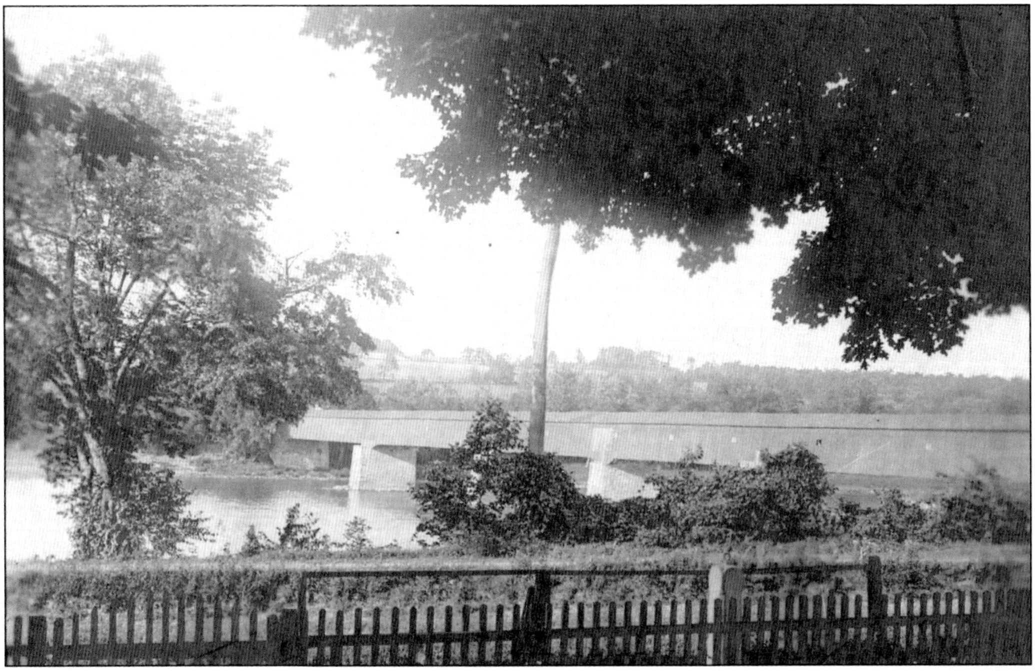

This view of the Centre Bridge is from the yard of the Fell's Boarding House in Centre Bridge, Pennsylvania. Austin L. Davison Jr.'s aunt Mary Bowlby, in addition to being post mistress of Centre Bridge, ran the boardinghouse. Although the photograph is undated, the presence of the covered bridge places it prior to the bridge fire in 1923. (Courtesy of Carl Cathers.)

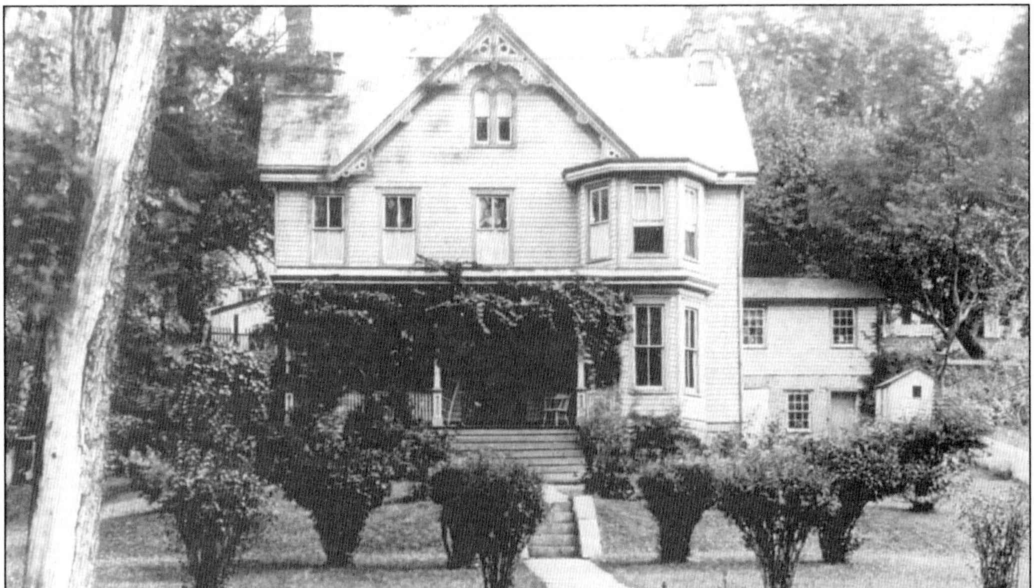

This house still stands in Stockton next to the Stockton Inn on the left. When this picture was taken, it was the residence of Charles Smith, who ran the Prallsville Mills with his brother Joseph Smith under the business name of J. W. Smith's Sons. (From the collection of Carl Cathers, courtesy of the Delaware River Mill Society.)

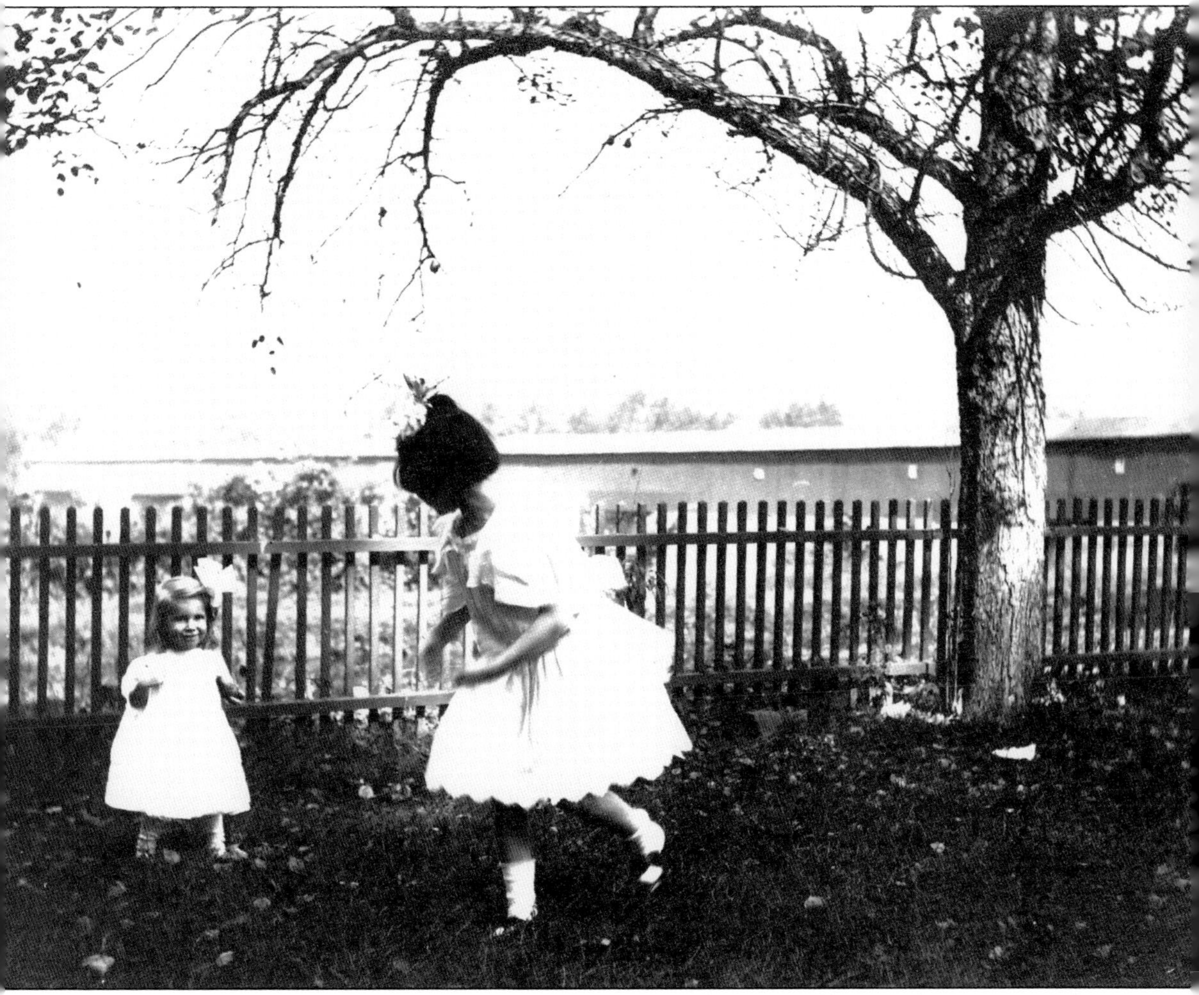

Davison's older brother Lloyd Fell Davison plays in the yard of the Fell's Boarding House with his older sister Florence Davison in this idyllic 1904 photograph. Their father Austin owned the general store on the corner of Bridge and Main Streets across from the Stockton Inn. It was in his store that the great fire of January 26, 1905, which destroyed almost a dozen properties, started. The February 2, 1905, *Democrat-Advertiser* reported that the cause of the blaze was thought to be mice nibbling on the stock of matches. The disaster occurred less than two years after the great flood of 1903, which left the Centre Bridge as seen in this photograph, as the only Delaware River crossing that was not destroyed between Easton and Lambertville. In less than 20 years, this bridge would also be gone. (Courtesy of Carl Cathers.)

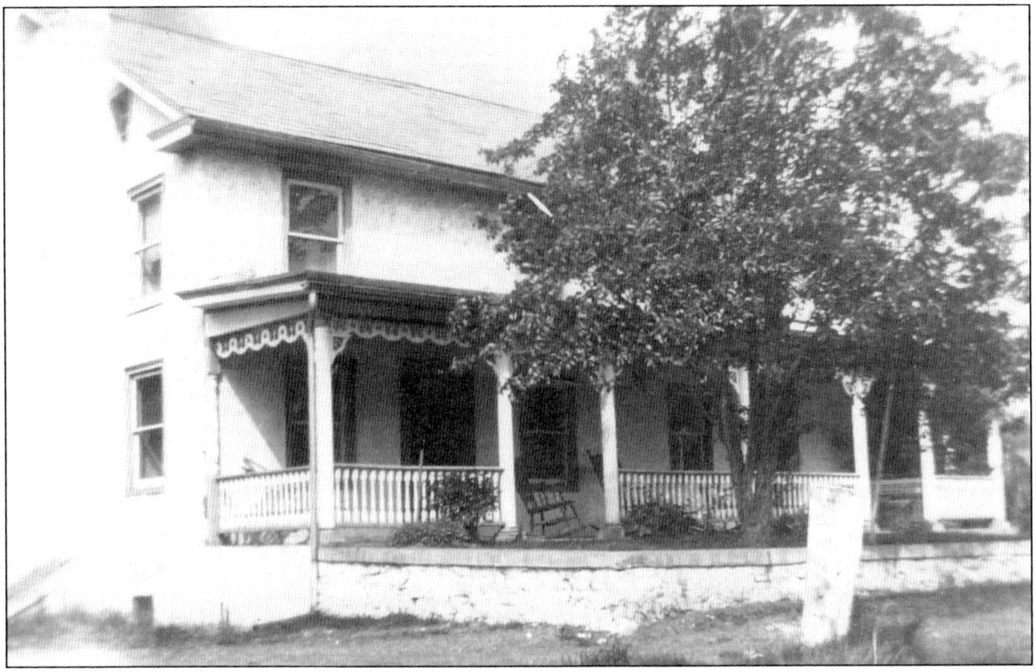

Joseph Howell operated his ferry from this location on Ferry Street and lived in this house. The river crossing generally signified the name of the early river towns on both sides of the river. For example, during the years that Howell operated the ferry, both Stockton and Centre Bridge were known as Howell's Ferry. (Courtesy of Carl Cathers.)

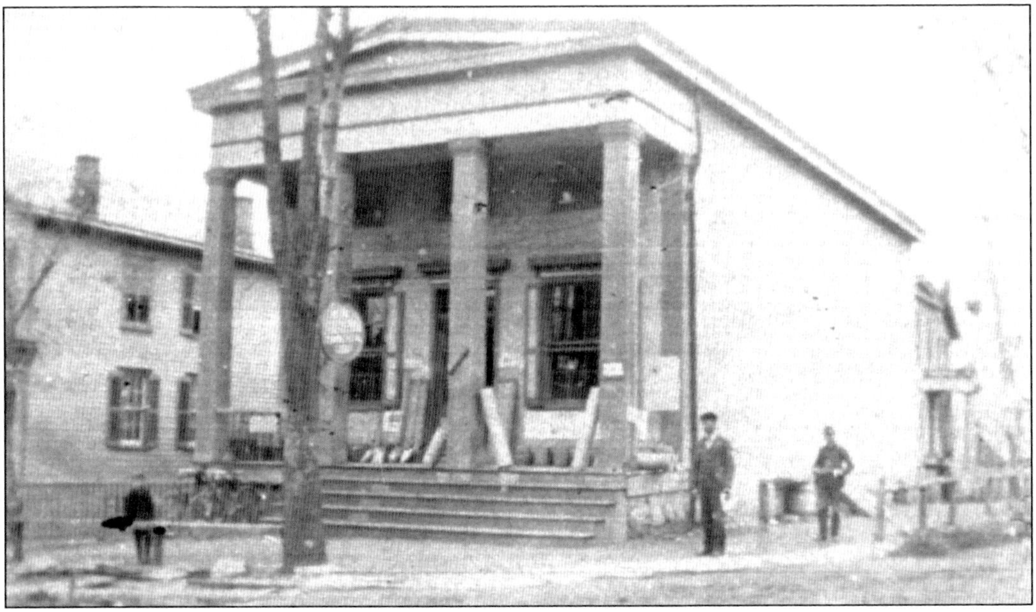

Built in 1850 on the corner across from Austin Davison's Store, this was the location of the W. P. Mason and F. E. Roberson general store. It was later converted to an appliance store, which added glass display windows. The store had a television on display in the window facing Main Street, where, before home televisions were common, the residents would gather to watch the fights on Friday night. (Courtesy of the Delaware River Mill Society.)

The Baptist church built in 1860 is seen here on a snowy winter day. Other denominations with long histories in Stockton include the Presbyterian and Catholic churches. Prior to the Catholic church being built in 1919, mass was held in a barn near the train station and then in Bodine's Hall in Stockton. (Courtesy of Edith McCloughan.)

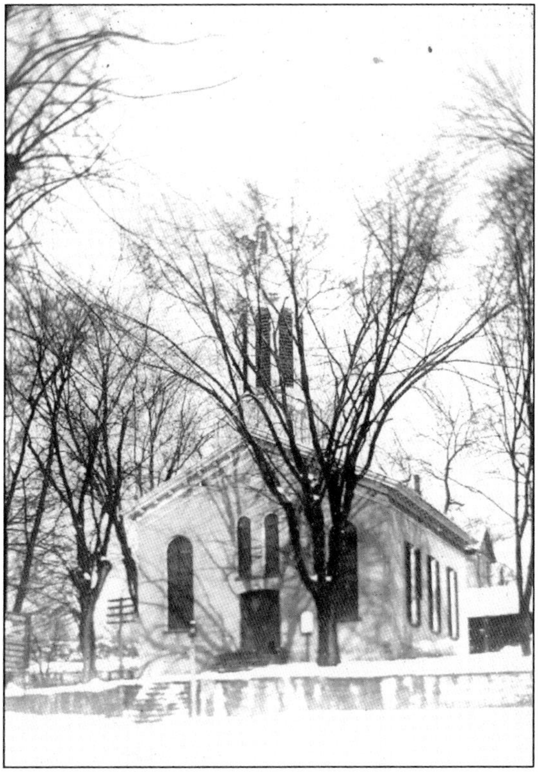

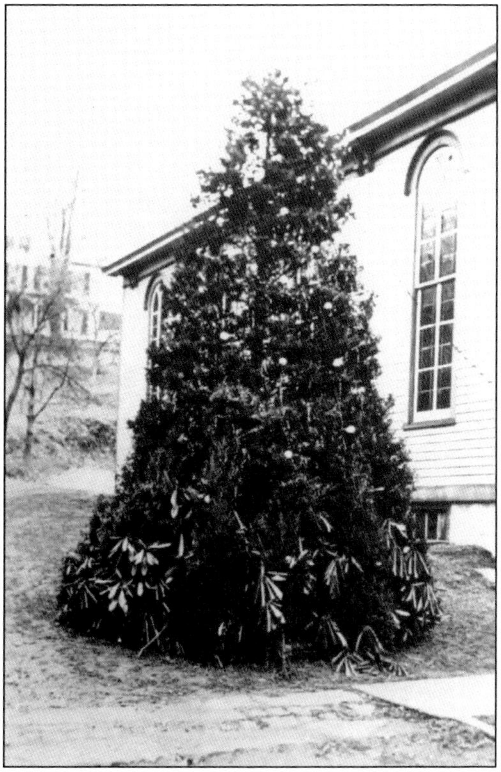

During the Christmas holiday of 1928, Stockton decorated its first community Christmas tree. Every Christmas, the civic committee would give the kids of the town an orange and hard tack candy. The tradition has continued with the tree's location changing from time to time over the years. (Courtesy of the Delaware River Mill Society.)

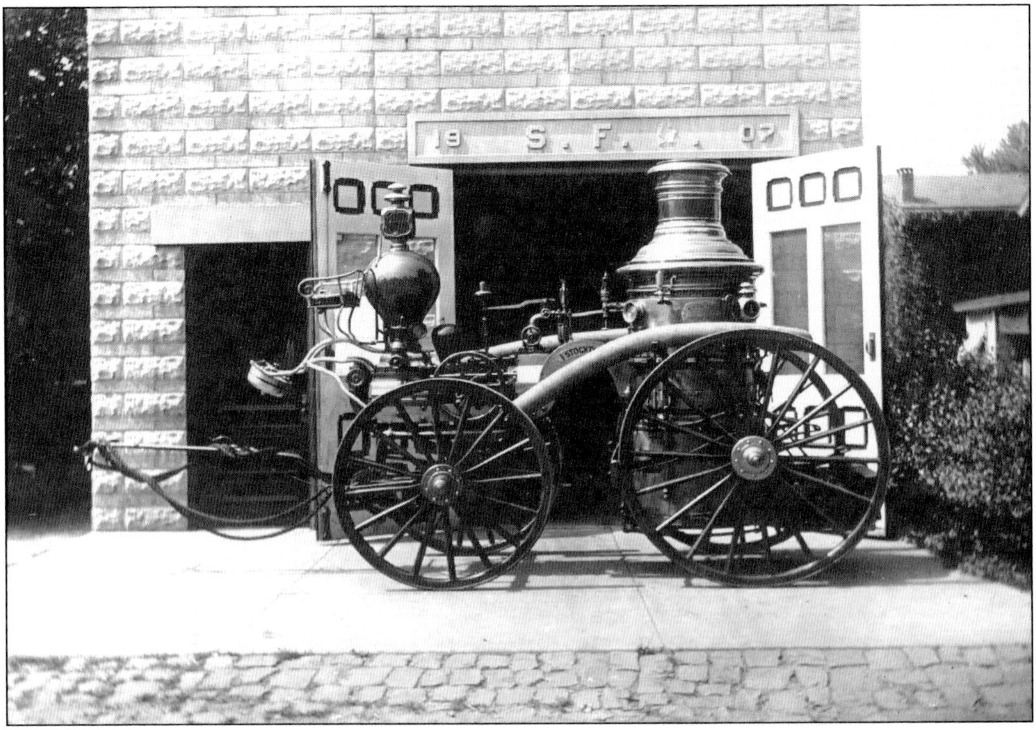

The Stockton Fire Department was formed in 1908 after the great fire of 1905. In response to the threat of fire to the community, the town voted in 1906 to start a fire company and purchase a fire engine. The first engine is pictured here and was purchased in 1908 and in use until 1923. (From the collection of Wesley Hendricks, courtesy of Carl Cathers.)

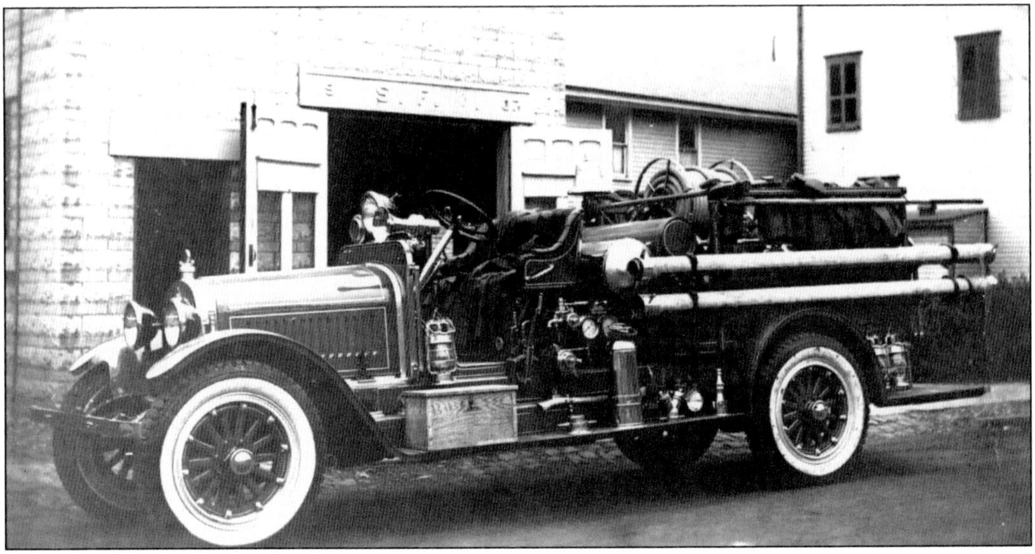

The second fire engine purchased by the fire department was a Stutz. It was rated to pump 500 gallons of water per minute and was purchased in 1923 for $7,500. The fire department building was constructed of cement block in 1908 and serves today as the borough hall. (Courtesy of the Delaware River Mill Society.)

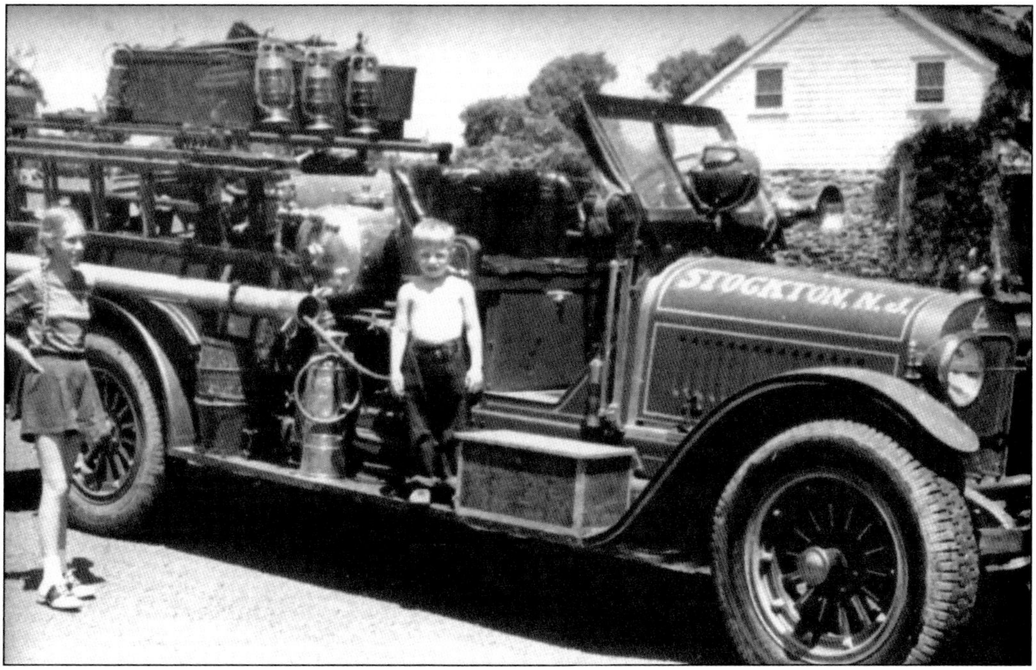

The Stutz was still in service in this *c.* 1941 photograph and is seen after responding to a call on Dilts Corner Road. Drawn to the fire engine like so many are, Steve Robinson and Jean Affleck stand with the truck. (Courtesy of the Delaware River Mill Society.)

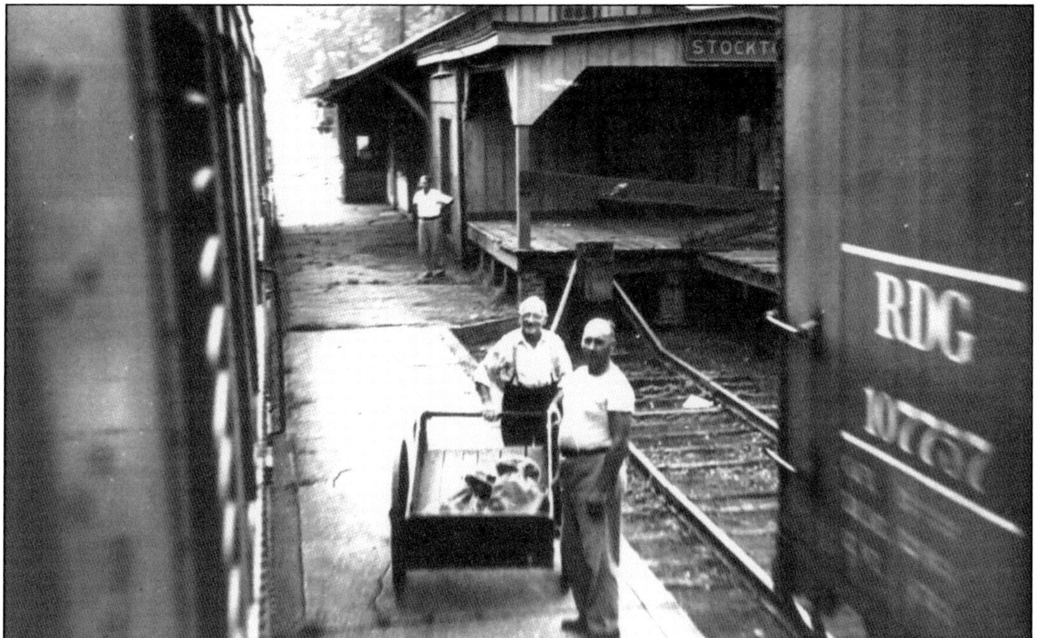

Two men deliver mail sacks to the train in this 1930s-era picture. The train was an integral part of the day-to-day life of Stockton residents. For example, every Friday there would be a barrel of live lobsters waiting on the covered area under the Stockton sign (top center of picture) for the weekend crowd at Colligan's Stockton Inn. (Courtesy of Carl Cathers.)

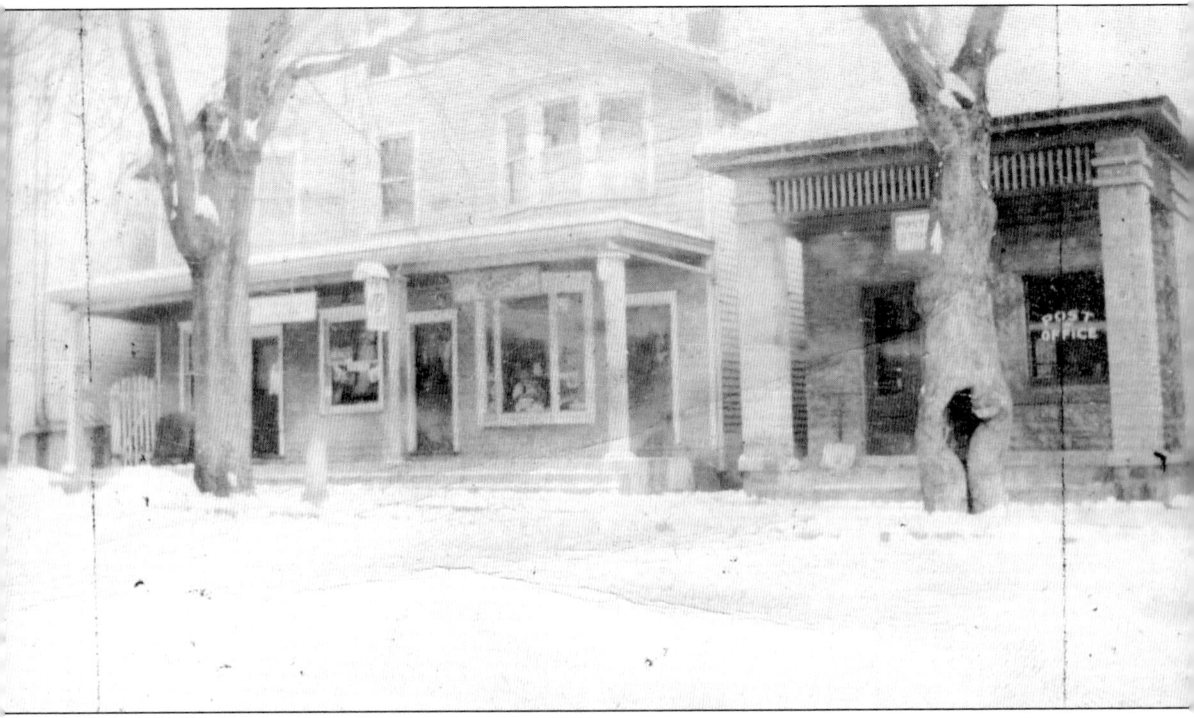

This snowy scene from the 1930s shows a store and eatery that sat next to the post office. It was first known as Lerue's, which was famous for its oyster stew. It later changed hands and became Bussy Mason's. The soda fountain was the place to go at 3:00 p.m. every day to get a soda and ice cream for 15¢ and read the ball scores in the *New York Daily News*. There was a sign over the old soda cooler that read, "We don't know where mom is, but we've got pop on ice." At lunch time, the schoolchildren would race down Skeeter's Alley between Bussy Mason's and the post office to be the first in line to pick up their mail before running home to eat lunch, and race back to school to get some playing time in before the 1:00 p.m. bell called them back into class. (Courtesy of Edith McCloughan.)

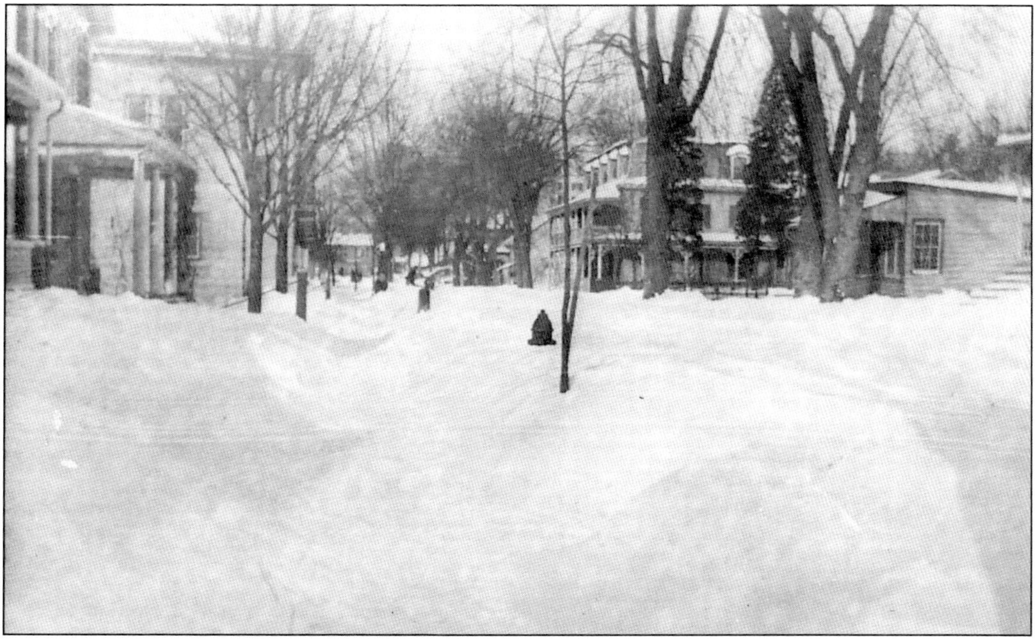

Here is the view looking north on Main Street after a winter storm around 1920. Durling's butcher shop is the first building on the right. William Durling made daily deliveries in the village by horse-drawn butcher wagon. Further up on the right is the Stockton Inn, and the tall square building at the top left corner is Davison's general store. (Courtesy of the Delaware River Mill Society.)

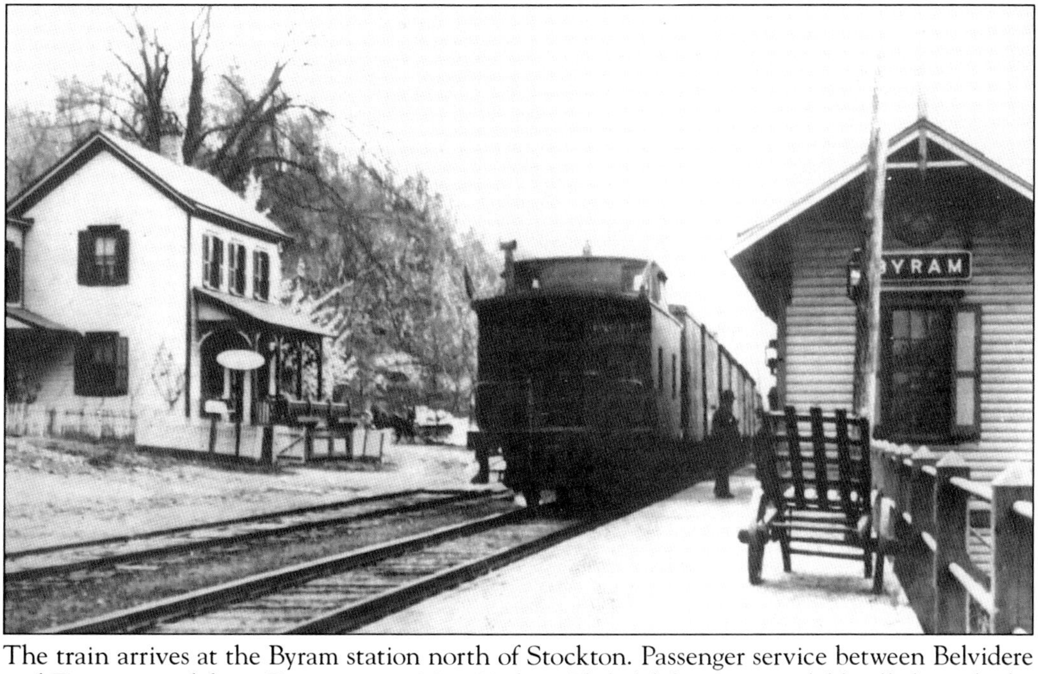

The train arrives at the Byram station north of Stockton. Passenger service between Belvidere and Trenton, and from Trenton onto New York or Philadelphia was available all through the day. Nine trains north and south serving 29 stops along the way ran from 7:25 a.m. to 10:00 p.m. (Courtesy of Carl Cathers.)

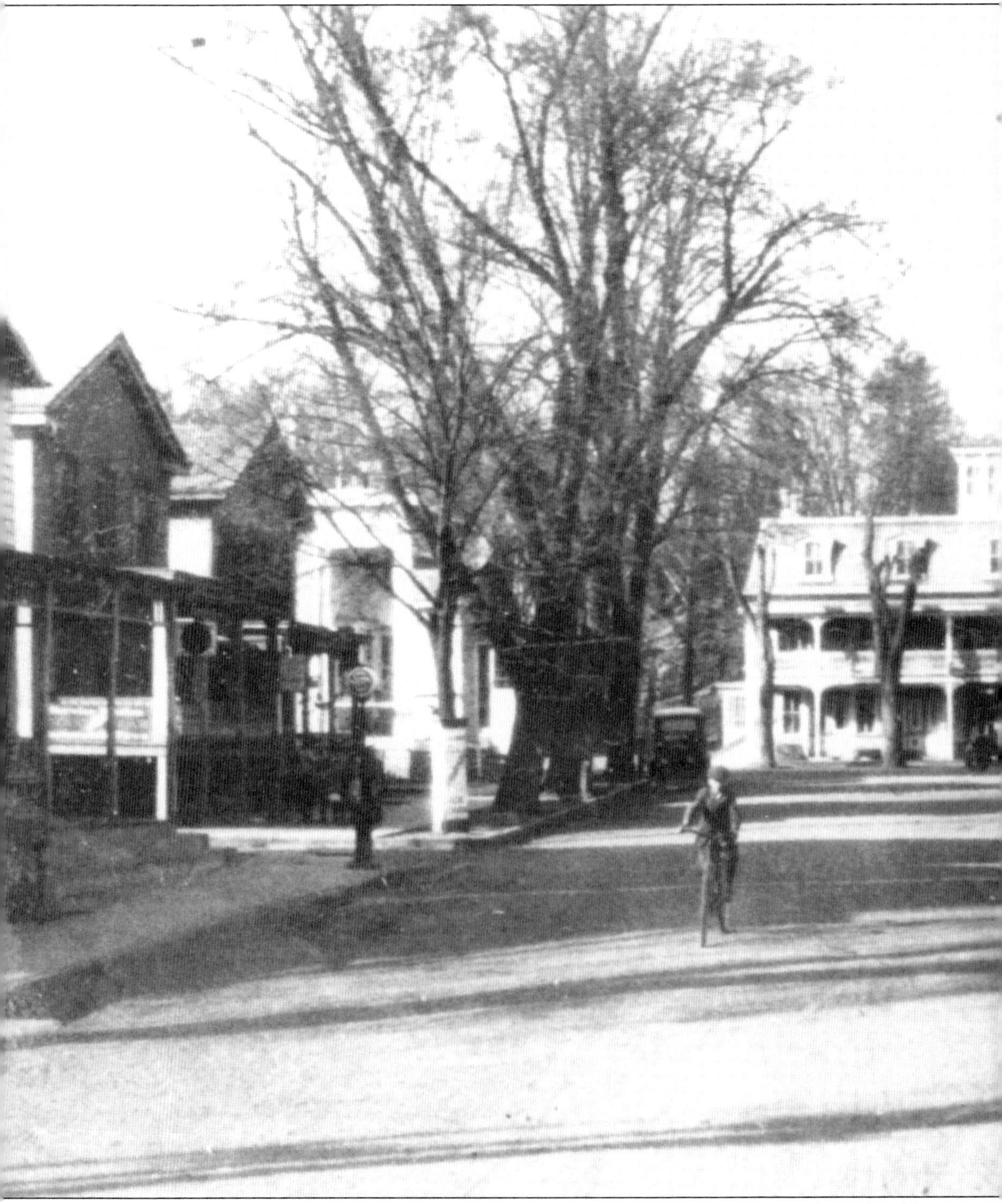

This view of Bridge Street looks toward the Stockton Inn around 1930. Based on the foliage on the trees and the light coats worn by the people in the street, it is late fall. With the cyclist riding toward the camera and past a sidewalk gas pump, a delivery truck at the inn, a group of pedestrians walking down the street, and the fellow resting against the post office porch pillar,

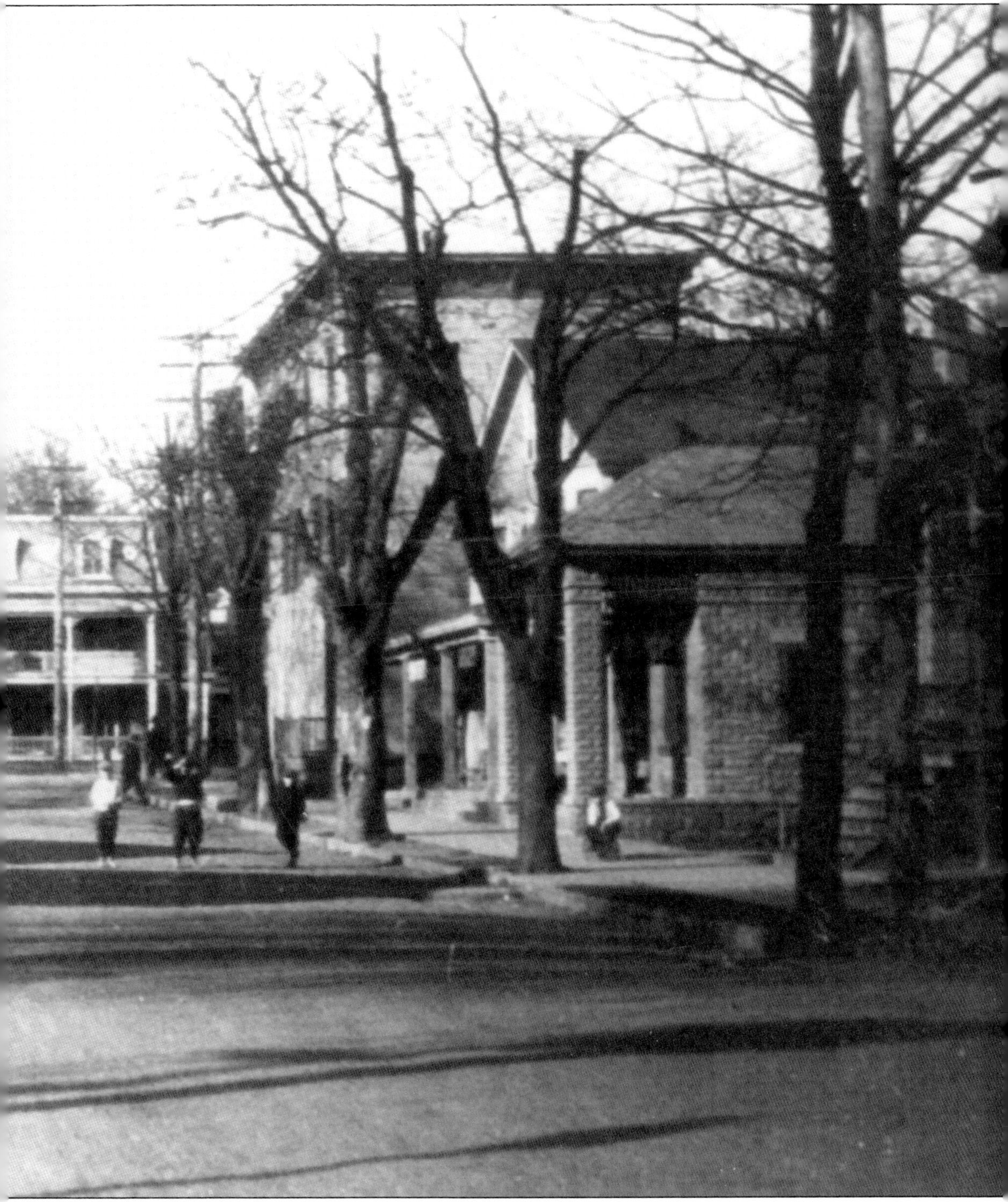

one can get the sense of this pristine and quiet town. The long shadows stretching across the street from the west indicate that the electric street light overhanging the scene will soon be called into service. (Courtesy of the Delaware River Mill Society.)

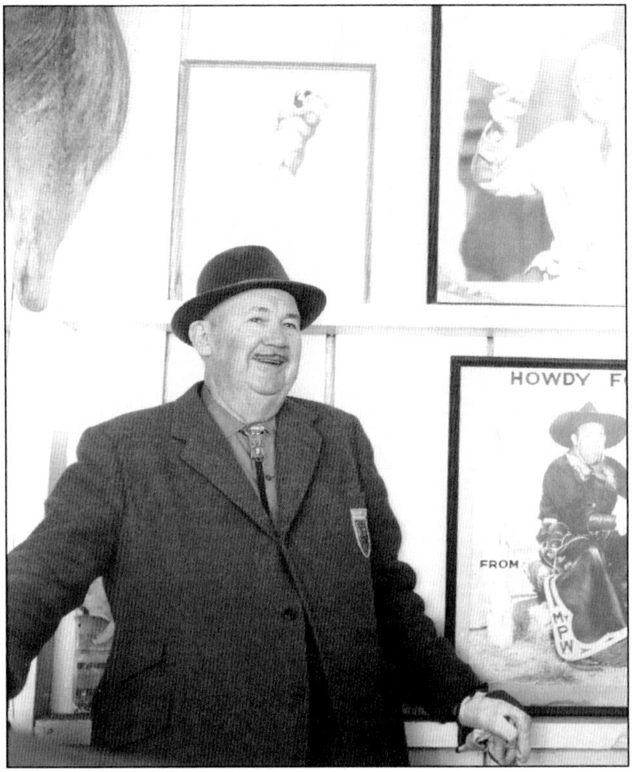

Paul Whiteman was the legendary band leader who introduced George Gershwin's "Rhapsody in Blue" to the public in 1924 with Gershwin at the piano. From 1949 to 1954, he hosted the *T.V. Teen Club*. Shot in Philadelphia, the show was a predecessor of *American Bandstand*. A regular at Colligan's Stockton Inn, he signed off every show with, "I'm off to Ma Colligan's." (Courtesy of Carl Cathers.)

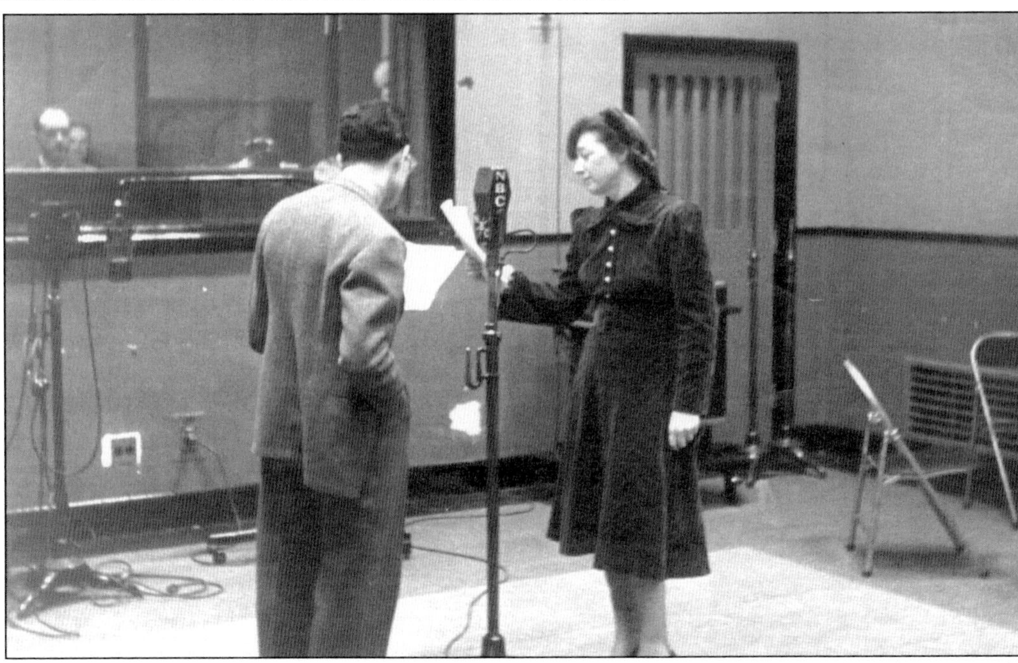

Anne Elstner Matthews is seen here doing a live broadcast of the *Stella Dallas Show*. A radio serial that ran for 18 years, Matthews missed only two shows and commuted from her home in Stockton via car and train. She and her husband John "Jack" Matthews owned the Letitia House built by John Prall Jr. (Courtesy of Carl Cathers.)

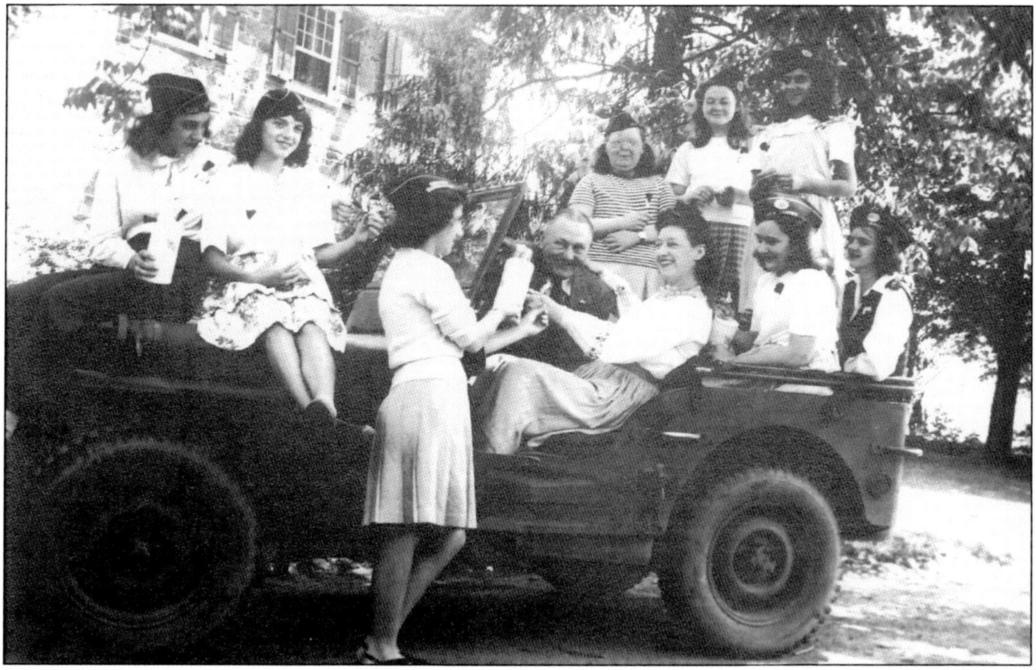

During the war years, Anne spearheaded a number of community projects in support of the war effort. In this shot taken in front of her home while sitting in the driver's seat of her husband's jeep, she's seen with Mayor Emmert Wilson and a group of young volunteers for a war bond drive. (Courtesy of Carl Cathers.)

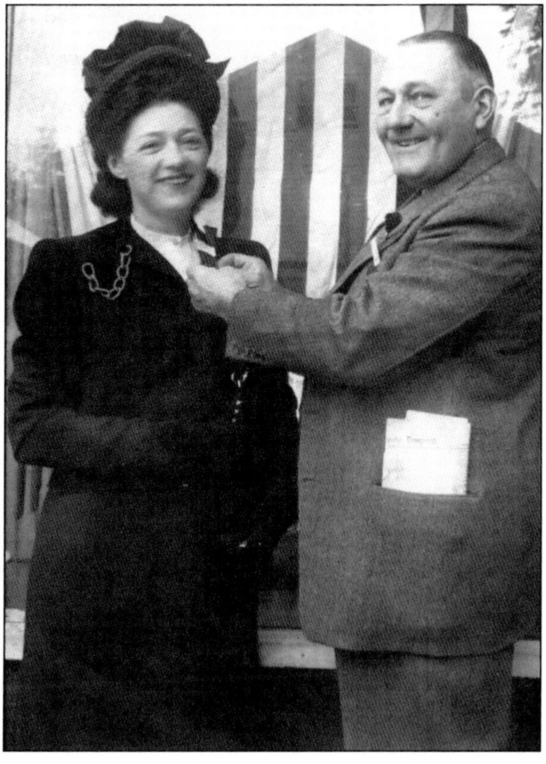

Wilson presents Anne with an award for her work with the schoolchildren to support saving for war bonds. During World War II, books using 25¢ stamps were used to promote saving for bonds. Anne provided every child in the school with a book that included the first 25¢ stamp. Note the *Hunterdon County Democrat* folded in Wilson's suit pocket. (Courtesy of Carl Cathers.)

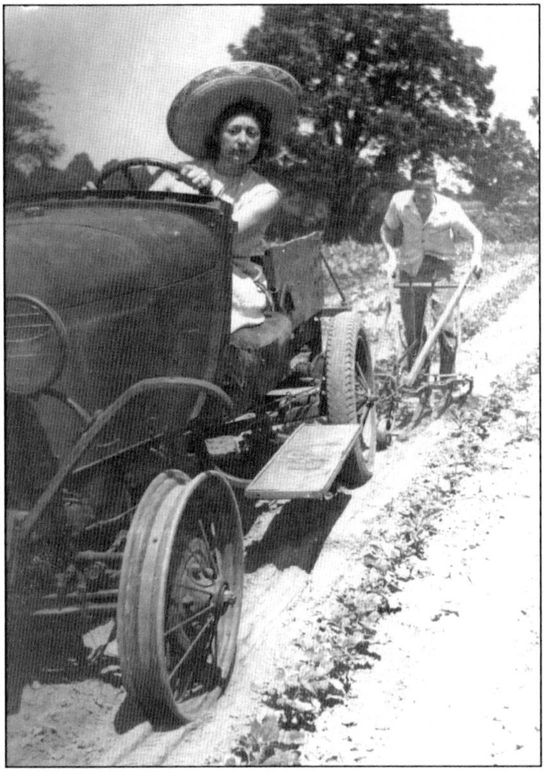

Another aspect of wartime life was the victory garden. Here Anne Matthews uses an old Ford Model A as a tractor pulling a one-horse cultivator guided by Carl Cathers. Because of the scarcity of rubber tires as replacements, the front wheels were run on their rims after the tires had worn out. The old car was restored in 1990. (Courtesy of Carl Cathers.)

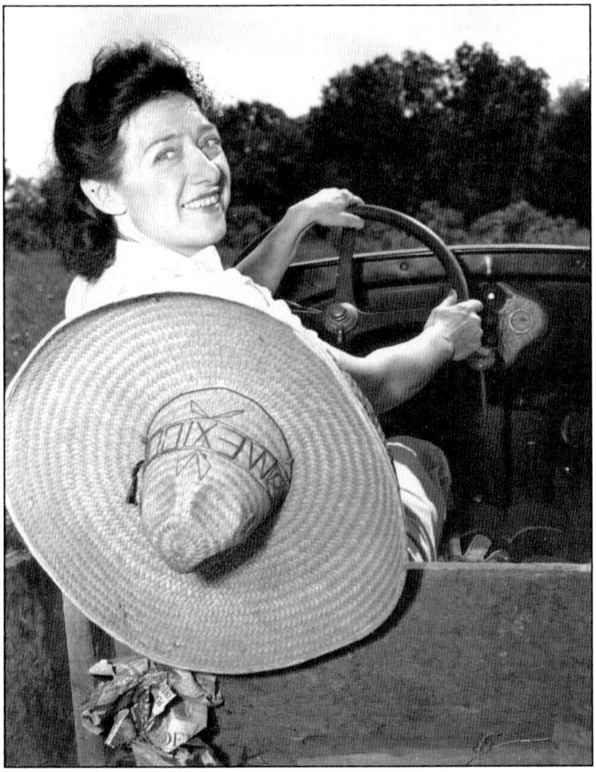

Anne Matthews and her husband Jack bought the Letitia House in 1940 for $10,000 and called Stockton home throughout the rest of their lives. The townsfolk knew her as Stella Dallas, after her radio character, and they led normal lives punctuated by visits from friends like Helen Hayes and Lefty Gomez, who once brought along baseball legend Cy Young for a visit. (Courtesy of Carl Cathers.)

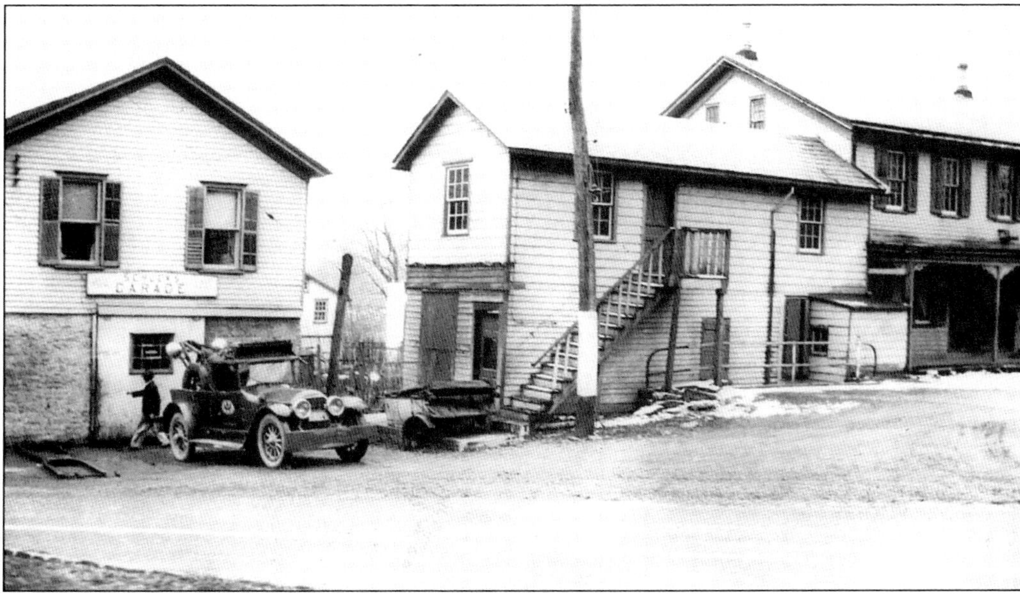

Pictured is Schuck's Garage in 1935 with the tow truck parked in front. A mechanic in the 1930s had to be able to fix more than just cars. Anton "Tony" Schuck fixed everything from cars, to tractors, to kids' roller skates. He even fabricated the stand for Robert Goddard's prototype rocket when the space-age pioneer chose Stockton to test one of his rockets. (Courtesy of the Delaware River Mill Society.)

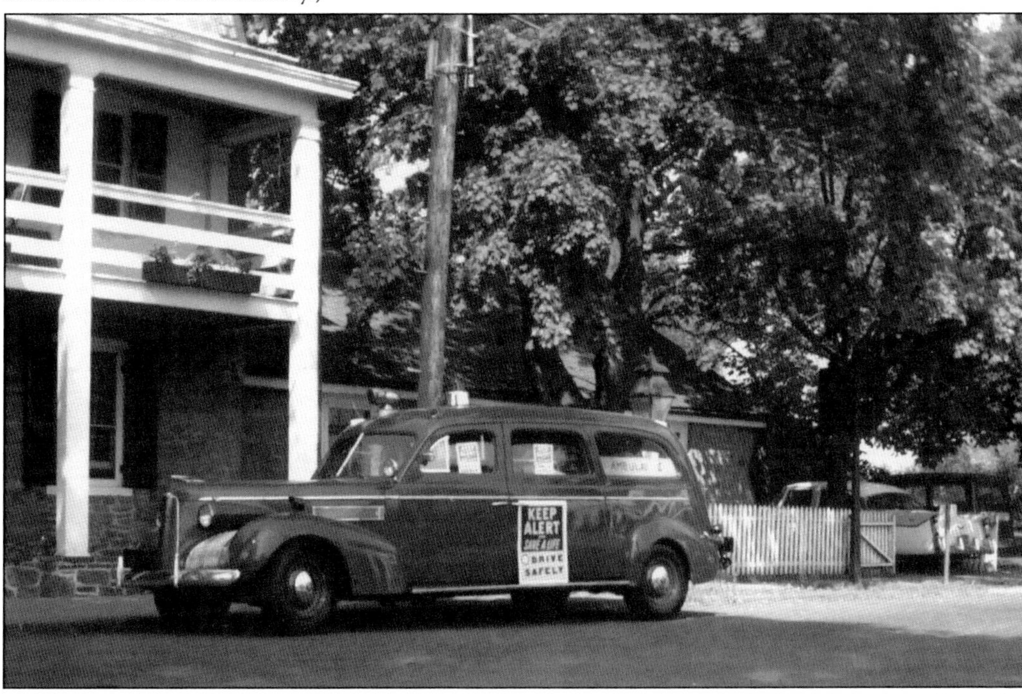

Fulfilling a community need, the fire department formed the Stockton Fire Company First Aid Squad in 1958. Neighboring Flemington's rescue squad was buying a new ambulance and offered their old 1939 LaSalle ambulance to Stockton for the newly formed squad's use. (Courtesy of the Delaware River Mill Society.)

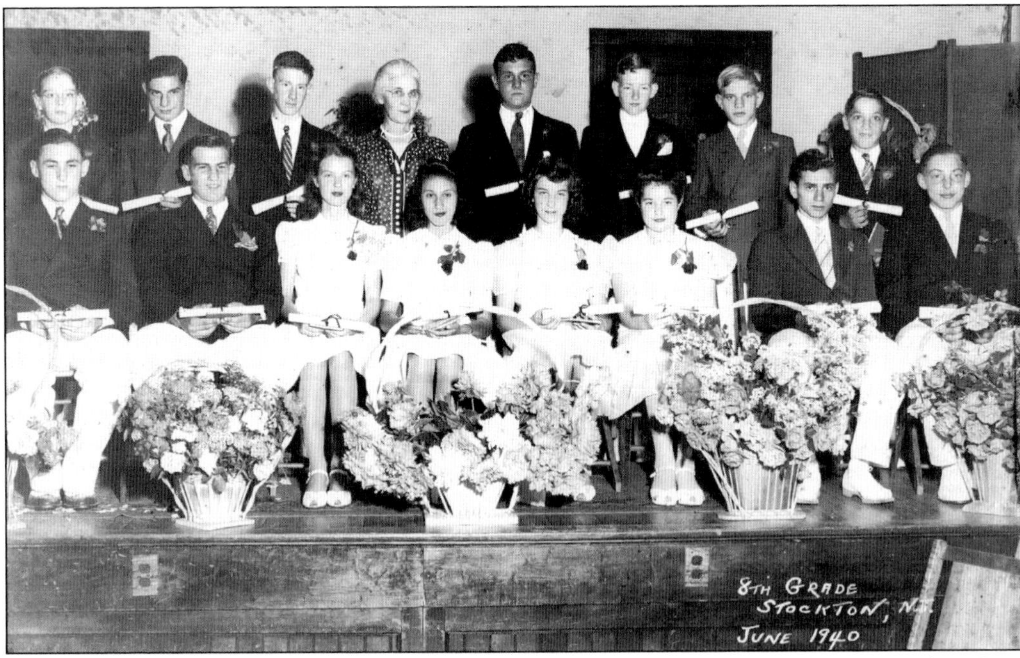

The Stockton School eighth grade graduating class of 1940 each had a nickname, such as Ding Dang, Lippo, and Skeeter. Their given names are, from left to right, (sitting, first row) Donald Palmer, Carmen Vallani, Naomi Errico, Coriela Giacondo, Rose Palmiere, Barbara Allen, Michael Pennett, and Kenneth Palmer; (standing, second row) Raymond Dilts, Peter Capizzi, Richard Naylor, Ada Reading (principal), Joseph Vallani, Carl Cathers, Wesley Hendricks, and Donald Souzzo. (Courtesy of Carl Cathers.)

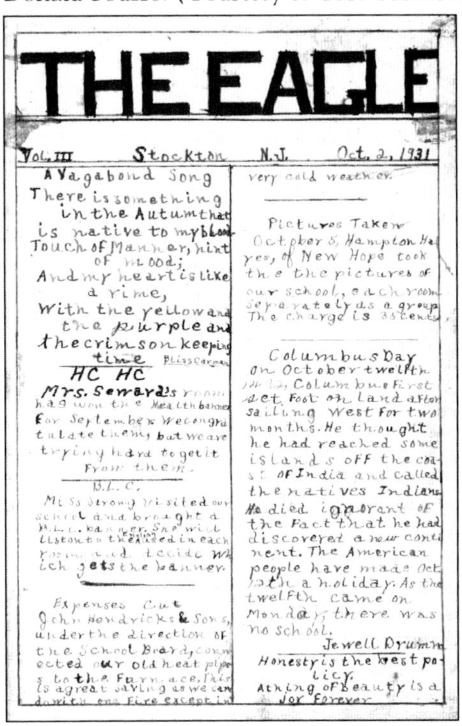

THE EAGLE

Vol. III Stockton N.J. Oct. 2, 1931

A Vagabond Song
There is something in the Autum that is native to my blood. Touch of Manner, hint of mood; And my heart is like a rime, With the yellow and the purple and the crimson keeping time
Bliss Carman

HC HC
Mrs. Seward's room has won the Health banner for September. We congratulate them, but we are trying hard to get it from them.

B.L.C.
Miss Strong visited our school and brought a B.L.C. banner. She will listen to the English used in each room and decide which gets the banner.

Expenses Cut
John Hendricks & Sons, under the direction of the School Board, connected our old heat pipes to the Furnace. This is a great saving as we can do with one Fire except in very cold weather.

Pictures Taken
October 5, Hampton Hayes, of New Hope took the the pictures of our school, each room separately as a group. The charge is 35 cents.

Columbus Day
On October twelfth 1492, Columbus first set foot on land after sailing West for two months. He thought he had reached some islands off the coast of India and called the natives Indians. He died ignorant of the fact that he had discovered a new continent. The American people have made Oct. 12th a holiday. As the twelfth came on Monday, there was no school.
Jewell Drumm

Honesty is the best policy.
A thing of beauty is a joy forever.

The *Eagle* was the Stockton School's hand-printed newsletter, put out monthly by the students. This is the front page of the October 2, 1931, issue, which cites on the last page the enrollment and attendance figures for the school as, "114 pupils Percentage of attendance 95%." Carl Decker was the editor-in-chief, Edith Wilson and Isabelle Hoffman were the assistant editors, and Horace Cathers was the printer. (Courtesy of Carl Cathers.)

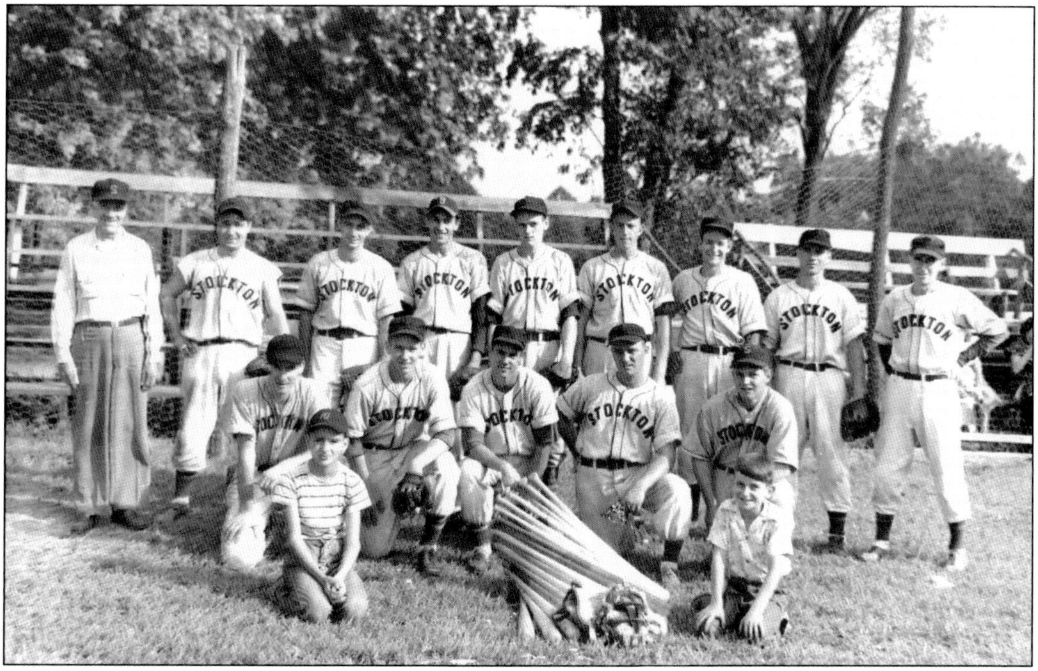

Each town had a baseball team, and this is a picture of the 1950 Stockton team. Boys grew up following scores and playing "shove up" in the school yard. Shove up had nine players with three batters and the rest in the field. When a batter struck out, he would move to right field and the rest of the players would "shove up" and rotate positions. (Courtesy of Carl Cathers.)

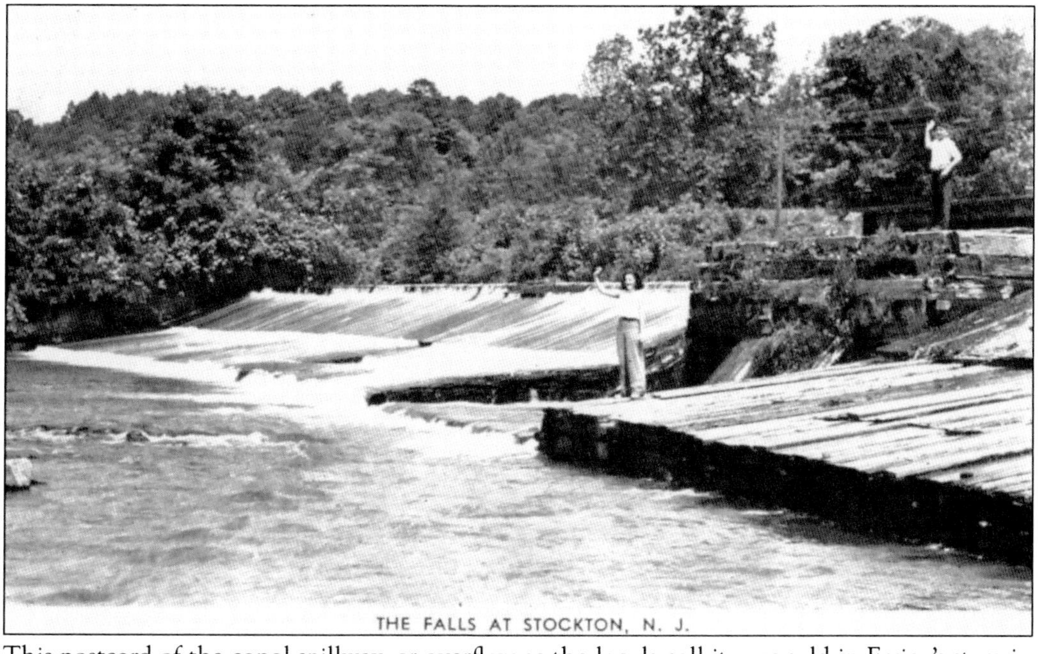

This postcard of the canal spillway, or overflow as the locals call it, was sold in Errico's store in Stockton. Not coincidentally, the young man stranding on the "stone box" is Leonard Errico and the young woman is Eleanor Errico; they are brother and sister. Their family owned the store in which the postcard was sold. (Courtesy of the Delaware and Raritan Canal Commission.)

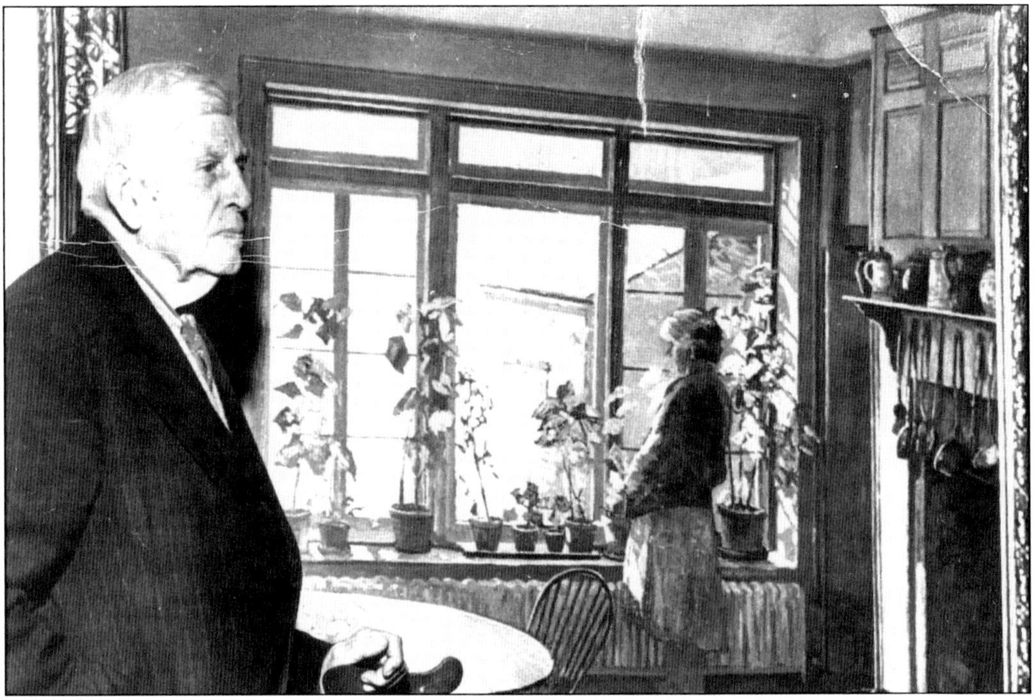

Edward Redfield (1869–1965), the well-known Pennsylvania impressionist, stands in front of his painting "South Window" at his home in Centre Bridge in this c. 1960 photograph. Considered one of America's greatest impressionist painters, he was good friends with Anne Matthews and a stylistic influence on many painters including Austin L. Davison Jr. (Courtesy of Carl Cathers.)

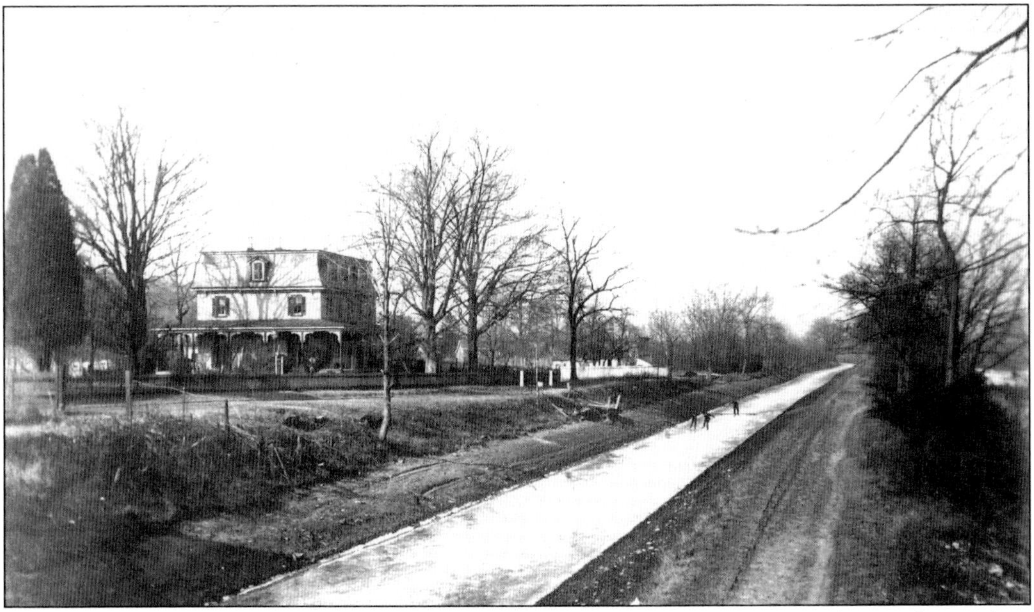

Redfield acquired the Fell's Boarding House for his home. The story goes that in his earlier, leaner years, Redfield would build a snowman near the canal and place a hat on its head. As the coal boats passed, the crews would try to knock the hat off of the snowman using pieces of coal. Redfield would then collect the free coal for his own use. (Courtesy of Carl Cathers.)

Austin L. Davison Jr. sits under one of his paintings in his home in Stockton. As a child, he would hide behind a tree and watch Redfield paint. Davison was influenced by Redfield's style and copied his technique of dabbing the canvas with the brush rather than using strokes. (Courtesy of Carl Cathers.)

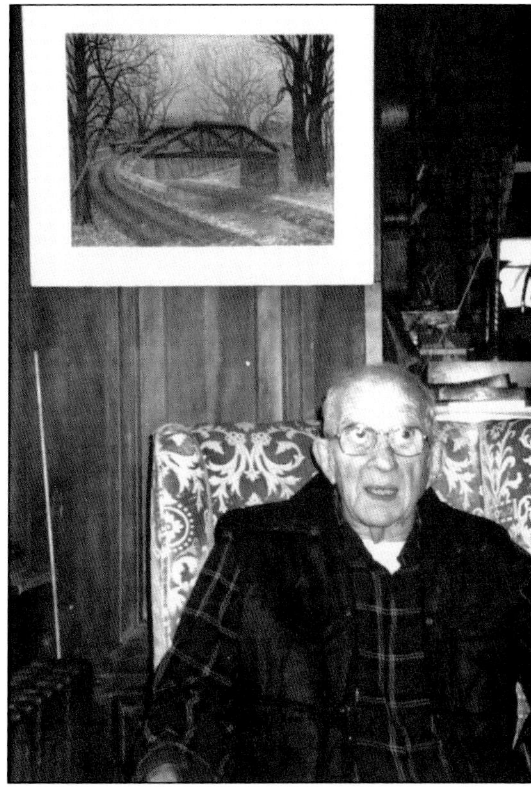

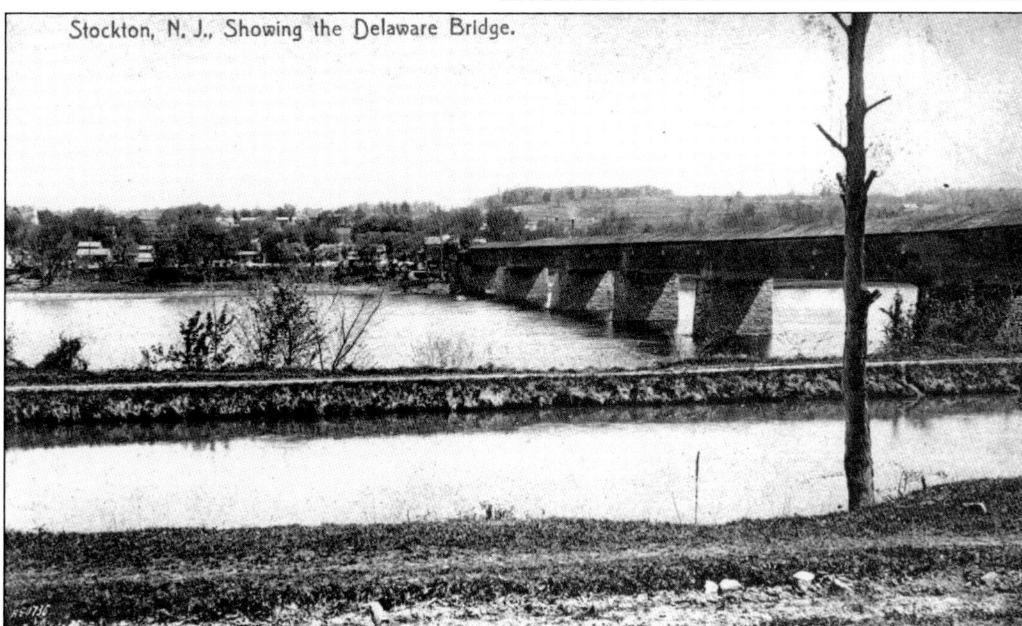

It is perhaps the coexistence of the serene beauty and crushing power within the very same river that draws and inspires so many people. The peaceful river here is the same river that, in the flood of 1841, shoved the bridge off its piers and gave George B. Fell a wild ride down river that did not end until he was rescued 15 miles away. (Courtesy of Carl Cathers.)

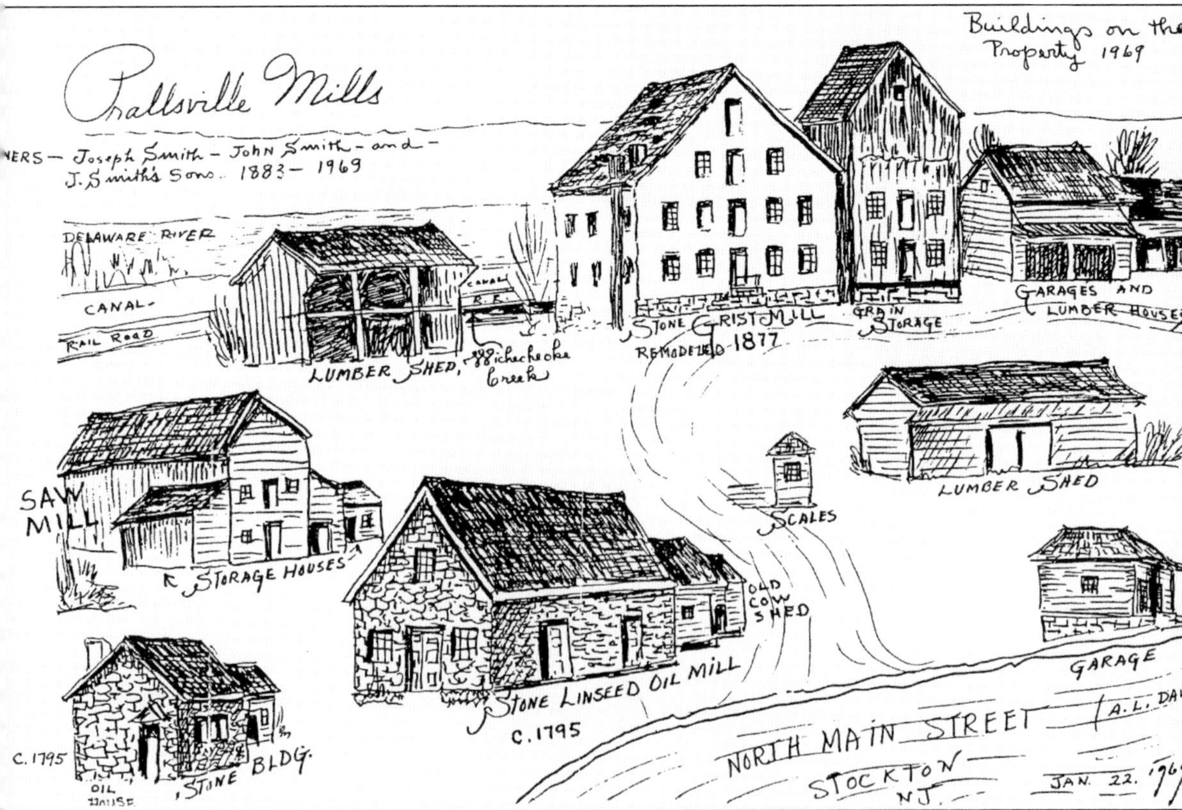

Austin L. Davison Jr. was very interested in local history and did a great deal of detailed research on the subjects of Stockton and river mills. He drew this picture of the buildings in 1969 with an eye toward recording the state of the property at that time. Since then, the small wooden structure attached to what he refers to as the "oil house" and "stone building" is gone. The wooden structures attached to the linseed oil mill are also gone. The garage at the edge of North Main Street, which was of no historical significance, has been torn down. The building in the upper right corner marked "garages and lumber houses" is now the office for the Delaware and Raritan Canal Commission. This building has also been used as an icehouse, horse stables, and a garage. (Courtesy of Carl Cathers.)

Five

Mishaps, Fires, and Floods

The people of Stockton are not resilient by accident—they have earned it. For a town as small as Stockton, it has seen its fair share of extreme challenges and disasters. The people of Stockton always bounce back and are living proof of the old adage "What doesn't kill you makes you stronger."

In 1888, quarry foreman James Wafer, wearing the wedding ring he was going to give to his fiancée, went into the powder magazine at 25 minutes past seven to get a can of fine powder. The article in the *Democrat-Advertiser* the following week written by L. R. Runkle described what happened next. "Two minutes later there was a great cloud of white smoke, a belch of fire 50 feet high and a noise like a hundred thunderstorms."

James Wafer, some surmise, possibly spilled a bit of powder on the floor and inadvertently crushed it under the heel of his boot, setting off the most destructive black powder explosion ever known in New Jersey. The powder magazine was reduced to splinters and replaced with a hole 12 feet square and 10 feet deep. All that was found of poor Wafer was his ring three quarters of a mile away and his mustache and upper lip in an apple orchard 500 yards from the explosion.

The explosion was so violent that it broke virtually every window in Stockton as well as a few in Lambertville. The shock was felt as far away as New Brunswick, and it rattled dishes in Newtown, Pennsylvania, some 14 miles away. The surprise was that exploding 300 cans of blasting powder and 250 dynamite cartridges killed only one man. The blast demolished a dozen buildings and did considerable damage to Stockton and injured six men.

Stockton recovered and moved on. But there would be more challenges to come from the river, the sky, and some mice chewing on matchsticks.

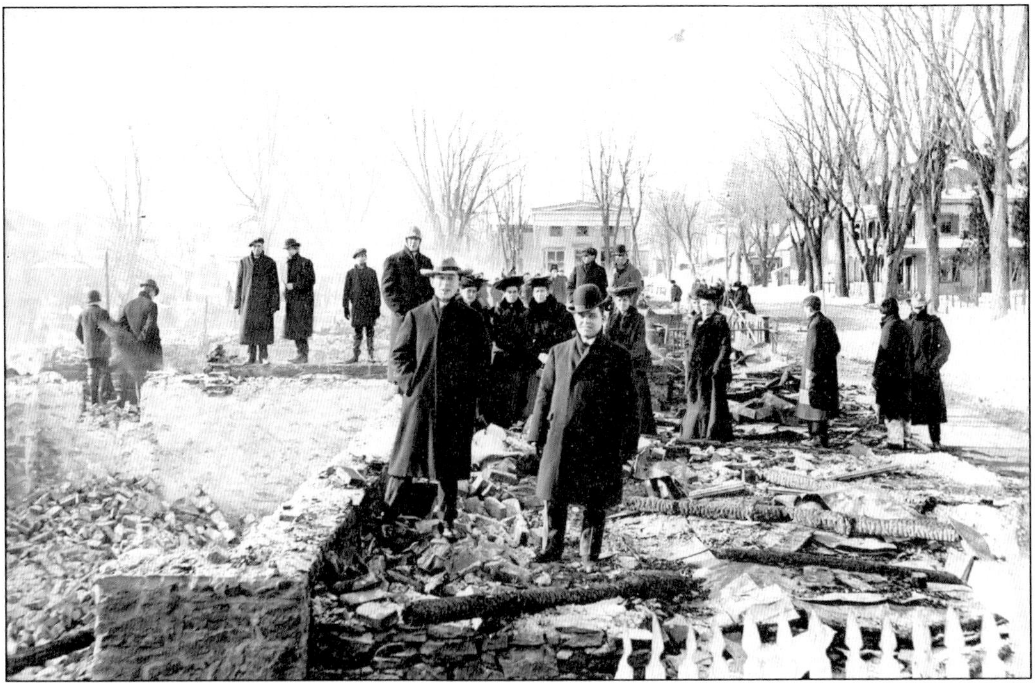

Less than two years after the flood of 1903, a devastating fire tore through the heart of Stockton on January 26, 1905, at 2:00 a.m. with temperatures at minus two degrees, in a blinding snow storm with high winds. This shot is looking north on Main Street. (Courtesy of Carl Cathers.)

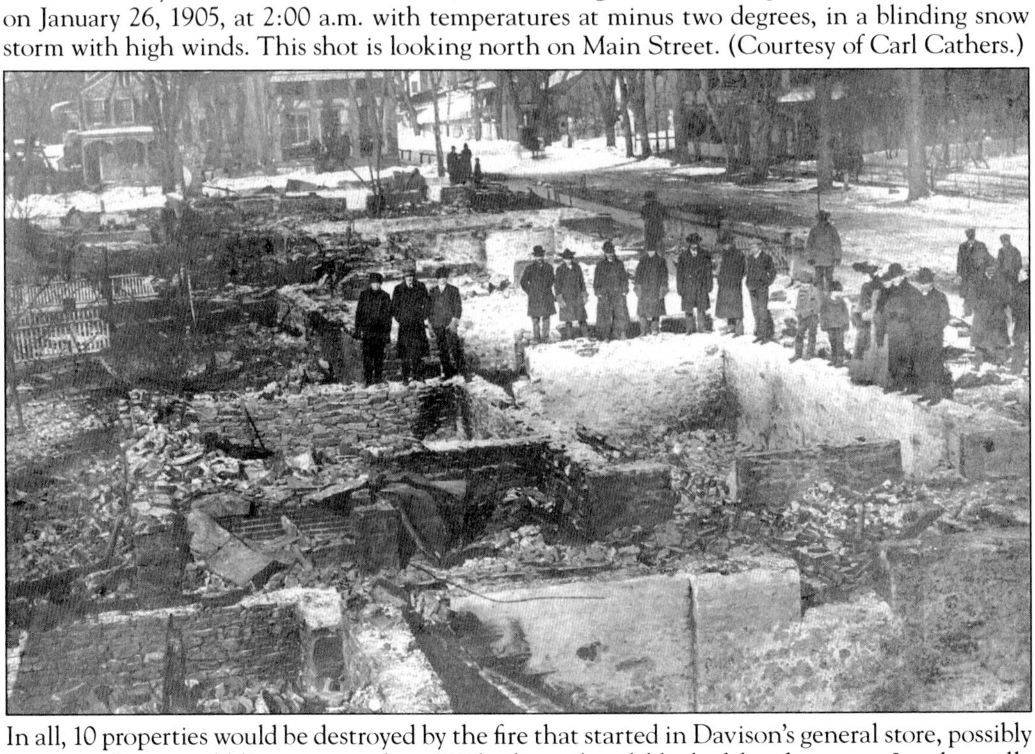

In all, 10 properties would be destroyed by the fire that started in Davison's general store, possibly because of mice nibbling on matches. With the railroad blocked by the snow, Lambertville and Trenton fire companies could not quickly reach the town. In the end, only foundations remained. (Courtesy of Carl Cathers.)

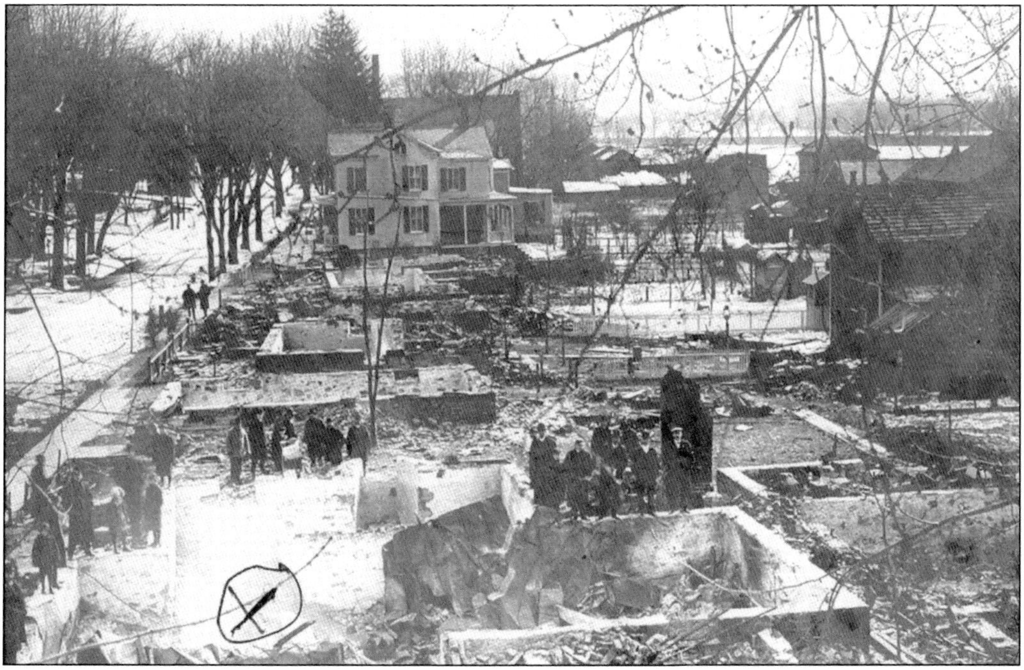

Columbia Fire Company from Lambertville arrive at 5:30 a.m. In three and a half hours, the fire consumed nine buildings to their foundations with the tenth almost gone. The *X* on the photograph marks the spot where the fire began at Bridge and Main Streets looking south down Main Street. (Courtesy of Carl Cathers.)

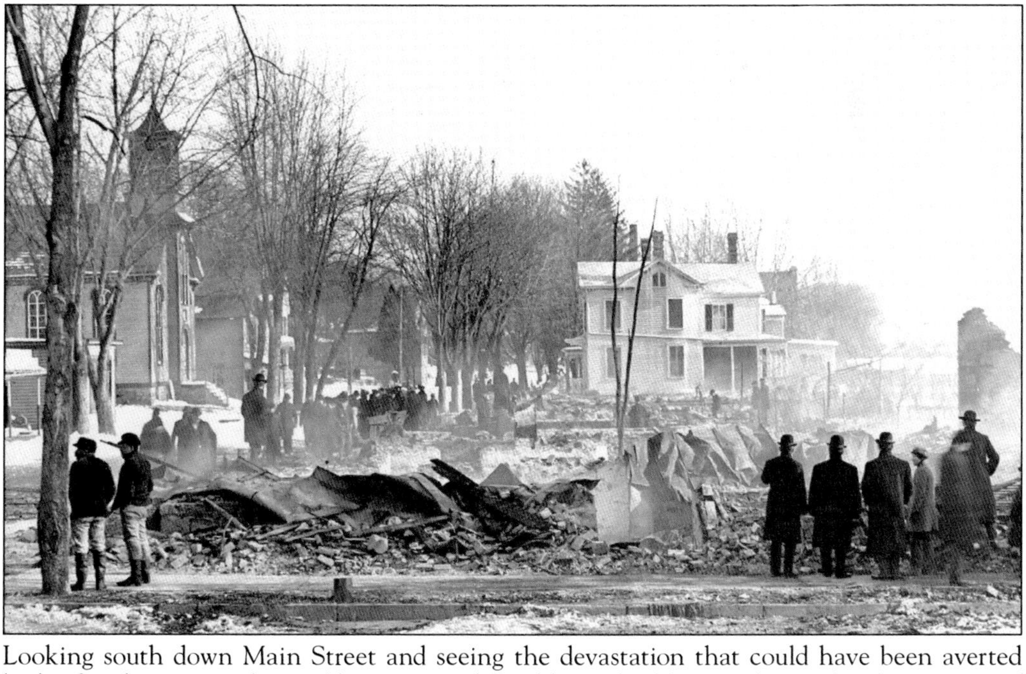

Looking south down Main Street and seeing the devastation that could have been averted had a fire department been able to respond quickly to the blaze explains why the citizens of Stockton voted the very next year to establish a fire company and buy a fire engine. (Courtesy of Carl Cathers.)

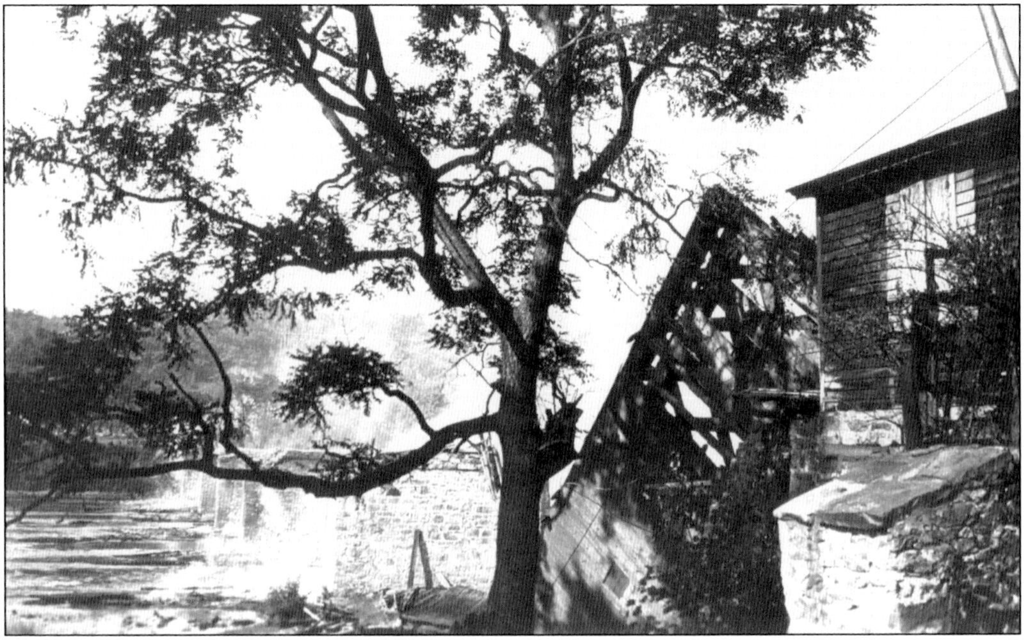

On July 22, 1923, lightening struck the center span of the covered bridge between Stockton and Centre Bridge, setting a fire that quickly engulfed the rest of the structure and sent it into the river. Although there were men on the bridge, no one was seriously hurt. (Courtesy of the Delaware River Mill Society.)

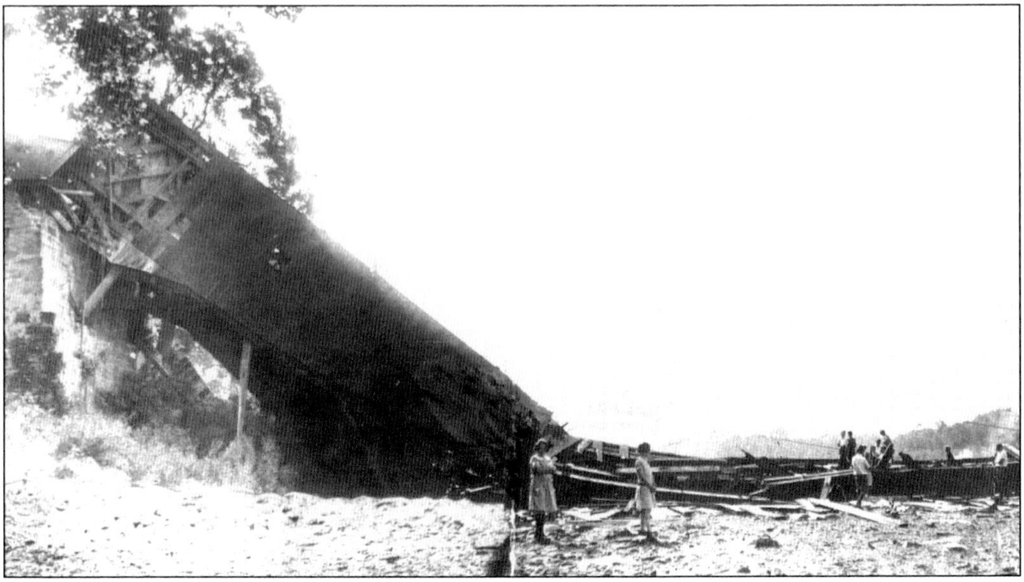

The next day people were still trying to assess the impact losing the bridge would have on their lives. As it turned out, they would have time to adjust, because it would be four years before the new steel bridge would be open in 1927. (Courtesy of Carl Cathers.)

Rivers flood and the Delaware River is no exception to this rule. On October 10 and 11, 1903, the waters rose high enough to destroy all of the crossings between Easton and Lambertville, with the exception of the Stockton bridge. This shot of Lambertville is taken from the foot of Coryell Street before the bridge was taken. (Courtesy of Carl Cathers.)

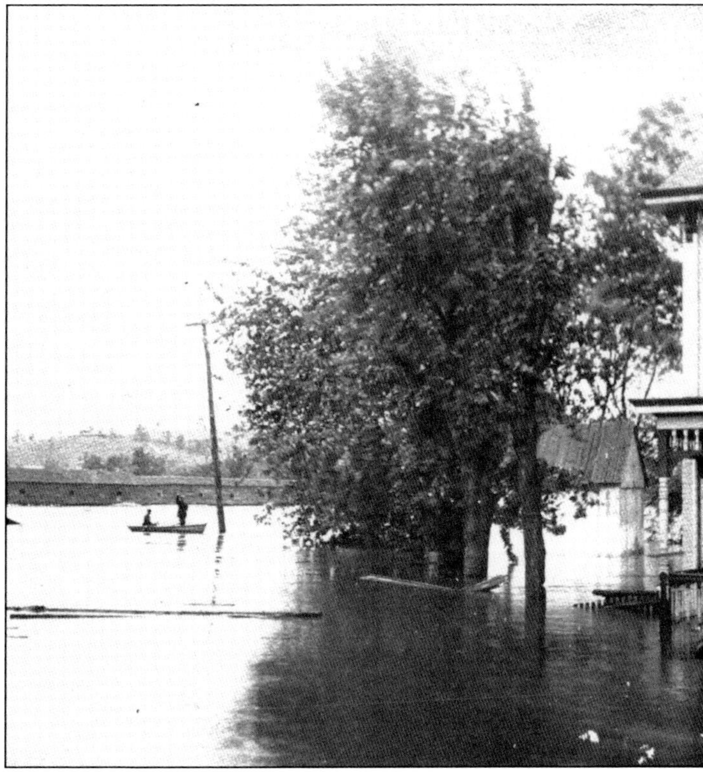

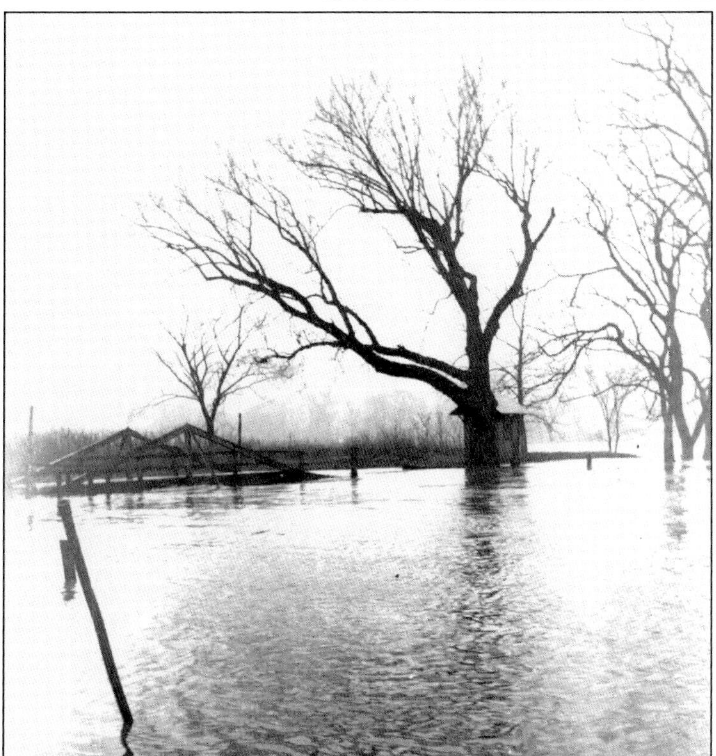

The flood of 1936, while not as high as the flood of 1903, still had enough strength to do a good deal of damage. Looking at the Prallsville lock, the water is up to the deck of the canal bridge, and George Price's tool shed has become an island. (Courtesy of Carl Cathers.)

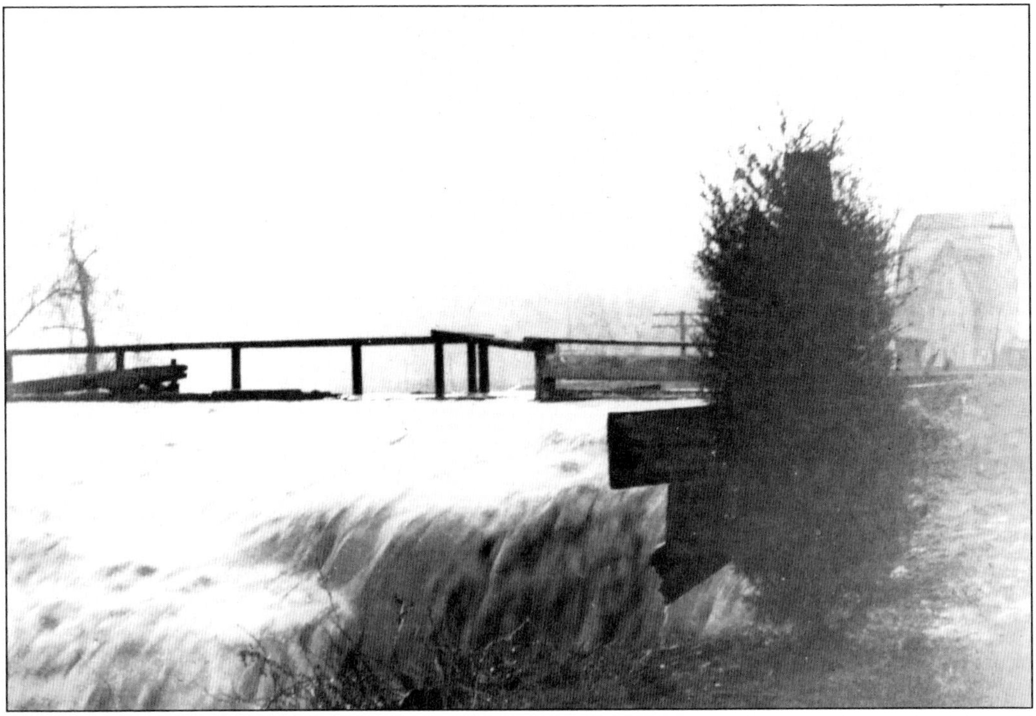

The 1936 floodwater is overflowing the canal and locks and racing through the yard of the old quarry office, which is now the Cathers homestead. The gristmill and silo at the Prallsville Mills complex can be seen in the upper right of the picture. (Courtesy of Carl Cathers.)

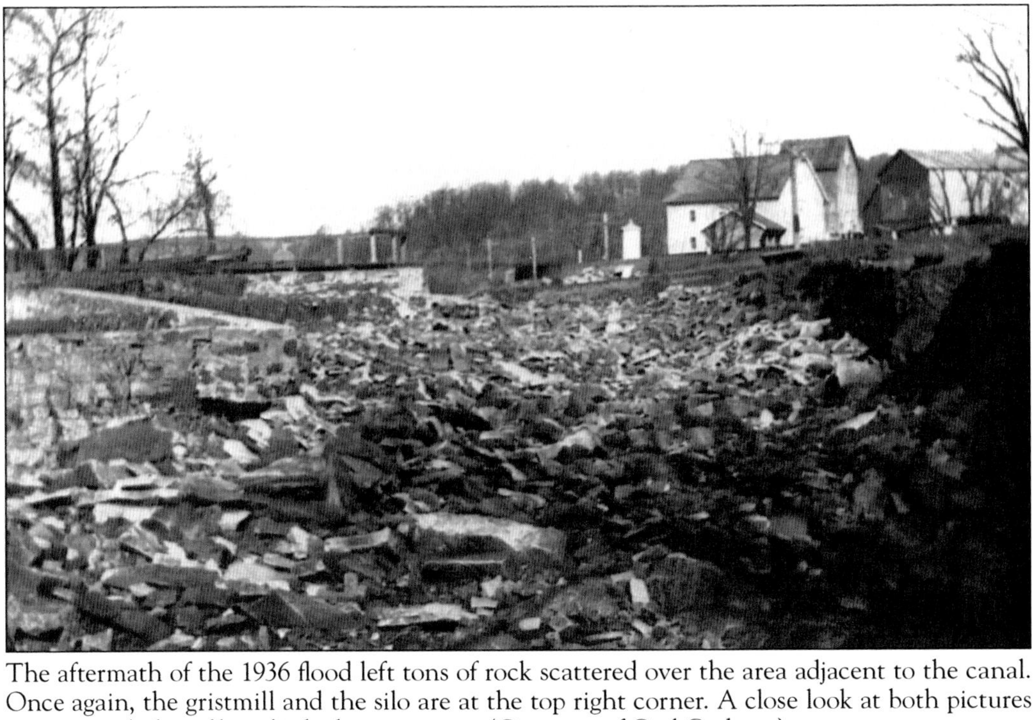

The aftermath of the 1936 flood left tons of rock scattered over the area adjacent to the canal. Once again, the gristmill and the silo are at the top right corner. A close look at both pictures gives a good idea of how high the water was. (Courtesy of Carl Cathers.)

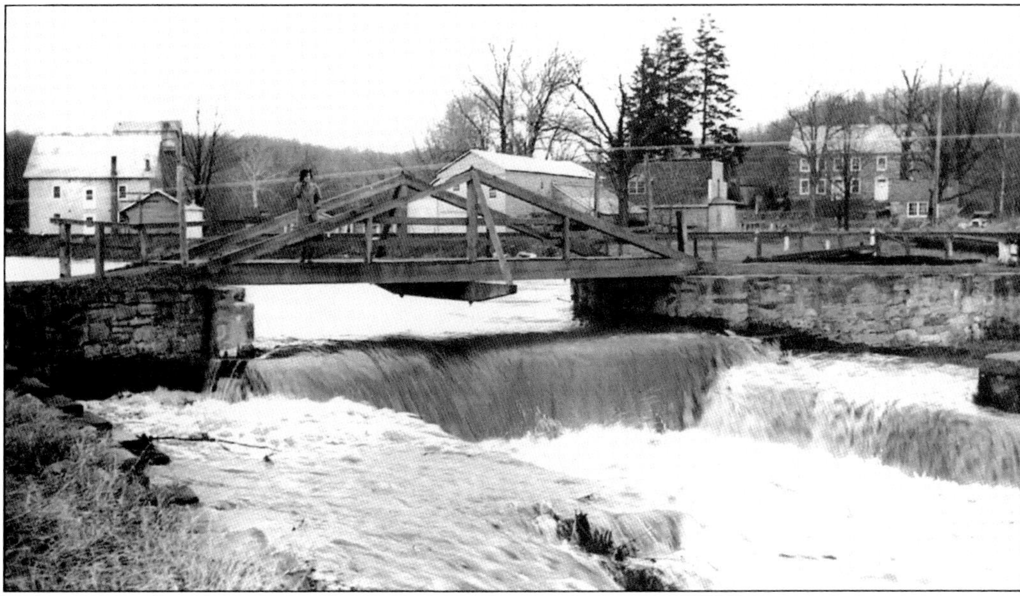

In this shot, the water has not yet risen to the deck of the canal bridge during the 1936 flood. Water pours past the lock, which did a great deal of damage to the lock gates and mechanism. The gristmill and the silo are on the left. (Courtesy of Carl Cathers.)

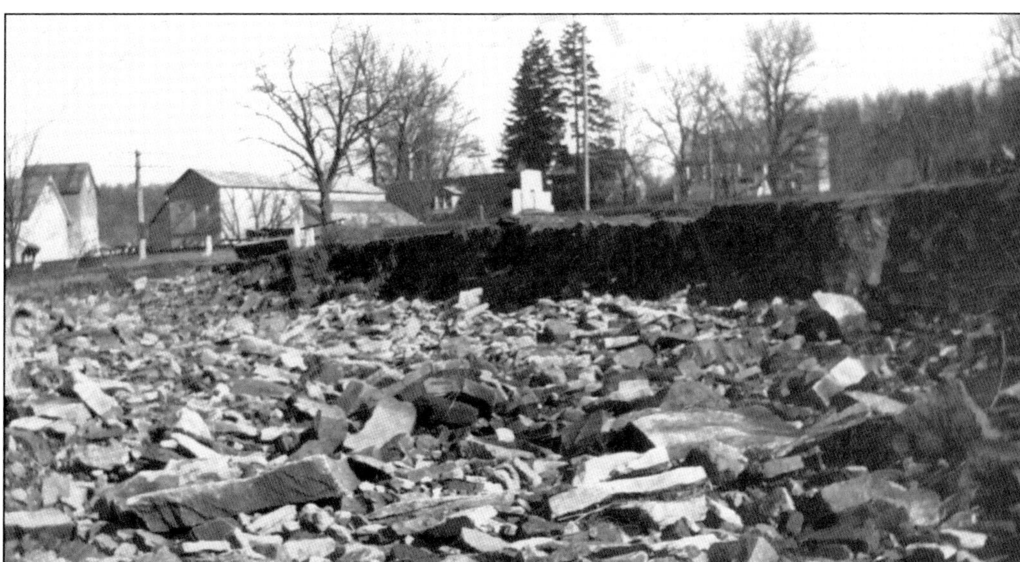

The rock bed left behind covers the entire yard of the Cathers home. The stones remained where they were and the area was covered with soil in order to reclaim the yard. While the 1936 flood was big, the biggest flood to ever hit Stockton was yet to come. (Courtesy of Carl Cathers.)

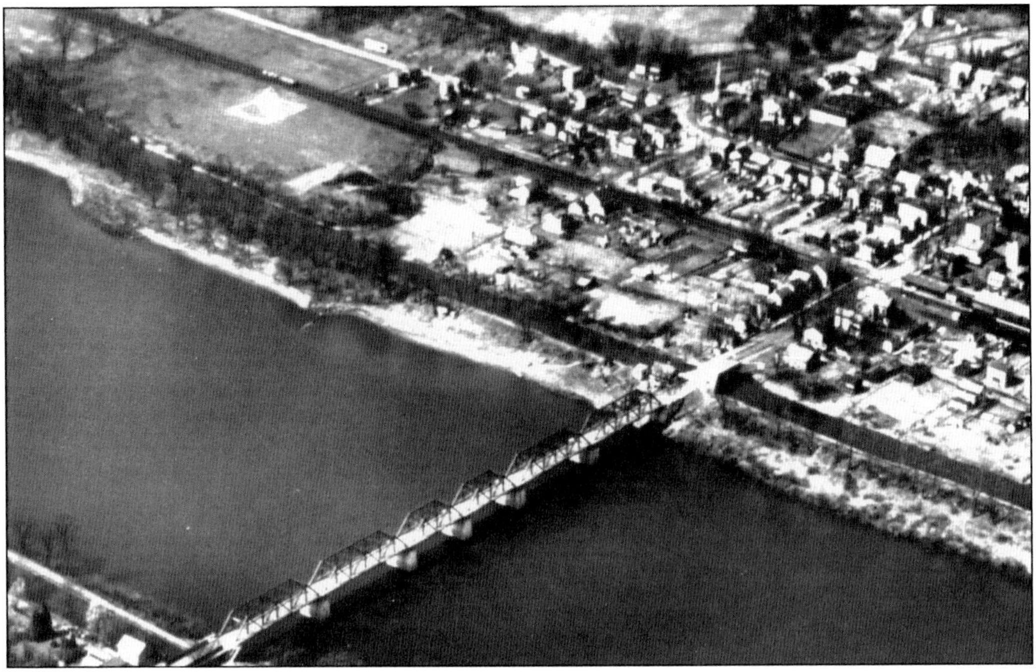

The above aerial shot, taken during a period of normal water levels, provides a stark contrast to the aerial shot taken at the height of the 1955 flood caused by Hurricane Diane. The flood of 1955 crested two feet above the all-time high of the 1903 flood. The entire lower part of Stockton was flooded right up to the porch on the Stockton Inn. The flood caused by Hurricane Diane was responsible for close to 200 deaths along the eastern seaboard and over a billion dollars in damage, giving Diane the distinction of being the first hurricane to ever reach the billion-dollar mark. (Courtesy of the Delaware River Mill Society.)

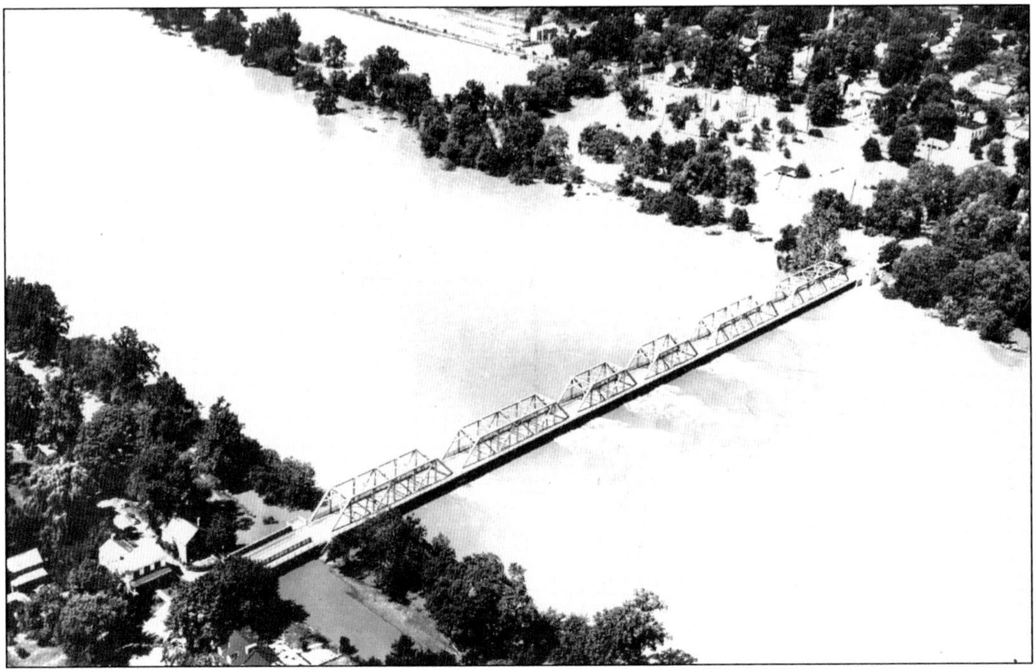

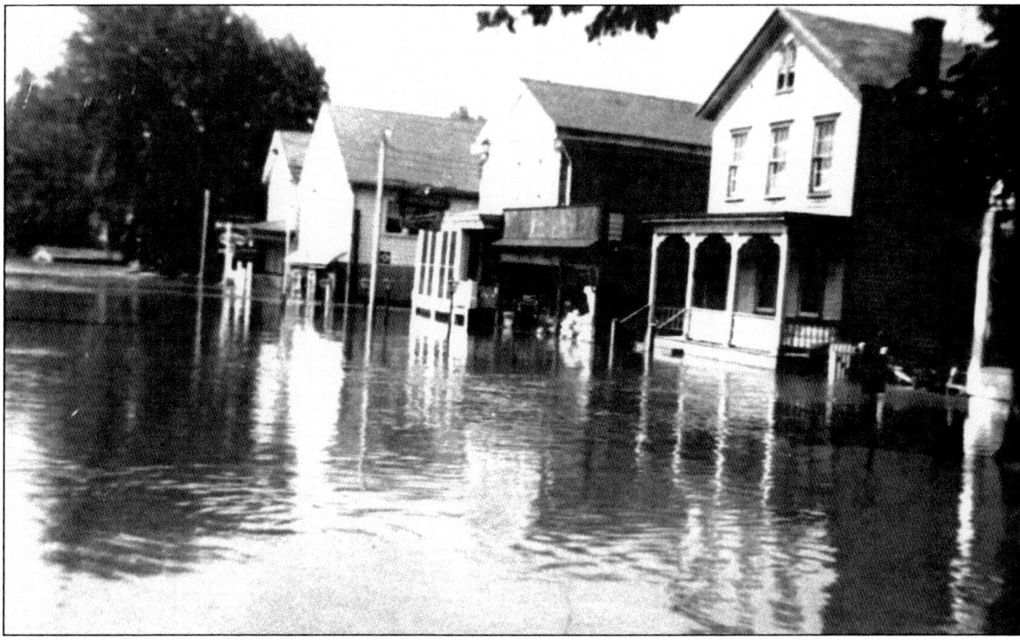

The area worst hit in Stockton was between the railroad tracks and the bridge. The flood was a result of two hurricanes, Connie and Diane that dropped three to seven inches of rain on the area in two successive weeks, overwhelming the streams and river. (Courtesy of the Delaware River Mill Society.)

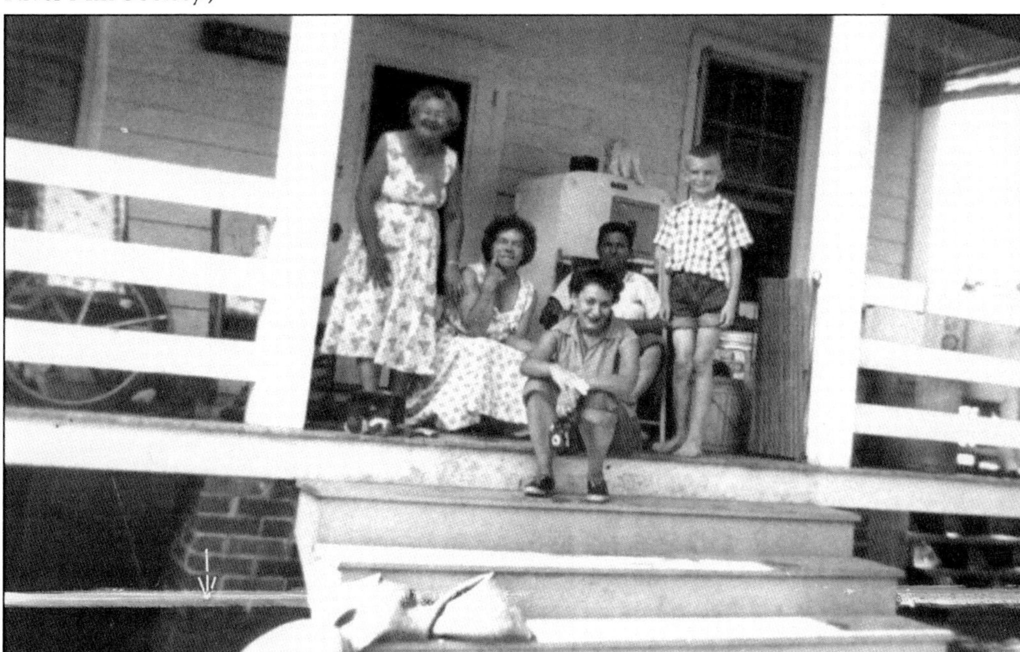

Local residents watch the water rise from their porch. The picture has been marked with a white line showing where the water was at the time. The people on the porch are, from left to right, Mary Soriero, Catherine Errico Pennett, Jeane Palmer, Frank Pennett, and Bobby Brisson. (Courtesy of the Delaware River Mill Society.)

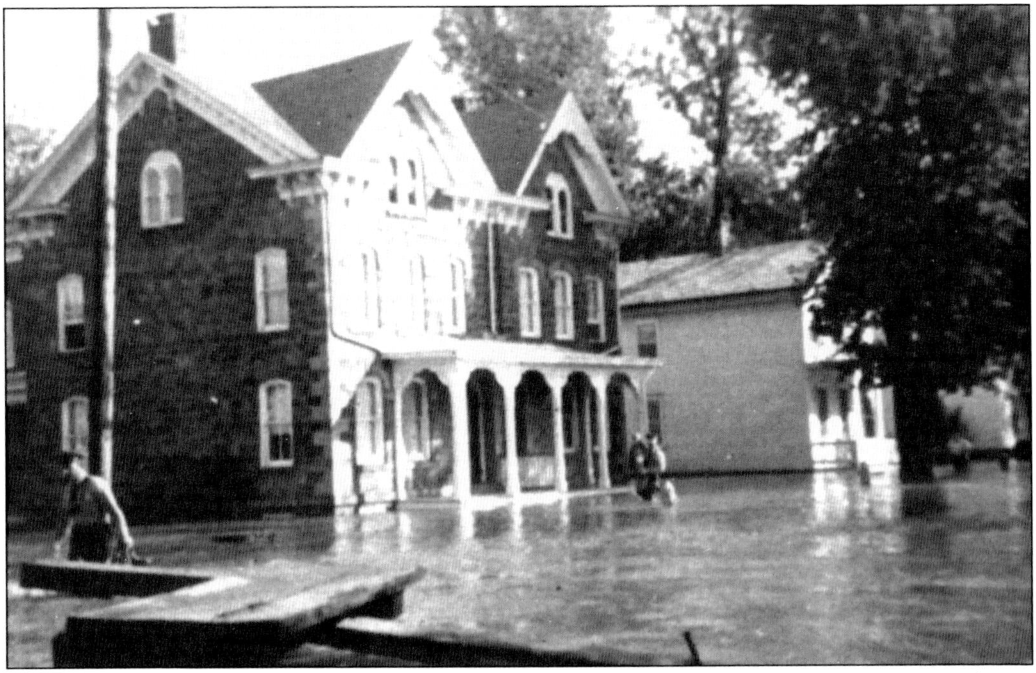

This shot is looking down the south side of Bridge Street toward the bridge as some people are moving through the thigh-deep water. Once the water subsided, the work of cleaning the river mud and silt from everything the water had covered began. (Courtesy of the Delaware River Mill Society.)

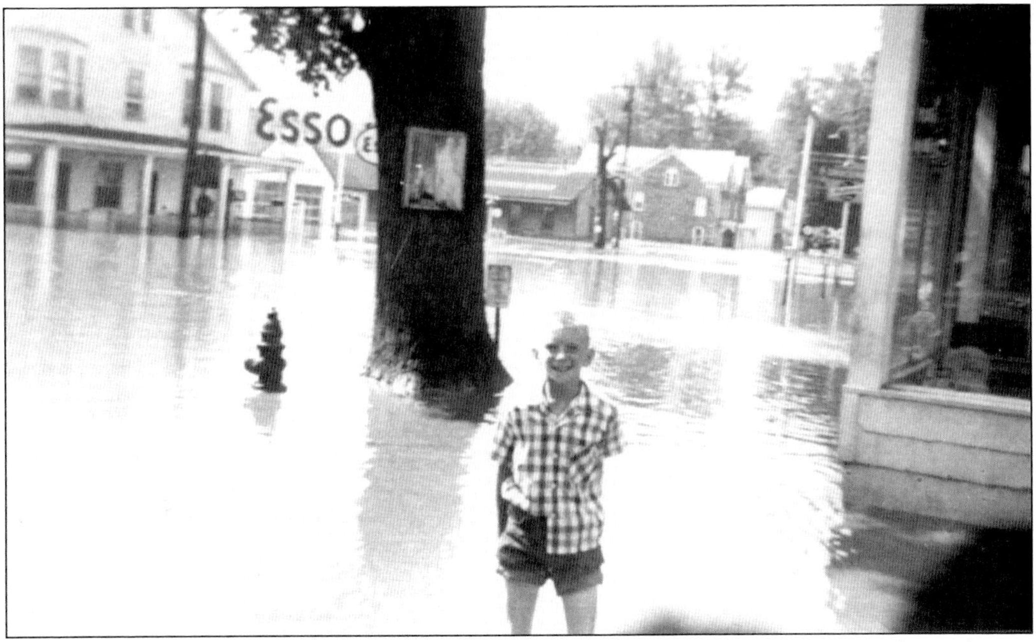

Bobby Brisson is seen here standing at the corner of Bridge and Main Streets next to the appliance store. While the water appears to not be too deep where he is standing, the house beyond the train station behind him appears to have water to the middle of its first floor. (Courtesy of the Delaware River Mill Society.)

Six

Prallsville Mills Today

John Prall Jr., a revolutionary war veteran, purchased a small mill and decided to develop a village around it. Over the years, the site reaped the benefits of the river's waterpower and the accessibility provided by first the canal and later the railroad. What remains today is a significant representation of an 18th-, 19th-, and early-20th-century American village industrial complex.

It was the location of the Prallsville Mills that contributed to its success, and in the end, it was its location that almost spelled its demise. The fate of the mill property was unclear after closing its operations in 1968. The natural beauty of the site and its easy accessibility made it an excellent candidate for development. If not for the vision of conservationist Donald B. Jones, who bought the Prallsville Mills in 1969 for the purpose of transferring it to the state for preservation, the mill might have been lost.

At the same time, a group of citizens formed the Delaware River Mill Society with the purpose of furthering the preservation of the mill complex. The property was transferred to the NJDEP in 1973 and leased to the Delaware River Mill Society who maintain and operate the site.

The Prallsville Industrial District, which includes the mill complex and surrounding village, was placed on the National Register of Historic Places in 1979. Today the Prallsville Mills complex is a center for history, the arts, ecotourism, and a variety of community and recreational activities.

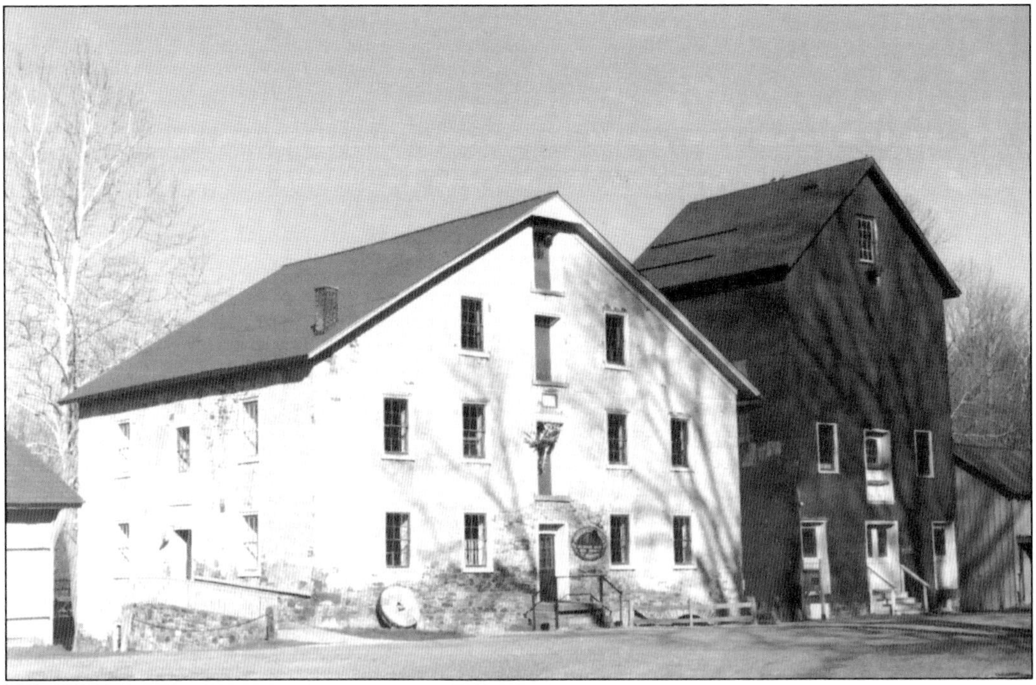

Location has allowed the Prallsville Mills to grow and prosper. Now as a part of the Delaware and Raritan Canal State Park and the center point of the Delaware River New Jersey Scenic Byway, the mill is poised to continue that growth and success. (Courtesy of the Delaware River Mill Society.).

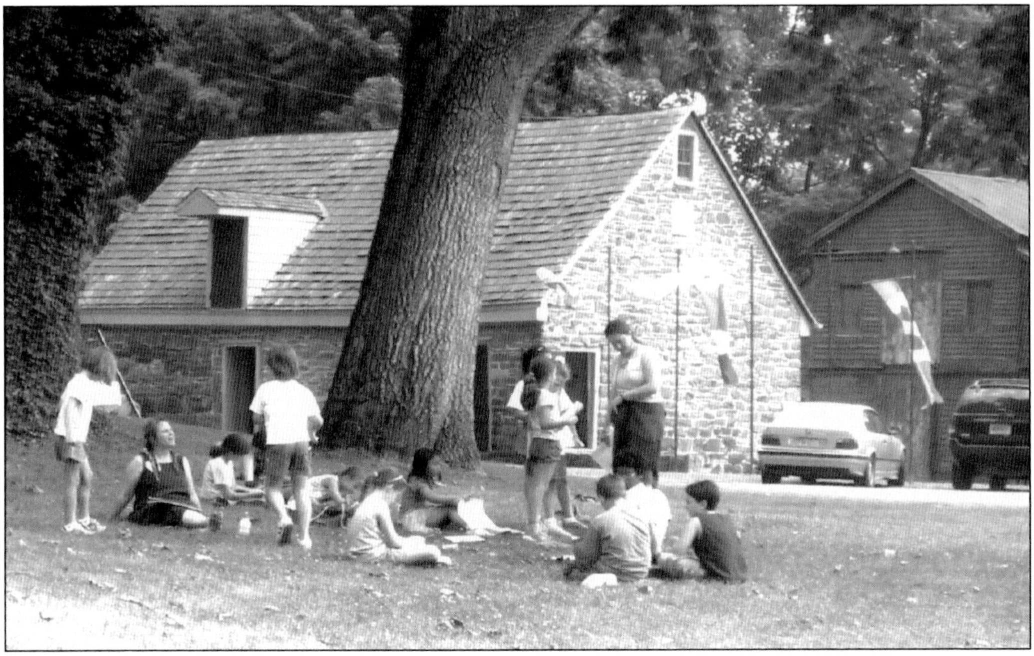

A variety of programs and events as well as plenty of open space in which to wander and points of interest to explore make the Prallsville Mills a center for history, the arts, ecotourism, and a variety of community and recreational activities. (Courtesy of the Delaware River Mill Society.)

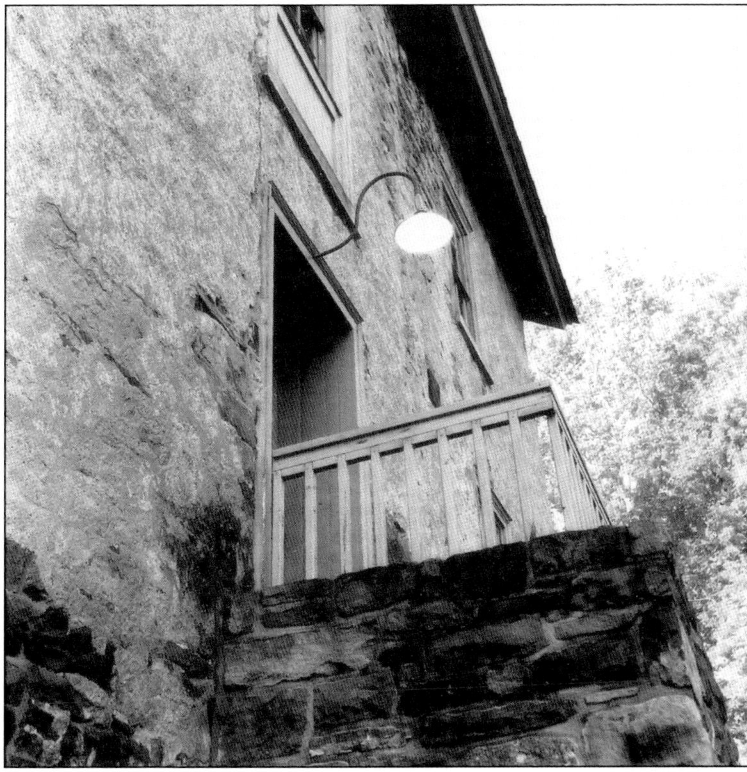

The gristmill that once ground grain into flour and feed is now home to art shows, historical tours, conservation workshops, children's camps, weddings, music, film, and professional theater. The surrounding area beckons hikers, bicyclist, water sports enthusiasts, painters, hobbyists, and folks that just want to sit back and relax to come and enjoy. (Courtesy of the Delaware River Mill Society.)

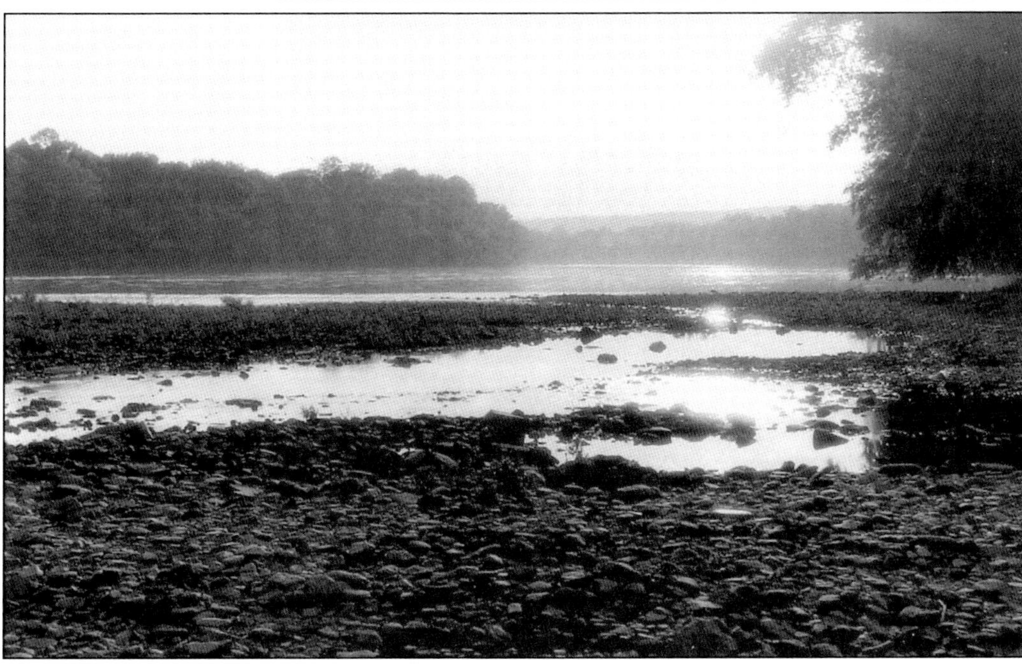

In the end, of course, it is the river. For those that build their lives in a river community, it is the power and the majesty of the river that ties it all together. There is danger in a river that thrills the senses and there is beauty—beauty that speaks to each of us in its own unique way, like so many moonlit diamonds on the water. (Courtesy of the Delaware River Mill Society.)

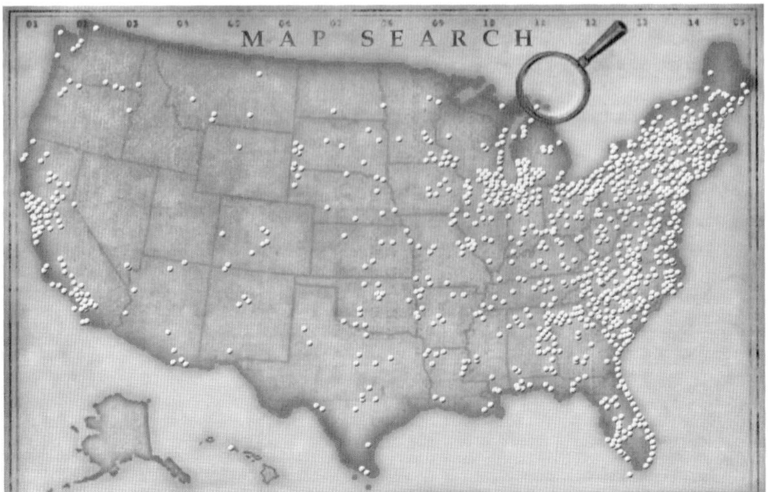
MAP SEARCH